Energy

A Guidebook

Dr Janet Ramage is a Visiting Lecturer in the Energy and Environment Research Unit of the Open University and also teaches at the University of Westminster and at King's College, London.

Energy

A Guidebook

Janet Ramage

Oxford   New York

OXFORD UNIVERSITY PRESS

1997

Oxford University Press, Great Clarendon Street, Oxford OX2 6DP

Oxford New York

Athens Auckland Bangkok Bogota Bombay Buenos Aires
Calcutta Cape Town Dar es Salaam Delhi
Florence Hong Kong Istanbul Karachi
Kuala Lumpur Madras Madrid Melbourne
Mexico City Nairobi Paris Singapore
Taipei Tokyo Toronto

and associated companies in
Berlin Ibadan

Oxford is a trade mark of Oxford University Press

© Janet Ramage 1983, 1997

First published 1983
Second edition 1997

British Library Cataloguing in Publication Data
Data available

Library of Congress Cataloging in Publication Data
Ramage, Janet, 1932–
Energy, a guidebook / Janet Ramage. — 2nd ed.
Includes bibliographical references and index.
1. Power resources. 2. Power (Mechanics) I. Title.
TJ163.2.R345   1997   333.79—dc21   96-52364
ISBN 0–19–288022–5

1 3 5 7 9 10 8 6 4 2

Typeset by Best-set Typesetter Ltd., Hong Kong
Printed in Great Britain
on acid-free paper by
Mackays of Chatham plc
Chatham, Kent

For Heinz, my favourite renewable resource

PREFACE

PREFACE

This is a new edition of a book originally written fifteen years ago. Much of the content of the original edition remains, of course, but this is not the 1983 book with additions. It is an account of the world of energy as it appears in the mid-1990s.

For readers familiar with the original book—teachers and lecturers in particular, who have been using it in their courses—a brief explanation of the revisions may be helpful. Some of the changes were obviously necessary: world and national energy data have been brought up to date, as have other facts and figures about the ways we use energy. In other areas, little change was required. The past fifteen years have seen no revolution in the basic science underlying our energy systems. More surprisingly perhaps, there have been no technological revolutions either: a few improvements in efficiency here and there; some additions to the ever-growing family of experimental wave-power devices; but nothing totally new and unexpected.

The major changes of recent years have been of a different kind: in the topics that are seen as important, the technologies that are receiving attention, and the issues that are being debated. Oil supplies still concern those whose job it is to be concerned, but today the discussions tend to be relegated to the financial pages. Fifteen years ago the great debate was whether coal or nuclear power would be the successor when the oil wells ran dry; but the issue of global warming and events at Chernobyl have made these alternatives rather unfashionable at present, and we now find governments and other major organizations looking seriously at the potential for entirely different energy resources. It has never been the intention in this book to follow every passing fashion, and many of the revisions are driven not by newspaper headlines but by the attempt to convey the ideas more clearly. Nevertheless, these changes in attitudes were a factor in the decision to devote one chapter to a general account of all fuels, traditional or renewable, and their uses. A new chapter discussing some of the ways we use energy and how we might use less in the future again brings together related items that were originally somewhat scattered. Comments by readers have led to separate chapters on costs and resources, and these later parts of the book, not surprisingly, show the greatest changes. Nothing dates more quickly than our view of the future, and for this and the above reasons, the last few chapters have been restructured and largely rewritten.

In preparing this revised edition I have benefited greatly from many responses to the original book: from colleagues teaching the subject in schools, colleges and universities, and from others who have used the book over the years. I would like to thank in particular the undergraduates who attended the original energy courses at the then City of London Polytechnic, and the participants in the Physics for Teachers programme, who taught me at least as much as I taught them. In the preface to the first edition, I was happy to thank my colleagues in the Department of Physics of the City of London Polytechnic for many years of stimulating discussion and constant learning. The debt remains, but the thanks must now be in retrospect. The Department of Physics was closed in the late 1980s, together with other survivors of the original Sir John Cass College—casualties of a market-oriented approach to higher education which sees nothing amiss in a polytechnic or university with no role for the physical sciences.

I am most grateful to the University of Westminster, which provided a refuge for the Physics for Teachers course until that too became the victim of financial cuts, and to the university's Department of Biological and Health Sciences, to whom I owe the continuing pleasure of meeting a lively class of students every week. Another, entirely unanticipated, pleasure of recent years has been the opportunity to join the Energy and Environment Research Unit of the Open University. Many of the changes in this new edition have their origins in discussions with EERU colleagues, whose expertise and enthusiasm have made working at the OU a constant delight. My warmest thanks are due to them all.

The editors at the Oxford University Press have demonstrated their usual friendly efficiency, and I'd like to thank Caroline Cory-

Pearce and Elizabeth Stratford in particular, who have tolerated delays with great patience, made sense of the mélange of old and new material, corrected errors, identified omissions and generally brought order to the book. Any remaining disorder is of course entirely my responsibility.

In recent years it has been particularly pleasing to meet people, now working professionally in the energy field, whose introduction to the subject was the first edition of this little volume. Naturally, I hope that the book will continue to be the beginning of a career for some readers. But this is not its main purpose. It is intended as a guidebook for anybody who wants to know a little about the world of energy, and it will have achieved its real aim if, at the end, each reader comes to view the pronouncements of all the experts with an informed, interested, and slightly sceptical eye.

J.R.
June 1996

CONTENTS

CONTENTS

LIST OF FIGURES

LIST OF TABLES

LIST OF ABBREVIATIONS*

A	amp
AC	alternating current
AGR	advanced gas-cooled reactor
atm	atmosphere
bbl	barrel
BIG/GT	biomass integrated gasifier/gas turbine
Bq	becquerel
BTU	British thermal unit
BWR	boiling-water reactor
°C	degrees Celsius
cal	calorie
Cal	*see kcal*
CANDU	Canadian deuterium-uranium reactor
CCGT	combined-cycle gas turbine
C_D	drag coefficient
CHP	combined heat and power
Ci	curie
CIG/GT	coal integrated gasifier/gas turbine
COP	coefficient of performance
C_R	coefficient of rolling friction
cu m	cubic metre
d	day
dB(A)	decibels (acoustically weighted)
DC	direct current
DFR	demonstration fast reactor
EJ	exajoule
EU	European Union
°F	degrees Fahrenheit
FGD	Flue gas desulphurization
ft	foot

* For definitions see Appendices A and B.

g	gram
gal	imperial gallon
gal(US)	USA gallon
GDP	Gross Domestic Product
GW	gigawatt
GJ	gigajoule
h	hour
HAWT	horizontal-axis wind turbine
J	joule
K	degrees Kelvin
kcal	kilocalorie
kg	kilogram
km	kilometre
kV	kilovolt
kW	kilowatt
kWh	kilowatt-hour
LMFBR	liquid metal fast breeder reactor
LWR	light-water reactor
m	metre
MBq	megabecquerel
Mbd	million barrels a day
mg	milligram
MJ	megajoule
mm	millimetre
mpg	miles per gallon
mph	miles per hour
mSv	millisievert
MSW	municipal solid wastes
Mt	million tonnes
Mtce	million tonnes of coal equivalent
Mtoe	million tonnes of oil equivalent
MW	megawatt
μg	microgram
μSv	microsievert
OTEC	ocean thermal energy conversion
OWC	oscillating water column
p	pence

PFR	prototype fast reactor
PJ	petajoule
ppm	parts per million
PV	photovoltaic
PWR	pressurised-water reactor
R & D	research and development
s	second
sq ft	square foot
sq m	square metre
STIG	steam-injected gas turbine
Sv	sievert
t	tonne
tce	tonne of coal equivalent
THORP	thermal oxide reprocessing plant
TMI	Three Mile Island
toe	tonne of oil equivalent
TW	terawatt
TWh	terawatt-hour
u	unified mass unit
UN	United Nations
V	volt
VAWT	vertical-axis wind turbine
VOC	volatile organic compound
W	watt
y	year

PROLOGUE

Well-known expert: World Primary Energy Consumption at the present moment of time is ten terawatts. In accordance with our high-growth scenario . . .

Voice: Please.

Expert: . . . demand is projected to reach eighty terawatts in the year 2030. Question?

Voice: Please, what is a terawatt?

Expert: 1 000 000 000 000 watts. With a fossil fuel production potential of five hundred million barrels of oil equivalent per day . . .

Voice: Please, how many terawatts in a barrel of oil—er—equivalent?

Expert: . . . we obtain a high-probability prognosis of a non-negligible shortfall on the long-term time horizon. Your question is incorrect.

PART I

The Present

1

The Global Picture

The Problem

Energy matters. Many of us pay good money for it, and many more of us walk for miles every day to find it. Some of us become very cross when we can't get it, and some of us even go to war over it. None of us could survive without it.

This book had its origins at a time when the world had just suffered two energy crises. These affected so many people that they brought home to us just how important our energy supplies had become. The consequences were different in different parts of the world: some people could no longer afford to heat their houses, others went hungry because they couldn't buy oil for cooking, and a few could only fill their petrol tanks on Mondays, Wednesdays, and Fridays. But whatever the local effects, the result was that the energy supplies which many people had come to take for granted were suddenly a matter of public concern. It needed a crisis to bring this about, but a few thoughtful people had been trying for many years to draw attention to the fact that our supplies were finite—there is only so much oil under the ground. These people had looked at the way we were using ever more each year and had asked how long it could go on, but no one had taken much notice of them. One effect of the 1970s crises and sudden price rises was to halt the seemingly inevitable growth in oil consumption (Fig. 1.1(a) and (b)), but a little calculation shows that we'd be foolish to think that this has solved all the problems. We have used as much oil since the first edition of this book was written in 1980 as in the whole of history before that year.

(a) World oil production

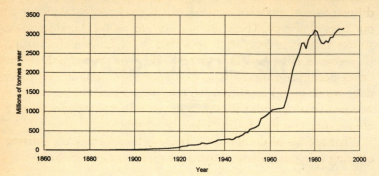

(b) The price of a litre of crude oil

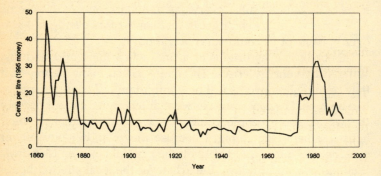

(c) UK coal production

Fig. 1.1 A short history of energy, 1860–1995

These concerns have been joined in more recent years by a different set of anxieties centred on the environmental effects of our uses of energy. These are not new, of course. London's first smoke abatement legislation appeared in the fourteenth century. (It seems to have had little effect despite the imposition of the death penalty for lighting a coal fire.) What *is* new is that these days we do things on such a large scale. Six hundred years ago it was just London; today it may be the world's atmosphere that we are ruining, and that could be less reversible.

What are we to do about it? There is no shortage of 'experts' offering solutions. Some of these are quite straightforward:

The nuclear future. World energy demand could be met by 100000 power stations using breeder reactors. The electricity would provide all our needs, including the production of hydrogen as a fuel for vehicles. By the time the plutonium runs out we shall have fusion power. Nuclear plants produce no carbon dioxide or acid rain, so there is nothing left to worry about.

The solar future. All our problems are the result of the system, which is dominated by huge multi-national companies and is therefore bad. We must return to a low-technology way of life, riding our bicycles and rising and going to bed with the sun, which will warm our modest and energy-efficient dwelling. We can build our own wind turbines, weave our own ethnic garments, and grow our own grass.

Then of course there are those who deny the whole problem. If we just ignore it, it will go away, soon to be replaced by next year's fashion in disasters.

How are we to know which expert to believe? We are offered a variety of unappealing solutions to problems that may or may not exist, and it's not surprising that many of us are uneasy. Opinion is confused with fact all too often in the energy debate, and the religious fervour of the advocates of one or another solution makes rational analysis difficult. But it is definitely not the moral of this book that we should give up in despair. Quite the reverse. If it has one, it is that the world of energy is not some inaccessible place wrapped in impenetrable mystery, but an area open to any reasonable person. Anyone who can count and add can follow the figures. And if we make sure not to get lost at the beginning, and advance carefully step by step, there is no reason why the science and technology should present much difficulty.

This is the programme for the first two parts of this book. Part I looks at our present sources and uses of energy, with the occasional glance back at the past. To illustrate the figures, and so that we won't become too parochial in our outlook, we compare the energy patterns of four countries: Britain, Switzerland, the USA, and India, to see where they obtain their energy and what they do with it. Then in Part II we move on from where and what to how, and look at the energy technologies. The best way to understand the systems we use is to understand the science behind them. As we look at each energy source and how it is used, we try gradually to build ourselves a picture of the physical world and its laws; finishing, we hope, with a clear enough view to be able to assess both our present technologies and those on offer for the future.

So much for the facts and figures and the technology, the essential background; but the energy debate is about more than these simple things. It involves economics and politics, and value-judgements about the sort of world we want to live in—much more difficult subjects. To ignore these in making decisions would be as foolish as to ignore known facts about the physical world. We do not have, as with the laws of physics, a firm basis for including them in our calculations, but they must enter when we plan for the future. The three graphs of Fig. 1.1 illustrate just a few of the problems in doing this. If you had been an oil company analyst in the early 1970s, what development plans would you have recommended? Or if you had been asked in the latter part of the nineteenth century to predict the demand for Britain's coal in, say, 1950, what would you have said?

So in Part III—when we come to attempts to determine how much oil there is, or how we are changing the environment, or how much anything costs, or where we are going from here—we are on much less sure ground and must proceed with extreme caution. Nevertheless, by investigating these questions, and seeing what a few people have to say today about possible futures, we might learn to appreciate the issues and the uncertainties, and to look equally carefully at the pronouncements of the experts and the fashionably easy answers.

And the rest is questions. This book offers no grand solutions. It is a guidebook to the world of energy, an attempt to point out and explain the most important features. Like many guidebooks, it includes warnings against hazards and doesn't entirely resist the temptation to award stars, but the choice of destination must be made by the traveller. Only you can decide where you want to go.

Numbers of Things

Any serious discussion of energy must be quantitative. Take the statement

My car uses very little oil.

In driving a thousand miles, or standing in the garage? Compared with Saudi Arabian exports or with a horse? This trivial example illustrates two requirements. In order to compare quantities we must be able to measure them, i.e. we need units (gallons, or litres, or tonnes); and then we must know which type of quantity we are discussing (gallons per mile, gallons per year, or just gallons).

One of the happier consequences of the continuing energy debate has been a growing appreciation of the advantages—evident to scientists for the past century or so—of having one agreed unit for energy. Even the United Nations Expert Group on Energy Statistics, which, according to its report, 'focused on problems of terminology and definitions of boundaries that arose in the elaboration of the conceptual and methodological approaches to be adopted in the development of energy balances' eventually untangled its language enough to suggest that international and national statistical offices should 'consider adopting the joule.' But open a book on energy resources and what do you find? Tonnes (or tons) of oil or coal, cubic feet of gas, kilowatt-hours, terawatt-years, therms, calories, and Calories. All these units still appear, and if we want to follow the energy debate as it is carried on in the real world, we have no option but to come to terms with them. Accordingly, one aim in this first chapter is to introduce the art of 'energy arithmetic'—of converting between different ways of specifying quantities of energy.

The need to use extremely large numbers can also lead to problems. Most of us can visualize a dozen objects, perhaps even a hundred, but who can picture 12 000 000 000 000? We cannot avoid using very large numbers, but we can at least try to make them more manageable, perhaps by using special names, or special ways of writing them. (Appendix A explains these methods and can be used as a glossary for terms such as terawatt or megajoule.) Then we can try where possible to convert very large numbers into quantities we can grasp. If the world rate of energy consumption is 12 million million watts and the world population is nearly 6000 million people, then the per capita consumption is about 2000 watts. And this, as we shall see, is equivalent to roughly a gallon of oil a day for each man, woman, and child. So we'll start by looking more closely at the 12 million million watts. It is after all the central fact for any book on energy.

World Energy Consumption

The world is consuming primary energy at a rate of about twelve terawatts.

The above statement raises at least four questions.

Question 1: How is Energy Consumed?

One of the most fundamental laws of physics states that energy is conserved. The total quantity stays constant. You cannot create energy or destroy it. If you have ten units of energy at the start, you have ten units of energy—somewhere—at the finish. In this sense, we never consume energy. It is however a matter of great practical importance that energy can take many different forms, and what we can do—and have done at least since our ancestors first used fire—is to devise means of converting from one form to another. When we talk of consuming energy this is what we mean: converting from the chemical energy stored in wood, coal, oil, or gas, from nuclear energy, from the gravitational energy of water stored in a reservoir, or the kinetic energy of the wind, into heat or electrical energy or light or the kinetic energy of a moving vehicle. *Consumption is conversion.*

Question 2: What is Primary Energy?

The answer to this is a little less clear-cut. Essentially, primary energy is the total energy 'contained' in the original resource. Our main present resources are the fossil fuels (coal, oil, and natural gas) and the biofuels such as wood, straw, dried dung, etc. (The energy content of the food we eat is not customarily included in the count.) To these we can add the energy provided by hydro-electric or geothermal plant and other 'renewables' such as solar or wind power, and by nuclear power-stations. The rather arbitrary nature of the criterion becomes evident if we consider solar energy. It counts if special systems such as solar panels or photovoltaic cells are used, but not if we simply warm ourselves in the sunshine. Nevertheless, drawing demarcation lines need not be too serious a problem—and no one has yet passed a law forbidding common sense, even in this field.

Question 3: What are Twelve Terawatts?

The important point to notice here is that a watt (or a terawatt) is a *rate* at which energy is used and not a unit of energy itself. Technically a watt is a unit of **power**, of energy per second:

• One watt is by definition one joule per second.

Thus a 750-W electric heater is converting electrical energy into heat (and perhaps some light) at a rate of 750 joules in each second. Appendix A then tells us that a megawatt (MW) is a million watts, and a terawatt (TW) is a million megawatts, a million million watts.

Conversely, a kilowatt-hour (kWh) is a unit of energy:

TABLE 1.1. *Power and energy*

Power	
1 watt	= 1 joule per second
1 kilowatt	= 1000 joules per second
1 kilowatt	= 3 600 000 joules per hour
Energy	
1 kilowatt-hour	= 3 600 000 joules
1 kWh	= 3.6 MJ

- One kilowatt-hour is the amount of energy converted in one hour at a rate of one kilowatt.

One kilowatt is 1000 joules per second, so it follows that 1 kWh must be 3.6 MJ (Table 1.1).

All of which leads us to an alternative version of our original statement:

> The world is converting the energy of its primary resources into other forms of energy at a rate of about 12 million megajoules in each second.

This would be more illuminating if we had a better picture of the amount of energy called one megajoule. We therefore postpone the very important fourth question for a few pages in order to look at some amounts of energy.

Per Capita Energy Consumption

12 TW divided equally between all the inhabitants of the world gives each of us, as we have seen, 2 kW of primary power. This does not mean, however, that we can each run a 2-kW heater continuously, even if we want to use our entire personal supply for that, because each kilowatt of electric power delivered would probably need nearly 6 kW of primary input. So if you run your heater for an average of about eight hours a day, you are consuming your fair share of world energy. Nothing left for production of food or clothing, for TV or travel, or to build a roof over your head.

It will be no surprise to learn that world energy is not distributed in fair shares. Table 1.2 shows production and consumption
patterns for different parts of the world, data which surely provide food for thought. As we'll see in Chapter 3, comparison of per
capita energy consumption and per capita annual income shows a
not unexpected correlation, but we must nevertheless look carefully at the easy conclusion that rising living standards necessarily
mean the consumption of ever more energy each year.

TABLE 1.2. *World comparisons*

	Percentage of world total			Per capita consumption compared with world average
	Population (%)	Energy produced (%)[a]	Energy consumed (%)[a]	
Industrialized countries	23	55	70	three times
Rest of world	77	45	30	one-third
Selected regions				
USA and Canada	5	23	28	six times
Europe	15	30	35	twice
Middle East	2	14	4	twice
Africa	13	7	3	one-quarter
Selected countries				
Bangladesh	2.1	0.04	0.06	one-thirtieth
Brazil	2.8	0.7	1.3	one-half
Canada	0.5	3.8	2.7	six times
China	21	9.7	9.6	one-half
CIS[b]	4.9	14	9.9	three times
India	17	2.3	2.7	one-sixth
Japan	2.2	0.5	6.1	three times
Kenya	0.5	0.002	0.025	one-twentieth
Switzerland	0.12	0.06	0.26	twice
United Kingdom	1.0	2.7	2.7	three times
USA	4.6	19	25	six times

[a] These figures do not include contributions from non-commercial 'biofuels' (see Ch. 2).
[b] Commonwealth of Independent States, i.e. Russia and ten other states which were earlier
within the USSR.

Energy Equivalents

Moving from energy consumption to energy supplies, we'll see in this section how energies can be expressed as equivalent amounts of two important fuels. We also look at a few other energy units.

Oil

Some of the most accessible annual data on world energy are published by the major oil companies. So we should not be surprised to find that their favoured unit for energy is the **tonne of oil equivalent** (toe). When oil is burned, whether in a furnace or an internal combustion engine, its chemical energy is converted into heat energy (a process discussed in more detail in Chapter 4), and 1 toe is simply the heat energy released in burning one tonne of oil. The value varies a little between crude oils from different sources, but a generally accepted average is 42 000 MJ (42 GJ).

Another measure of quantity of oil and correspondingly of energy is the **barrel**. This odd unit, alien in a world of pipelines and supertankers, comes from the size of the barrels used to carry oil from the world's first drilled well in Pennsylvania in the 1860s. One barrel of oil is 42 US gallons or 35 Imperial (British) gallons—about 159 litres. The density of crude oil varies, but on average there are about 7.3 barrels to the tonne. The energy released in burning one barrel of oil (1 boe) is therefore about 5700 MJ.

We have seen that the world is consuming primary energy at a rate of 12 TW. Remembering that a watt is one joule per second, a little arithmetic converts this into a daily consumption of roughly 1 million million million joules (1 EJ), which is equivalent to

180 Mbd (million barrels daily).

Further arithmetic shows that world annual consumption of primary energy is about 380 EJ, which is

9000 Mtoe (million tonnes of oil equivalent).

This of course includes all forms of energy. Actual world oil production is some 65 Mbd or 3200 Mt a year, accounting for a little over a third of the above total.

The energy content of one (Imperial) gallon of oil is about

160 MJ, which is a little less than the world-wide average per capita daily consumption of primary energy. So the average person uses the energy equivalent of just over a gallon of oil a day. Of course the fortunate European receives about twice this, and the average American five times as much.

Coal

For many years until the mid-1980s, official British statistics expressed all forms of energy in **tonnes of coal equivalent**, a unit which still appears in some tables. Coal is a much more variable material than crude oil, and world-wide its energy per tonne ranges from less than 20 GJ to over 30 GJ. The figure of 29 GJ per tonne is often adopted as an international average, and is the one used in this book unless otherwise specified. (Significantly, UK statistics now tend to use tonnes of oil equivalent.)

Some Other Units

Before the general adoption of the joule, two other units commonly used by scientists were the **calorie** and the **British thermal unit** (BTU).

- One calorie is the heat energy needed to warm one gram of water by one degree Celsius and is equal to 4.19 joules.
- One BTU is the heat energy needed to warm one pound of water by one degree Fahrenheit and is equal to 1055 joules.

Derivatives of these two include the therm (100 000 BTU) and the kilocalorie, written kcal or Cal, and some countries continue to use these units, notably the USA.

The Cal became familiar as the unit for the energy content of food, which leads to a further way of looking at our consumption of primary energy. If we assume that the daily food energy needed to support an adult is about 2000 Cal, we find that the average European is using the energy equivalent of some forty people. A further look at Table 1.2 shows that the number of such energy servants you have at your command depends very much on where you live, reflecting in large part the extent to which your society uses the muscle-power of machines.

On Facts and Figures

There remains one final question about the statement that the world consumes primary energy at a rate of 12 TW:

Question 4: How do we Know?

Before venturing further into the sources of energy, we should perhaps discuss the sources of data. Where do the figures come from? The first answer is that we find them in official statistics, technical journals, and similar publications such as those mentioned in the Further Reading. But one shouldn't believe everything one reads in books (or anything in newspapers) and a couple of examples might bring out the importance of knowing exactly what the figures mean and whether they are reliable. Consider, for instance:

> The UK chemical industry consumes 14 per cent of energy used by industry in the UK.

> the [chemical] industry used over 15 per cent of the energy required by all manufacturing . . .

> the gross energy input [to the chemical industry] being . . . 20.5 per cent of the total industrial energy consumption . . .

Three quotations from the same issue of a technical journal. Are they disagreeing about the facts, or talking about different things?

Or consider the figures for world oil production. Crude oil is effectively traded on a world market, so the data are probably better than for any other form of energy. Nevertheless you can read that world production in 1994 was

	3197.126 million tonnes
or	3209.1 Mt
or	24 373 612 thousand barrels

The third presents a slight problem unless we know the number of barrels in a tonne to one part in 24 million. Adopting the generally accepted world average of 7.33 gives us yet another total:

$$3325.1858 \, \text{Mt}$$

Of course if the barrels per tonne are really known only to one part in 733, at best we should say 3325 Mt; but the original authors do not seem to have been inhibited by discrepancies of 100 or even 100000 times their claimed precision.

In collecting international data there is also the particular problem of governments who publish wishful thinking, or of those who decline to publish at all. (A feature of many energy studies until the late 1980s was the strange geographical entity known as WOCA. It was of course the World Outside the Communist Areas.) Apart from such political issues, care is always needed in interpreting published figures, for reasons which we can characterize under the headings 'definitions' and 'conversions'.

Definitions

World data usually start as national statistics, and with some 200 countries it is hardly surprising that the terminology doesn't always match at the seams. Does 'production' include energy used by the producer? Does 'consumption' include energy used for transmission of energy? The problems are illustrated by the many pages of explanatory notes associated with any official statistics. For instance: 'Hard coal mines consumption: this heading covers only coal used as a direct source of energy within the coal industry: it excludes the coal burned in pit-head power stations (which is included in 'consumption for transformation, thermoelectric plants)'. Without this, how are we to interpret the statement that precisely 74.65 per cent of Britain's coal is used for electricity generation? In the absence of the pages of explanation surely it would be better to say, 'About 75 per cent', or even, 'Roughly three-quarters'.

A further mismatch appears in comparing figures for production and consumption. One would hope that any difference would be accounted for by changes in stocks, but when production data come from producers and consumption data from consumers this is by no means always the case. In recent UN data, for instance, total (world) exports of crude oil exceeded imports by 15 million tonnes. Some of it may be on the high seas—in ships, one hopes—but the figures do illustrate a problem. (Other authors avoid this particular difficulty and balance their books by including entries for 'unidentified trade'.)

Conversions

We have already seen several examples of conversion between different energy units, but have not bothered too much about the nature of these relationships. On inspection we find that we have used the word 'equivalent' in a number of different ways, and it is important to distinguish these.

First, there are cases where the conversion between units is exact. One watt is exactly one joule per second because that is how it is defined; and 1 kWh is therefore exactly 3.6 MJ because there are exactly 3600 seconds in an hour. Then there are relationships which although not exact are known very precisely and may be regarded as universal. The conversions between joules, therms, and calories are examples.

When we come to quantities such as the heat content of a fuel, matters are not quite so simple. The heat content of a particular piece of coal can be measured to great accuracy, provided the conditions are carefully specified: 'Take one kilogram of dry coal at room temperature, crush it and burn it completely to produce carbon dioxide, water and ash, cool these products back to room temperature and measure the heat energy extracted.' With similar care we might measure the solar energy reaching a particular roof in the course of a particular day. But it is hardly practicable to use these methods for the lifetime output from an entire coal-mine or solar panel. In the real world it becomes essential to use average values. The problem is that not everyone uses the same average. If your tonne of coal equivalent and average solar intensity are not the same as mine, our discussion is likely to end in confusion. So the rule for data in this category is to make sure we know what the figures mean before using them.

Finally, there is the question of attainable conversion factors. How many kilowatt-hours of electrical energy are in practice obtained from each cubic metre of gas in a power station or from a particular wind-farm on an average day? The answers to these questions depend on our current technology and may well change. But we cannot ignore them because they are already there: hiding even in such apparently simple data as primary energy production. And their effect is not always small. When one source states that 3 per cent of a nation's primary energy comes from nuclear power but another says 10 per cent, they may be in complete agreement about the facts and 'merely' using different conventions. (We'll look at some of these in Chapter 2.)

The Units We Use

The advantages of using one set of clearly defined units are obvious—but we must take care that concern for precision and consistency doesn't become a strait-jacket. We need to appreciate the other terms used in the real world, not only to assess the present situation but to grasp the implications of projections and scenarios for the future. And there is another reason. Specifying carefully that the mass of a vehicle is 760 kg and its speed is 36.2 metres per second has the advantage that you can easily show that its kinetic energy is half a megajoule (see Chapter 6). But describing it as a three-quarter-ton car travelling at 80 mph certainly conveys a better picture to most of us. In the chapters which follow, therefore, I adopt a middle route:

- I'll normally use the accepted units (metres, kilograms, and seconds, and their multiples shown in Appendix A), but with translation into everyday quantities where this might add meaning.

- The joule, being the accepted unit for energy, is normally used. However, the convenience of the kilowatt-hour, not only for electrical energy but for household fuel consumption (in the UK), makes it an obvious choice in these contexts. Other energy units (Mtoe, etc.) may occasionally appear as well as joules in situations where they are commonly used.

- Except where otherwise stated, I use a standard set of factors to convert between the different units (kilometres and miles, joules and kWh, etc.). These are given in Appendix B.

- The number of digits used in quoting values is normally determined by the reliability of the data, but I'll often use more approximate values where there is no loss of essential detail.

2

Primary Energy

Introduction

To plan for the future you need to know about the present. Whether your aim is to safeguard world energy supplies in 2050 or reduce your household heating bills for next year, it is well to know how much energy is being used today, in what forms and for what purposes. It may also be useful to know how the situation has changed over recent years.

These are subjects of the next two chapters. We start with the world as a whole; then, in order to see the detail within the broad picture, we look at the changing scene in four countries: Britain, Switzerland, the USA, and India. This choice is not entirely arbitrary. The two European countries provide interesting contrasts with their very different geographical conditions and energy resources; the USA must be important in any study, as the major consumer and perhaps the extreme towards which we are all moving; and India illustrates well the potentialities and problems of a country still developing its nation-wide energy systems.

The World

The contributions from the main primary resources are shown in Fig. 2.1 and Table 2.1, and the picture is clear enough. We have reached a situation where oil contributes more than a third of all our energy and the fossil fuels together account for over four-fifths. Indeed, if we exclude the biofuels, the fossil fuels account

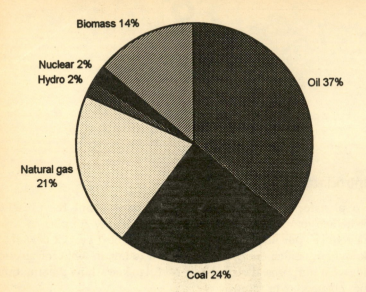

Fig. 2.1 World primary energy 1994

for 95 per cent of the total 'commercially traded' energy. Fig. 2.2 shows how consumption of these non-renewable and carbon-dioxide-producing energy sources increased over a 40-year period. The dramatic rise in the use of the two favoured fuels in the first twenty years is obvious: in 1973 we consumed four times as much oil and over five times as much natural gas as in 1953. With this pattern apparently destined to continue indefinitely, it is no surprise that the sudden doubts about future supplies and the doubling of oil prices in 1973 led to panic and disarray. As we have already seen in Fig. 1.1(a), the crises of the 1970s, followed by economic recession in the early 1980s, did bring the growth in oil consumption to a halt—but only temporarily. The more prosperous mid-1980s saw the start of a return to the old rate of rise, and as Fig. 2.2 shows, despite all the crises, the increase in world primary energy consumption between 1973 and 1993 was nearly as great as the total consumption in 1953.

It is perhaps worth noting that world population roughly

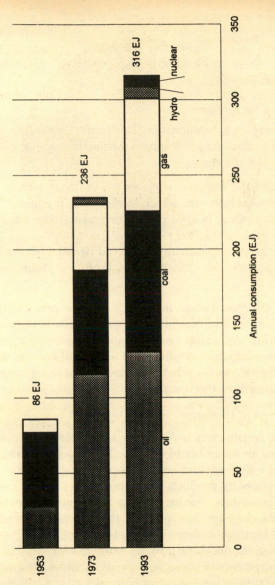

Fig. 2.2 World primary energy 1953–1993
This graph does not include biomass as the past contributions are too uncertain.

doubled between 1953 and 1993 whereas primary energy consumption increased four-fold; so our galloping consumption is due as much to our increasing individual appetites as to our growing numbers. We'll look at these facts and some of their implications again later.

Interpreting the Figures

Before moving on to some national patterns, we need to investigate a little more closely the figures for the three minor contributions to the world's energy:

- *Biomass*: all the material such as wood, plant wastes, dried dung, urban refuse, etc., which started as living matter and is burned to produce heat or power, or perhaps converted into a liquid or gaseous 'biofuel';
- *Hydroelectric power*: equivalent to about twenty Niagara Falls;
- *Nuclear power*: from a world total of over four hundred reactors.

Specifying the contribution from each of these raises problems, and the main point of the following paragraphs is to provide a warning. When you compare one country with another, or compare the contributions from different sources of energy, it is important to know exactly what the experts are talking about and how they have done their sums.

The Question of Biomass

The most uncertain entry in Table 2.1 is undoubtedly the biomass contribution, for a number of reasons. These fuels are often 'non-commercial'—they are garnered in surrounding forests or fields, or arise as waste by-products of other activities and are used on site, or are home-grown or bartered for other goods or services. In other words, they are not formally traded, so the economists' methods of keeping track are not available.

For much of the developing world, biofuels are essential for life. Without some means of cooking, people can starve. And as deforestation becomes an increasing problem, it may be very important to know how much of the world's energy comes from biomass, if

TABLE 2.1. *World primary energy, 1994*

The total annual primary energy is about 370 EJ, equivalent to just under 9 billion tonnes of oil a year, or a constant year-round supply of energy at a rate of 12 billion kilowatts (12 TW).

Energy source	Quantity in customary units	Energy (EJ)	Percentage contribution	
			To total energy	Commercial energy only
Fossil fuels				
Oil	3200 million tonnes	136	37	42
Coal	3450 million tonnes	91	24	28
Natural gas	2100 billion cu m	79	21	25
Fossil fuels total		*306*	*82*	*95*
Power-station output				
Hydro	2300 billion kWh	8.4	2.3	2.6
Nuclear	2200 billion kWh	7.9	2.1	2.5
Biomass[a]		52	14	—

[a] Biomass includes such a variety of sources that no single 'customary unit' is appropriate. See also the discussion of this contribution in the text.

only in order to seek alternatives. In the past decade, detailed studies in a number of countries have led to an increased appreciation of the large role it plays. The figure used here, representing about one-seventh of the world's total primary energy, is accepted as the best current estimate. It may yet turn out to be much too low.

'Primary Electricity'

Table 2.1 shows hydroelectricity and nuclear power each contributing roughly eight exajoules to world primary energy. But elsewhere you will find tables giving about three times this figure for these two sources, or yet others showing about 8 EJ for hydroelectricity but 24 EJ for nuclear power. The basic fact, agreed by all, is that they produce respectively 2300 and 2200 billion kWh of electricity a year—roughly the same totals. As mentioned in Chapter 1, the discrepancies are the result of different conventions in defining the corresponding 'primary energy':

- One method converts the billions of kWh directly into joules. This gives the figures in Table 2.1.
- The other method is intended as a measure of the value of the resource as replacement for fossil fuels. The output is therefore multiplied by a factor of about three, which in the present case would give 'effective' primary energy inputs of 26 and 24 EJ for hydro and nuclear respectively.

You may well ask why we talk about the output at all. Shouldn't it be the input which counts as primary energy? Unfortunately there are difficulties with this. We'll be looking at the details later, but a brief summary will illustrate the problem. Of the three main types of power-station, hydroelectric plant converts nearly all the energy of the incoming water into electrical energy, whilst nuclear and most fossil fuel plants convert only about a third of the heat produced by their fuel into useful electrical output. For hydro-plant this means that the 8 EJ of output needs not much over 8 EJ of 'primary' input. However, it is argued that using this figure in a diagram such as Fig. 2.1 would underrepresent the 'true value' of hydroelectricity compared with the other fuels.

Nuclear power poses a different problem. The output can be measured, but as we shall see in Chapter 8, the corresponding 'primary energy input' is by no means as easy to define. So in this case again, the 24 EJ represents the fossil fuel energy input which would be required to provide the same output as the nuclear plant.

Each convention has its merits. The lower (output) figure has the advantage of telling the truth: it shows what we actually measure. But does it properly represent the value of the resource? Another point is that neither convention tells us whether the plant actually produces that extra 16 EJ as waste heat. The fact that nuclear plant produces waste heat but hydro does not is the reason given for recent changes in UK statistics, which now use the high figure for nuclear and the low figure for hydro. Of the other data sources mentioned in the Further Reading, the United Nations statistics use the lower, electrical output figure for both, whilst the *BP Statistical Review* adopts the same policy as the UK data. In this book we follow the UN and adopt the 'what you get' policy:

- The primary energies shown here are simply the electrical output for both hydroelectricity and nuclear power, given in kilowatt-hours, or where necessary directly converted into other energy units.

Britain

The contributions to primary energy production and consumption in the UK in 1994 are shown in Fig. 2.3. Comparison with Fig. 2.1 shows that the relative proportions of oil, coal, and gas used in Britain are not unlike the pattern for the world as a whole. As the world consumption of commercially traded fuels is dominated by the industrialized countries (Table 1.2), this broad similarity shouldn't surprise us. The main difference is, of course, that the biofuels do not contribute significantly to British energy supplies. Nuclear power plays a somewhat greater role, and hydroelectricity a much smaller one—for obvious geographical reasons. (Note that the percentages shown are rounded to the nearest 1 per cent, and contributions appreciably less than this do not appear in these diagrams.)

Looking at Fig. 2.4 we see that total consumption rose fairly steadily by 1½–2 per cent a year in the twenty years before the oil crisis of 1973, and since then has done little but rise and fall with the state of the economy. The more striking features appear in Fig. 2.5. In 1953 we see not merely a coal-producing country but a coal-based country. Apart from a little oil—mainly for motor vehicles and stationary diesel engines—everything ran on coal: coal-fired power-stations, coal for process heat in foundries and factories, coal fires in the home, and (with no natural gas yet) coal gas for cooking. Moreover, the diagram reveals Britain as a net exporter of coal—as indeed she had been for a century or more, and continued to be into the 1970s. In the peak years of the 1920s and 1930s, UK annual coal exports were greater than today's entire coal production, and at the start of World War II their energy value was more

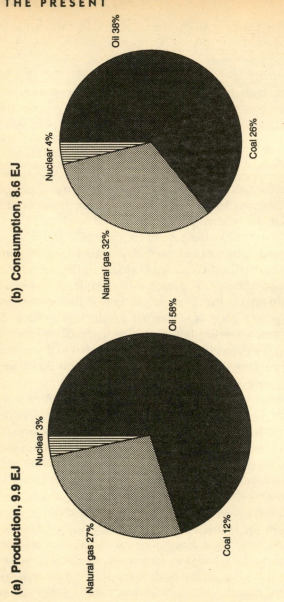

Fig. 2.3 Primary energy production and consumption, UK 1994

(a) Production, 9.9 EJ

Nuclear 3%

Natural gas 27%

Coal 12%

Oil 58%

(b) Consumption, 8.6 EJ

Nuclear 4%

Oil 38%

Coal 26%

Natural gas 32%

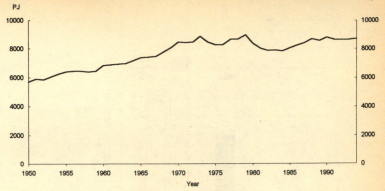

Fig. 2.4 UK primary energy consumption, 1950–1994

than twice that of oil imports. But in the post-war period the attractions of oil and natural gas reduced the demand for coal, as in many industrialized countries, and although overall world demand continued to rise, overseas markets were lost to cheaper coal from other sources. Production fell steeply, as we saw in Fig. 1.1, and with ever-rising oil imports, Britain became for the first time in her history a net importer of energy.

This is the situation in 1973, shown in Fig. 2.5. Coal is just about in balance, and natural gas production has begun; but imported oil accounts for almost half the country's total energy consumption. This was soon to change again. With the development of North Sea oil, the balance tilted once more. Oil production grew rapidly throughout the later 1970s, and by the end of the decade oil had overtaken coal as the major energy producer. Since then, the energy value of oil exports has continued to exceed that of imported gas and coal, and Britain has again been a net exporter of energy. Meanwhile coal, mainstay of the Industrial Revolution and predominant for more than two centuries, has fallen to third place in both production and consumption. A final point worth noting is that Britain is the only one of the four countries in our brief studies whose total energy consumption has slightly fallen in recent years. How much this is due to conservation efforts and how much to other factors are questions we shall return to later.

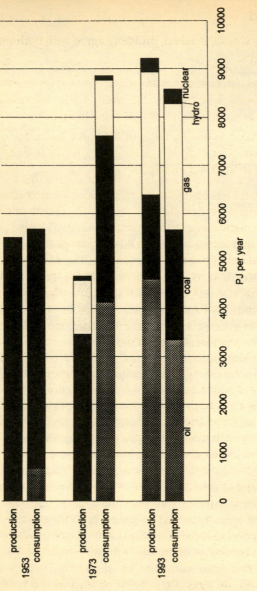

Fig. 2.5 Production and consumption by source, UK 1953–1993

Switzerland

Most people would, if asked, probably agree with both the following statements:

> The possession of adequate energy resources, and in particular self-sufficiency in oil and natural gas, is critical for the economic well-being of any country today.

> Switzerland is one of the world's more fortunate countries, with a sounder economy, stronger currency and higher standard of living than almost any other.

Yet Switzerland has essentially no fossil fuel resources: no coal, no oil, no gas. Fig. 2.6 shows the situation, with more than two-thirds of energy demand being met by imported fossil fuels.

There are, of course, some who will argue with the second of the above statements, Swiss commentators in particular, but it remains the case that by any reasonable measure of well-being—personal income, proportion of the population above the poverty level, nutrition, housing—Switzerland has for many years stood as a counter-example to the easy generalization that energy self-sufficiency is essential for economic survival.

Again the historic data of Fig. 2.7 are in many ways even more striking, but the story they tell is very different from Britain's. We see the Switzerland of 1953 as a country with roughly the same per capita energy consumption as present-day India. The comparison is not quite as absurd as it may seem. The Swiss were still largely a rural people, with many small peasant farmers using human and animal power rather than machines. There was, of course, some industry, and an urban population that was mainly concentrated in a few large cities. And there was a well-established tourist industry bringing money into the country. Just like India today— until we take note of two very significant differences: the population of present-day India is nearly two hundred times greater and the average income is some thirty times smaller than the Swiss level forty years ago.

Switzerland in 1953 may have been relatively less developed, but observe the change in the following twenty years. While

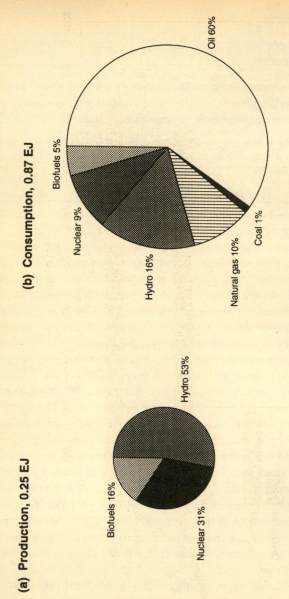

Fig. 2.6 Primary energy production and consumption, Switzerland 1994

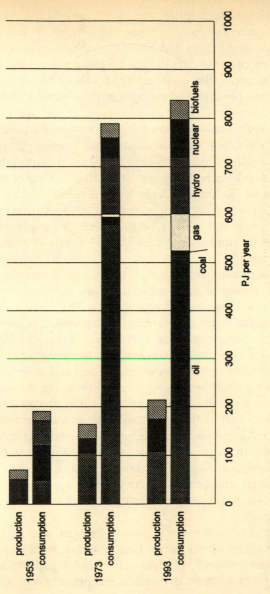

Fig. 2.7 Production and consumption by source, Switzerland 1953–1993

Britain's energy consumption was increasing by a half, Swiss consumption was rising to four times that of 1953. In this sense at least, Switzerland in 1973 had become a typical European country; and as the more recent data in Figs. 2.6 and 2.7 show, this remains the case. The population of Switzerland is about one-eighth that of the UK, so the per capita consumption of the two countries is not now very different.

The relatively small coal contribution reflects the absence of a coal-based past; but the low natural gas consumption is now changing rapidly, a consequence of the development of the trans-European pipelines bringing gas from Russia. One of the safer predictions for the future must be that the corresponding data for the year 2013 will show a big increase in this particular contribution. (Any prediction in the world of energy is fraught with danger, so caution requires the qualification, 'provided politics or war don't intervene.')

Switzerland does possess one important source of energy. About one-quarter of her land surface lies 1000 metres or more above the remaining three-quarters, and with a mean annual precipitation of the order of 1000 mm, the hydroelectric potential is considerable. For almost a century after the first installation (to light a hotel in St Moritz), power-stations drawing energy from the waters of the Rhine, Rhône, Inn, and Ticino and their tributaries provided a regularly increasing output. But, as Fig. 2.7 shows, the past couple of decades have seen very little further growth in hydro-power. Part of the reason is that the major sources have already been developed; but environmental considerations have also become an important factor, with growing concern about the construction of ever more dams in remote Alpine valleys. Environmental concerns—and the Swiss system of popular referenda—have also resulted in constraints on the growth of nuclear power.

The biofuels contribution shown in Figs. 2.6 and 2.7 includes two rather different resources. One is wood. With nearly 2000 square metres (half an acre) of forest per head of population, three-quarters of it in common ownership and publicly accessible, precise estimation of the amount of wood used for fuel is difficult, and data from different authorities can vary by 50 per cent or more; but there is agreement that this source provides at least a per cent or so of national energy consumption. The second biofuels contribution comes from rubbish. With legislation prohibiting local landfills, almost all domestic and other non-agricultural wastes are incinerated, the majority as input for power-stations.

The United States of America

The USA is everyone's favourite example of conspicuous consumption, in energy as in material goods. Consumption per capita is over five and a half times the world average and twice that of most other industrialized countries. As Fig. 2.8 shows, the country is a net importer of energy, mainly because oil is being consumed at about twice the rate of production. This shortfall has increased fairly steadily since the 1950s, except for a brief period in the late 1970s following the oil crises and the opening of the Alaskan fields. Comparison of Fig. 2.9 with the similar diagrams for the UK and Switzerland indicates further significant differences—as well as the sheer quantity. Natural gas, a familiar fuel in the USA well before its development in Europe, has experienced little or no growth over the past twenty years. However, coal production has increased—residual evidence of the sudden interest in this un-fashionable fuel in the late 1970s when it seemed that oil supplies might fail (see 'Secondary Fuels', in Chapter 4).

Overall, total energy consumption shows only a slight increase in the second period, but our diagram doesn't reveal the year-by-year detail. In fact, consumption fell for a few years around 1980, but during the past decade seems to have settled down to a modest but fairly steady rise of $1\frac{1}{2}$ per cent a year; not the continued reduction hoped for by the enthusiastic conservationists of the late 1970s, but less than half the rate of the preceding few decades. And we shouldn't forget that the USA is still a country whose population is increasing, currently at about 1 per cent a year, so

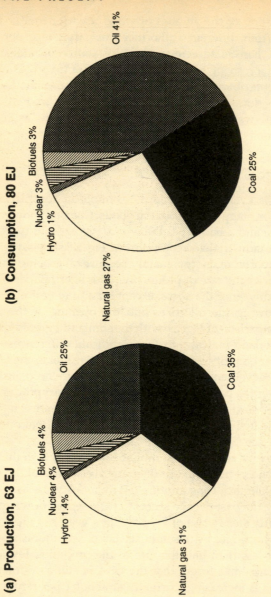

(a) Production, 63 EJ

Oil 25%

Biofuels 4%
Nuclear 4%
Hydro 1.4%

Coal 35%

Natural gas 31%

(b) Consumption, 80 EJ

Oil 41%

Biofuels 3%
Nuclear 3%
Hydro 1%

Coal 25%

Natural gas 27%

Fig. 2.8 Primary energy production and consumption, USA 1994

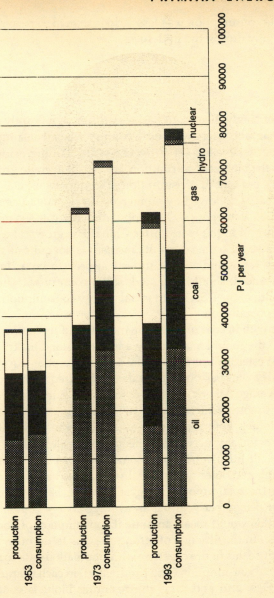

Fig. 2.9 Production and consumption by source, USA 1953–1993

per capita consumption was less in 1993 than in 1973, and is rising only slightly during the mid-1990s.

India

Not surprisingly, Figs. 2.10 and 2.11 differ significantly from the earlier diagrams. Here we have a country whose consumption has by no means levelled off in recent years. Putting aside for the moment the biofuels contribution, we see an average growth rate of about 5 per cent in consumption of 'commercial' fuels between 1953 and 1973, followed by an increase in the rate to nearly 6 per cent in the second period. The population (at over 900 million the second largest in the world after China) has grown at a rate of 2 per cent a year, so the per capita increase is not quite as great, but in energy terms India does indeed appear to be a developing country. And, it should be noted, still a country with little more than a tenth of the USA commercial energy consumption for three times the population.

The growth in coal production and use and its continued dominance of the commercial energy scene also stand in striking contrast to Western countries. A total oil consumption equivalent to about half a pint per person per day, compared with two gallons for the average American, is an obvious indicator of the extent of the use of motor vehicles in the two countries.

The biofuels contribution is, as always, the most difficult to estimate with any accuracy. The present view is that in India perhaps half this contribution comes from wood and half from dried dung and other agricultural wastes used as fuel. Most estimates of the total amount suggest between half a tonne and 1 tonne per person per year. At an average energy content of 15 GJ a tonne, this would mean an annual consumption of about 10 GJ per capita. In the absence of strong reasons to do otherwise, we therefore use this figure together with population data to calculate the national consumption (and production) in each year. As can be seen in Figs. 2.10 and 2.11, the resulting biofuels contribution amounts to approximately half the total energy consumption, but

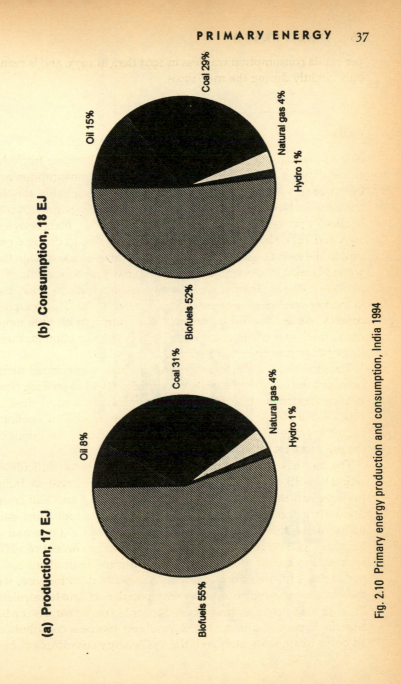

(a) Production, 17 EJ

Oil 8%

Coal 31%

Natural gas 4%

Hydro 1%

Biofuels 55%

(b) Consumption, 18 EJ

Oil 15%

Coal 29%

Natural gas 4%

Hydro 1%

Biofuels 52%

Fig. 2.10 Primary energy production and consumption, India 1994

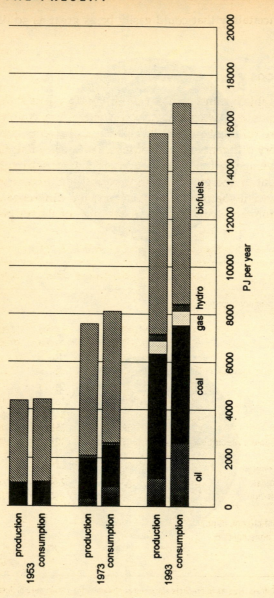

Fig. 2.11 Production and consumption by source, India 1953–1993

with an uncertainty that could easily be as great as 50 per cent either way.

Comparisons

A look at Table 2.2 and comparison of Figs. 2.3–2.11 shows that our four countries, chosen to provide interesting contrasts, do indeed have different present-day patterns of energy consumption and very different energy histories. There are a few similarities. The average Briton and the average Swiss use roughly the same amount of energy, although from rather different sources. Indeed, as we'll see in the next chapter, the difference can be accounted for entirely by the different sources of electric power in

TABLE 2.2. *National primary energy contributions, 1994*

	Britain	Switzerland	USA	India
National total primary energy (all in PJ)				
Production	9900	250	63,000	17,000[a] (7500)
Consumption	8600	870	80,000	18,000[a] (8700)
Average daily consumption per capita				
Oil	4$\frac{1}{2}$ litres	6 litres	10 litres	$\frac{1}{5}$ litre
Coal	3$\frac{1}{2}$ kg	$\frac{1}{9}$ kg	8 kg	$\frac{1}{2}$ kg
Natural gas	36 kWh	9 kWh	65 kWh	$\frac{1}{2}$ kWh
Hydro and nuclear electricity	4$\frac{1}{2}$ kWh	24 kWh	10 kWh	$\frac{1}{5}$ kWh
Biofuels	—	1 kg	—	2 kg
All primary energy				
in megajoules	*400*	*340*	*850*	*53[a] (26)*
in kilowatt-hours	*110*	*95*	*240*	*15[a] (7)*
Average annual change in per capita energy consumption				
1953–73	+2%	+6%	+2%	—[a,b] (+2$\frac{1}{2}$%)
1973–93	—[b]	—[b]	—[b]	+2%[a] (+4%)

[a] Including biofuels. Figures in brackets show the contribution from 'commercial' fuels only.
[b] Smaller than ±$\frac{1}{2}$%.

the two countries. No such changes, however, will remove the other main differences. No matter how we do the calculations, the average American continues to use about twice as much energy and the average Indian about an eighth as much as the average European.

There are a few signs of improvement. In our earlier period the disparities were actually increasing, with consumption rising more rapidly in the countries which were already using more energy. As Table 2.2 shows, this at least is no longer the case; but before we interpret the data as signs of a better and more equal world, we shall need to know much more. Is this apparent 'improvement' no more than the result of the recession in Western countries in the early 1980s, to be replaced by further increases during more prosperous periods? And should we be pleased to see growth in the use of energy, in any case? Fossil fuels may be causing catastrophic changes in climate. 'Biofuels' may mean the destruction of the Earth's remaining forests. What would be the consequences if countries such as India were to increase their consumption in the next twenty years as Switzerland did between 1953 and 1973? These are subjects to which we return towards the end of the book. First, we'll look in more detail at what we use all this energy for, and then, in the central part of the book, at how we use it.

3

Patterns of Consumption

Energy Balances

To the best of our knowledge, energy is conserved, so the total annual energy consumption of a nation, a factory, or a household must be equal to its total annual energy supply. If we draw up a balance-sheet with energy income on one side and expenditure on the other, then physics tells us that the books must balance. In this chapter we'll look at an energy balance-sheet to see the eventual fate of all the primary energy. By investigating a few of the details, and comparing the patterns of consumption of different countries, we'll try to identify areas where there is scope for reducing energy consumption, in order to return to them later.

Table 3.1 shows a much simplified energy balance-sheet for Britain in 1995. (The data have been rounded off, usually to the nearest 50 PJ.) On the supply side, we start with the figure for home production. Imports are then added and exports subtracted, also the non-energy uses of oil (as a lubricant, or raw material for plastics and other products of the petrochemical industry, etc.) and fuel used by foreign-going ships, traditionally not included in national consumption. The aim is to find the amounts of energy used, so we must allow for any changes in stocks: subtracting fuel stored and adding fuel used from stocks. The bottom line is then the actual consumption of each fuel. (Note that 'electricity production' is the output of UK nuclear and hydroelectric plants, and 'imported electricity' is that which comes from France through the link under the English Channel.) Finally, adding all the contributions, we have a total national consumption of 8500 PJ.

TABLE 3.1. *Energy balance-sheet, Britain 1995*

Supply	Oil	Coal	N. Gas	Elect'y	TOTAL
Production	6000	1350	3000	300	10700
Imports (+)	3000	450	70	60	3600
Exports (−)	−5000	−20	−40	—	−5000
Non-energy	−600	—	—	—	−600
Marine bunkers	−100	—	—	—	−100
To stock (−)	−200	300	−100	—	0
Consumption	3100	2100	2900	380	8500

Consumption	Liquid	Solid	Gas	Elect'y	TOTAL
Transport	2100	—	—	25	2100
Industry	300	250	550	350	1500
Domestic	130	150	1100	350	1700
Other	170	20	350	300	800
All sectors	2700	400	2000	1000	6100

Note: All data are in petajoules. Some totals may differ from the sums of the items, due to rounding of the data.

The right-hand part of the table now describes where it was used. The categories of consumer are fairly straightforward. **Transport** covers both public and private, carrying both people and goods, in road vehicles, trains, and planes (internal flights only). **Industry** is obvious; but note that this item doesn't include energy used by the energy industries themselves. **Domestic** includes all the buildings that people live in; and **other** is everything else: shops and offices, schools and colleges, farms, museums, etc. At this final-use stage, the categories of energy need to be changed slightly: 'liquid' now refers to all the oil products (diesel, petrol, heating oil, aviation fuel, etc.); 'solid' includes coke and smokeless fuels as well as coal; and 'electricity' now means all electricity, from power-stations of every type.

Having carefully tracked all the energy purchased by everyone in each sector, we obtain a figure of 6100 PJ for the total energy consumption. This is a great deal less than the 8500 PJ on the supply side, so it appears that our balance-sheet doesn't balance. This is of course, no surprise, because the two sides are not talking about the same thing. On the left we have primary energy and on the right, **final-use energy.** The difference between the two, well over a quarter of the original energy, is the energy 'lost' by the energy industries in converting the primary energy into the forms of energy that we, the consumers, want to use.

The consumption part of the table allows us to look at this final-use energy in two ways. The 'total' column on the right shows the amount going to each of the four sectors. It reveals, for instance, that we spend more energy on transporting ourselves and our possessions from place to place than we do on manufacturing things, or just living at home. Another way to divide up the final-use energy is shown in the four entries along the bottom line, 'All sectors'. A striking feature here is how little anybody wants in the form of solid fuels. This category would have looked very different back in the days of coal fires and steam trains, but even industry uses only a sixth of its energy in this form today. The demand for fuel for internal combustion engines and the preference for gas central heating are obvious, as is the ever-growing demand for electricity. (While total UK energy consumption has changed only slightly over recent years, electricity consumption continues to climb by a per cent or so each year.)

Figure 3.1 shows the data of Table 3.1 in graphical form: first the supply and then the consumption divided in the two ways described. The fourth column, on the right, offers yet another method. It asks what the energy is used for. This is much less easy to discover. The electricity company can't tell from the meter reading what you have been doing with each kWh you are about to pay for—you could have used it for cooking the dinner, watching TV, or trimming the hedge. How much of the consumption in an office block is used for lighting and how much to run computers—or to make coffee? Data like this must be obtained by surveys, by asking sample groups of consumers, and the results can be subject to quite large errors. Nevertheless, it is useful information. Consider 'low-temperature heat', for instance: the energy needed to keep us warm at home and at work, and to provide hot water. 'High temperatures' in contrast are the sort of temperatures needed for many industrial processes. If electricity, generated using high-temperature steam, is being used for purposes where all we need is gentle warmth, perhaps we have identified one area where a change would mean better use of energy. This is certainly a question to return to later.

A National Power System

A great deal of information is missing from the balance-sheet of Table 3.1. In particular, it tells us nothing about the reasons for the difference between the total primary energy consumption on the left and the total final-use energy on the right. For that we need a more detailed version, showing all the conversion processes in the middle. There are many of these processes, each involving some 'lost' energy: oil refining, conversion of coal to other solid fuels, pumping gas through pipelines, etc. But the chief culprit is the generation of electricity. The 1000 PJ of electricity we consume each year—nearly 5000 kWh per head of the population—accounts for about two thousand of the lost petajoules. So we'll look at the details for this case.

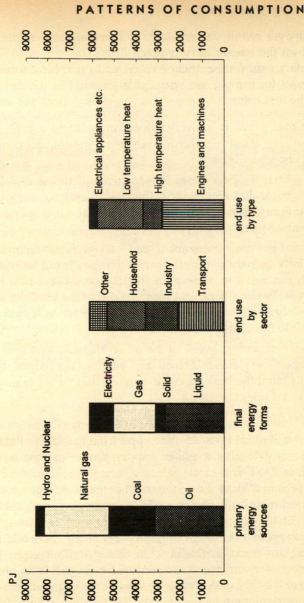

PJ

9000
8000
7000
6000
5000
4000
3000
2000
1000
0

Hydro and Nuclear

Natural gas

Coal

Oil

primary energy sources

Electricity

Gas

Solid

Liquid

final energy forms

Other

Household

Industry

Transport

end use by sector

Electrical appliances etc.

Low temperature heat

High temperature heat

Engines and machines

end use by type

Fig. 3.1 Patterns of energy use, UK 1995

Figure 3.2 has the information. Notice that it has two vertical scales: on the left we have terawatt-hours (billions of kWh), the customary unit for electrical energy, and on the right we have petajoules for comparison with Table 3.1 and Fig. 3.1. Let's start with the first column.

- The coal input to power-stations amounts to a little under 1500 PJ, or about two-thirds of the total annual coal consumption shown in Table 3.1.

- Then there is the nuclear input, currently the second largest contributor. In order to show this, we've adopted the UK convention in this case, entering an input of about three times the measured electrical output.

- Natural gas contributes about 500 PJ, a significant amount, particularly as only five years earlier the gas input would have been too small to appear on the diagram. (This twenty-fold increase between 1990 and 1995, a result of the 'dash for gas', is certainly another thing we'll return to later when we ask about possible future developments.)

- The oil etc. entry covers all the other 'thermal' power-stations (Chapter 5 explains this term), and includes not only oil-fuelled plants but those burning more than one fuel, or waste materials such as domestic rubbish.

Britain also has a contribution from hydroelectricity, as we saw in Chapter 2, but this is too small to appear in Fig. 3.2. We have then a total input to all the public supply power-stations of about 3000 PJ, or 830 TWh.

The second column shows the result of the next stage: an electrical output marginally under 300 TWh, or about 35 per cent of the input. All the rest has become waste heat—more than enough energy to provide central heating for every single household in the country! Unfortunately this is not just a result of incompetence in running power-stations; as we see in Chapter 5, it is an essential feature of the type of power-station we have, and such losses—or worse—are common to all countries that rely on fossil or nuclear fuels for their electric power. So, assuming that we are on the

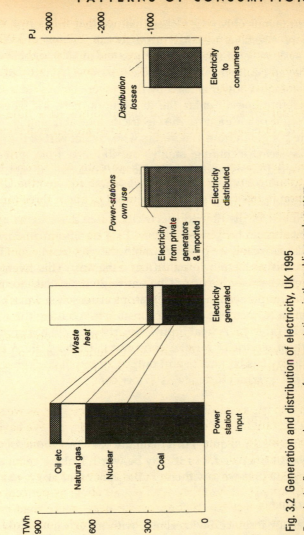

Fig. 3.2 Generation and distribution of electricity, UK 1995

Data in the first two columns are for power stations in the public supply system.
The heading 'oil etc.' includes plants burning mixed fuels and wastes.
The output of hydroelectric and wind-power plants is too small to appear separately on this scale.

whole in favour of saving rather than wasting energy, there are two more questions we shall need to ask: can we change our power systems, or if not, can we make use of all this heat?

We haven't quite finished with the losses yet. About 5 per cent of the generated power is used by the power-stations themselves, and therefore doesn't enter the distribution network. There are also a couple of additions to the electricity total at this stage. A few TWh are bought in from generators who are not part of the public power system, including small contributions from privately-owned wind-farms and small-scale hydroelectric plants. Then there are 15–20 TWh of net imports, arriving from France via a power cable laid under the Channel. The third column in Fig. 3.2 shows the total distributed electricity, after these items are all taken into account.

Finally, however, we have yet another loss: 5–10 per cent of the energy vanishes literally into thin air on the way to the consumers, again for reasons which can't be entirely eliminated, no matter how efficient the system. (These reasons are discussed in Chapter 7.) Ultimately, then, we find the consumers receiving the 1000 PJ we saw in Table 3.1. A total input of nearly 900 TWh has produced 280 TWh of electricity for the consumers. Under a third of the input energy has become useful output, or to put it another way, the overall 'system efficiency' is 31 per cent.

Other Countries

We shall not go into quite such detail for the other three countries discussed in Chapter 2, but it may be worth looking again at the consumption data we saw there, in the light of the above analysis.

Switzerland

Consider for instance Switzerland, with a per capita daily consumption (in 1994) of 95 kWh compared with 110 kWh in Britain. Then notice from Fig. 2.6 that hydroelectricity contributes about 60 per cent of the 'hydro and nuclear' total, say 14 kWh of the per capita 24 kWh. Now suppose the Swiss had to generate that electricity from fossil fuel or nuclear plant. They'd need an input of about three times the output, say 42 kWh; and the extra 28 kWh would raise their per capita consumption to 113 kWh, just about the same as Britain's.

Another difference between these two countries is in the proportions of oil and natural gas. As mentioned in the last chapter, this is largely a result of history. Having no coal, Switzerland never had a fully coal-based energy economy, and unlike Britain, didn't develop an extensive distribution system for gas from coal. Four or five decades ago, houses were mainly heated with wood, and nearly all electricity was hydroelectricity. Then, in the days of relatively cheap imported oil, this became the favoured fuel for central heating. As mentioned in Chapter 2, natural gas has become available only in recent years, and the distribution system has by no means reached all parts of the country yet, so oil and to some extent electricity, supplemented by wood, remain much more common than in Britain.

The USA

Comparison of the UK and the USA (Figs. 2.3 and 2.8) shows a remarkable similarity in the percentages of total consumption coming from the different sources. This is not perhaps surprising, as both countries have indigenous supplies of oil, coal, and natural gas. The American pattern of use is in fact fairly similar to that in Britain, with gas as the main heating fuel, oil used mostly for transport, and coal mainly in industry. A rather larger proportion of power-stations in the USA use oil or gas, but as we've seen, the UK use of gas is now growing rapidly. The main difference in the consumption shown in Figs. 2.3 and 2.8 is therefore in the total quantities of energy involved: 79 EJ for the USA compared with 8.6 EJ for Britain. In per capita terms, just about twice as much of every type of energy.

India

India, as we've already seen, is different from the other three countries in many respects. The large role played by the biofuels, providing energy for cooking and to a lesser extent heating for much of the population, is the most significant difference; but the pattern of the three fossil fuels also shows a contrast with the other countries. India has reasonably large coal reserves (enough to maintain present extraction rates for more than 200 years) and an established coal-mining industry which supplies her present needs and is growing at a few per cent a year. Figure 3.3 reproduces the two central columns of Fig. 3.1, for Britain, with the corresponding data for India, and we see at once the much greater use of solid fuels in India. Well over half the energy used by industry in India comes from coal, whereas in Britain the figure is about a sixth; and even more striking is the fact that 60 per cent of India's trains still run on coal.

India's proved reserves of oil and gas are much the same as those of the UK, but in both cases her annual production is about a quarter of the British—although it serves 15 times the population. Gas still plays a relatively small role, but output has risen rapidly over the past decade as this resource has been developed. Oil production, as in the USA, supplies about half the oil consumed, and India's known reserves are only enough to maintain even this production rate for about 30 years. As we've seen, the per capita total oil consumption is hardly more than a fiftieth of the American—and well under half of this tiny amount is used for motor vehicles. This raises a very serious issue for the future. If growing industrialization and a corresponding increase in the number of vehicles on the road were to bring Indian demand for oil to no more than a tenth of the present US level, it is easy to see that there would be a serious problem unless major further reserves are discovered. So yet another question we'll need to ask concerns the consequences in terms of energy supplies—and environmental effects too—if the countries of the developing world are ever to approach the present energy consumption levels of the industrialized countries.

Energy and GDP

The Gross Domestic Product (GDP) of a country is the total inland production of the national economic system; in other words, the value of everything the country produces in a year. We would

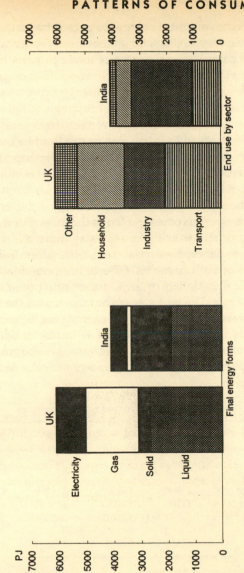

Fig. 3.3 Patterns of energy use, UK and India

The 50 per cent of India's energy supplied by biomass is not shown.
The population of India is about 15 times that of the UK.

obviously expect the amount of energy that a country consumes to be related in some way to this total, and common sense suggests that they might be proportional to each other: to produce twice as much output you'll need twice as much energy. This suggestion has caused much concern amongst world energy experts for many years, because it of course implies that if the people in the world's less prosperous countries are to improve their living standards, their demand for energy must increase in proportion; and where is all the energy to come from? Unfortunately, or perhaps fortunately, common sense has proved not entirely right. It is indeed the case that the poorest countries, those with the lowest national product in financial terms, use the least energy on the whole, whilst the very prosperous ones tend to use the most. But there are some interesting variations within this overall pattern.

Consider, for instance, Switzerland and the USA. Table 3.2 shows the GDPs of both countries. (The figures are obtained by converting the GDP in dollars or Swiss francs into pounds at the normal exchange rate. The next row of the table shows the figures in 'purchasing power' terms, taking into account the differences in the cost of goods in different countries.) To make comparisons easier, all the quantities are given per capita, i.e. the totals are divided by the populations, and the numbers are rounded off in

TABLE 3.2. *Energy and gross domestic product, four countries*

	Britain	Switzerland	USA	India[a]
Population (millions)	58	6.9	260	920
Annual per capita GDP				
Current exchange rate[b]	£10000	£24000	£14000	£180
Local purchasing power[c]	£10000	£15000	£15000	£800
Annual per capita energy consumption	150000 MJ	125000 MJ	300000 MJ	18000 MJ
Energy/GDP ratio[b]	15 MJ/£	5 MJ/£	21 MJ/£	100 MJ/£

Note: See the text for an explanation of this table.

  [a] Biofuels are not included in this table.
  [b] GDP converted to pounds sterling at the normal exchange rate.
  [c] GDP converted at a rate which takes into account its local purchasing power.

order to see the patterns more clearly. We see that the goods, services, etc. produced per person in the US are worth about £14 000 a year and in Switzerland £24 000. Using the data in Chapter 2, we can calculate the annual per capita energy consumption for the two countries, and the US figure is about $2\frac{1}{2}$ times the Swiss. So it appears that Switzerland produces goods, etc., worth more per person but uses less energy per person to do it.

A useful way to compare the 'energy efficiencies' of different countries is to divide the energy consumed by the GDP. The result is the **energy/GDP ratio**, which is effectively the amount of energy used in producing each pound's worth of national product: the megajoules per pound (MJ/£). The final line in the table shows this for our four countries. If the 'common sense' theory above were correct, with energy use proportional to GDP, every country would have the same ratio. Even with our small sample of four, this is very clearly not the case. Why not? The following are just a few of many possible answers:

- Some countries obtain their primary energy in more useful forms than others (hydroelectric rather than fossil-fuel power-stations, for instance).
- Some countries earn their GDP by less energy-intensive types of activity than others: agriculture rather than heavy industry, or commercial rather than industrial activity, and so on.
- Some countries use less energy than others for the same purposes (greater industrial energy efficiency, better insulation of buildings, etc.).
- Some countries use more energy than others to support economically non-productive activities (watching TV, going for a drive, reading a book).

We've already seen that the first of these may explain the difference in per capita energy use between Britain and Switzerland, but it doesn't explain how the average Swiss earns over twice as much for the same energy expenditure. How do the Swiss produce so much money with so little energy? Common sense again provides an explanation. Switzerland, as everyone knows, earns her money from tourists climbing up or sliding down mountains, from milk, butter, and cheese produced by Swiss cows grazing in Alpine meadows, and from rich Arabs grazing in Zürich banks. None of these activities is very energy-intensive, so the reason that Switzerland uses little energy is that she doesn't have much industry. Unfortunately common sense is wrong again. As we see in Fig. 3.4, industrial production contributes a slightly larger percentage to the Swiss GDP than to the British. Tourism does play a greater role in Switzerland, but the contributions from the agriculture and financial sectors show little difference. So we are left with the second and third of the above reasons. It is true that many (but by no means all) Swiss domestic and commercial buildings are better insulated; but the more severe climate tends to offset this. To analyse and compare industrial production in the two countries in terms of the types of product and the energy efficiencies with which they are produced would require more space than we can afford here, but it seems that countries such as Britain and the USA might learn something by a close inspection of Swiss methods.

India's energy/GDP ratio is much higher than the others. It is true that if we use the 'local costs' figure for GDP it comes down

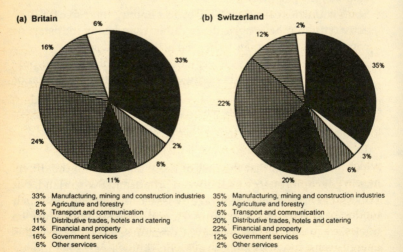

(a) Britain		(b) Switzerland	
33%	Manufacturing, mining and construction industries	35%	Manufacturing, mining and construction industries
2%	Agriculture and forestry	3%	Agriculture and forestry
8%	Transport and communication	6%	Transport and communication
11%	Distributive trades, hotels and catering	20%	Distributive trades, hotels and catering
24%	Financial and property	22%	Financial and property
16%	Government services	12%	Government services
6%	Other services	2%	Other services

Fig. 3.4 Contributions to Gross Domestic Product

to about the US value, and it is also the case that energy is often used less efficiently in less industrially developed countries, but this is to hide an important point. The essential and significant difference appears in the final column in Fig. 3.3. Well over half India's final-use energy (ignoring of course the large biofuels contribution) goes to industry. A developing country will use more energy per unit of output precisely because it is developing: developing its industries and developing an industrial infrastructure. Once more, it seems, we have a reason why energy consumption in the developing world is bound to increase, at least in the short term. Which raises another question: is energy conservation a luxury that only the wealthy can afford?

People Travelling

We'll finish this comparison of energy economies with a brief look at the second main destination of our primary energy: fuel for vehicles.

> *You consume 100 gallons of petrol a year driving to work every day in city traffic. Making the journey in a fully occupied Swissair airbus, your share would be less than 50 gallons. Aircraft are more energy-efficient than cars.*

True or false? We could equally well prove the reverse. On a reasonably clear road, four people in a small car could travel 50 miles on one gallon of petrol, i.e. the car achieves 200 passenger-miles per gallon. The average for commercial flights in modern aircraft (excluding Concorde) is about 40 passenger-miles per gallon. So aircraft are much less energy-efficient than cars.

Later, in Chapters 5 and 6, we'll investigate some of the factors which determine the energy efficiencies of motor vehicles; but here we look at the overall pattern. There are two aspects to this. We need to know how far people travel and we need to know the modes of travel they use. Data on walking, cycling, or riding horses are rather uncertain, so we'll confine ourselves to the main energy-using modes: road vehicles, aircraft, and trains.

There are some 600 million motor vehicles in use in the world, about one for every ten people in the entire population. At current rates of rise the number will reach a billion in less than 25 years. Consuming an average of 1½ gallons of fuel a day each, these vehicles account for about half the world's total primary oil consumption, a proportion which is also rising.

Comparison of travel patterns in our four countries brings few surprises. We saw in Table 2.2 that the per capita daily consumption of 'primary' oil is some 10 litres (2 gallons) in the USA but only about 5 litres in the two European countries, and a glance at Table 3.3 and Fig. 3.5 offers possible reasons for these differences. The average American travels 21000 km (13000 miles) in the course of a year, over four-fifths of it by private car and most of the rest by air. The Europeans use their cars for just as large a percentage of their journeys, but the total distance is only about two-thirds of the American. (Note that the total mileage for Switzerland includes cars passing through on business or holiday journeys, so the annual distance for the average resident is closer to the British figure than the table suggests.) The fact that the total US oil consumption is double the European but the car mileage is only 50 per cent greater obviously reflects the greater petrol consumption of American cars; but we must also remember that private cars are not the only consumers of oil products. In the US, they account for only a half to two-thirds of primary oil consumption, with the remainder used for air and some rail travel, the

TABLE 3.3. *Using the roads*

	Britain	Switzerland	USA	India
Population (millions)	58	6.9	260	920
Cars (millions)	20	3.1	144	3.0
People per car[a]	3	2¼	1¾	300
Total annual travel per person, all modes (km)	13000	17000[b]	21000	650
Percentage by car	88	85	84	10

[a] 'People' include all adults and children. In the USA there are now more cars than people with driving licences.
[b] Includes an appreciable contribution from traffic travelling between other countries.

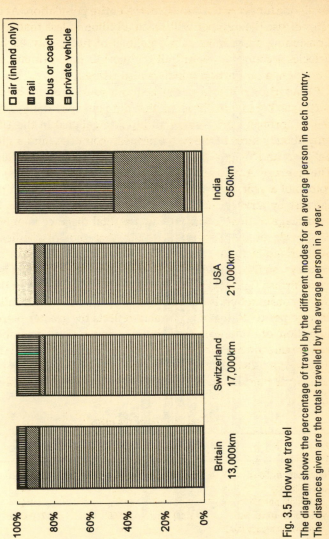

Fig. 3.5 How we travel

The diagram shows the percentage of travel by the different modes for an average person in each country.
The distances given are the totals travelled by the average person in a year.

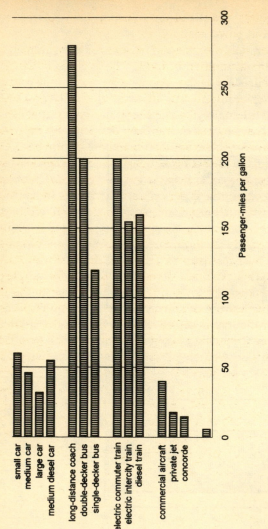

Fig. 3.6 Passenger-miles per gallon

The bars show the passenger-miles travelled for each gallon of petrol or the equivalent with average occupancy. The data for electric trains assume that the electricity is generated at normal power-station efficiency.

transport of goods, and all the non-transport uses, such as heating, input to oil-fired power-stations, etc.

The transport data also suggest reasons for the extremely small per capita oil consumption in India. The average Indian travels about a thirtieth as far as the average American in the course of a year but consumes only about a fiftieth as much oil. Fig. 3.5 reveals one important difference: the average Indian covers nine-tenths of his or her journeys by bus or train and one-tenth by car or plane, whilst the average American does just about the reverse. As Fig. 3.6 shows, even the least efficient bus with an average load carries a given number of people twice as far on a gallon of petrol as the 'best' car. Of course, the 50 per cent of the average Indian journey that is taken by train doesn't add proportionately to oil consumption, but another look at Fig. 3.6 shows that steam trains, however romantic, are hardly the most energy-efficient means of transport. Nevertheless, the consequences of these patterns of use for national oil consumption explain why there is pressure for people in the industrialized countries to adopt something closer to the Indian pattern, making less use of cars and more use of public transport. It is a salutary thought in the morning rush-hour that a full coach could easily be achieving twenty times the passenger-miles per gallon of a car with a single person in it—and occupying a much smaller road area per person.

PART II

Technologies

The first three chapters have built up a picture of the way things are. Now we move on from the energy of the world to the world of energy, and in the next few chapters look at why things are the way they are. Not, of course, why people behave as they do. If there is an answer to that difficult question, it's not in this book. Our concern is with the much simpler matter of why things behave as they do. What picture of the physical world and its laws allows the engineer to predict that massive coils of wire spinning at high speed will generate electric power; or that a suitable wafer of silicon lying in the sun will do the same?

To understand such matters is important not only for engineers. We all need to know about the energy systems we use—in order to use them as efficiently as possible, if for no other reason. Whether you are considering the merits of combined heat and power for the industry which you happen to control, or the advantages (or otherwise) of leaving the immersion heater on all night, an appreciation of the basic science at least clarifies the situation, and may even lead to a clear-cut answer. And there is the future. Most of us would like to reduce next year's fuel bills, a subject not unconnected with thermal insulation or the efficiency of the combustion process. Or on the larger scale, we might like to know how much useful energy we are likely to get from solar radiation, the wind, or the ocean waves. Scientific laws do not prescribe what we ought to do, but they can say what is possible—or more important, impossible—and can often tell us the likely consequences of our proposed actions.

This is not intended as a science textbook, and no single work could be a textbook of all the technologies from the gas turbine to the solar cell. The plan, therefore, is to be selective in order to avoid being superficial. We start with the basics, the picture of a physical world made up of atoms. By asking exactly what happens when we light the gas under the saucepan, we can see why burning fossil fuels must produce carbon dioxide. Heat is important for all energy systems (either we are trying to produce it or we are trying to get rid of it) and by investigating the difference at the atomic level between a hot object and a cold one, we might begin to understand why the power-station and the internal combustion engine waste two-thirds or more of the energy of their fuels. Looking at electric currents on a similarly detailed scale, we can see why energy is always wasted in power lines. A nuclear reactor, switched off, inevitably continues to generate heat; an ordinary 60-watt light bulb produces 56 watts of heat and only 4 watts of light. All these facts are fairly direct consequences of basic science.

On the other hand, the fact that a car engine is used most of the time at well under its already low optimum efficiency is a matter of technology. It is not an inevitable consequence of the laws of science but a result of requirements we put on the engine for other reasons. The same is true of other, broader questions, such as why we prefer gas to coal, or whether we could replace our present systems altogether and use energy from the sun, wind, waves, or tides. These too are technological matters—in the sense that factors such as convenience, economics, or environmental effects play an important role. Science, as always, sets limits to the possible, but issues such as these put constraints on the attainable.

4

Fuels

Introduction

This chapter discusses probably the oldest of all technologies: the burning of fuels to provide heat. Already familiar to our prehistoric ancestors, the combustion of fuels still accounts for nearly all our present-day use of primary energy. The term **combustion**, however, has a much wider meaning now than in the past. An internal combustion engine or gas turbine may not seem much like a wood fire, but as we shall see, the fuels used in these modern systems have much in common with a log of wood, and their combustion involves essentially the same basic processes. (The nuclear reactor, whose heat comes from an entirely different source, is the exception—see Chapter 8.)

We'll start, then, with some ideas about heat and heating and about the process of combustion, taking the fuels in turn: first the fossil fuels—gas, oil, and coal—and then the biofuels. A detailed look at large power-station boilers allows us to assess their emissions, the pollution problems these pose, and possible ways of dealing with them. Finally, we'll look at some of the methods for converting one fuel into another—obtaining oil or gas from coal, or wood, or even domestic rubbish.

Heating Things

What is heat? What is the difference between a cold object and a hot one? What happens as we heat a pan of soup over a flame, or water in an electric kettle? The simple answer is that heat energy is transferred from the flame or the hot element to the liquid and its container. But can we say more than that?

We'll come to the sources of the heat shortly, but let's start with the materials that are being heated. What is happening to them? The physicist's answer is that the extra energy is increasing the motion of their atoms and molecules. We'll look at atoms in more detail later, but for present purposes we need only to picture them as the extremely tiny particles from which everything is made. A **molecule** is a cluster of atoms—anything from two to many thousands of them. It is very important that when we think of materials as consisting of these tiny particles we have a dynamic picture in mind, not a static one. The air around us consists mainly of molecules of nitrogen and oxygen—and a lot of empty space. The distance between molecules is about ten times their size (it is their consequent freedom to move which makes air a gas and not a liquid or solid), and we can visualize the molecules of the air in the room as like a swarm of gnats, moving incessantly. Their average speed is high, about 1000 mph, and when the air is heated this speed increases, the change between ice-cold air and air on a very hot day being about 5 per cent.

For solids and liquids the detail is different but the effect much the same. The atoms of a solid cling together fairly closely (one reason why you don't fall through your chair), but not so closely that they cannot move. Each can oscillate in the space available between all its neighbours, and the hotter the material the more vigorous the oscillations. Our picture of a solid is thus of a quivering mass of particles. A little more energy and they start to leave their positions altogether. At first, they are still packed fairly closely but are able to slither between each other, so we have a liquid. Finally, when they break free altogether we are back with the gas.

For any material, then, there is a way of looking at two important quantities: **temperature** is simply a measure of the average speed of the atoms or molecules: 'hotter is faster'. And **heat** is the energy added or removed in order to change the temperature, to melt a solid, or to boil or freeze a liquid.

Burning

Where does the heat come from? To answer this question, we start with some more. What makes something a fuel? Why will wood burn, or oil, but not sand or sea water? What is 'burning'?

Let's start with a few well-known facts.

- Burning needs air—or to be precise, oxygen.
- The fuel and oxygen both disappear in the process, leaving other, different substances.
- Heat is produced—i.e. energy is released.

The 'different substances', the combustion products, are the result of chemical changes: rearrangements of atoms into different types of molecule. Our picture of combustion, then, is that the atoms making up the fuel molecules and the oxygen molecules rearrange themselves to form the new molecules of the combustion products. Notice that in this chemical change the total number of atoms of each type remains the same. Atoms are very persistent creatures, and only in nuclear reactions shall we see them change into other species. On the large scale, we call a material consisting entirely of one species of atom an **element**, and a material consisting of more than one species a **compound**. (Table 7.1 in Chapter 7 shows the elements, with some details of their atoms.)

The Fossil Fuels

As we have seen, more than three-quarters of the world's total energy consumption comes from the fossil fuels: natural gas, oil, and coal. As their name suggests, all the fossil fuels were originally living matter: plants or animals that were alive hundreds of million years ago, in the age of the dinosaurs. Coal seams, for instance, come from the accretion of layers of dead trees and other plants, initially protected from atmospheric decay by water, and ultimately compressed to a tenth or less of their original thickness. They range from a few inches to hundreds of feet thick and can lie thousands of feet under the surface of the Earth or so near that they penetrate it. Oil and gas have similar origins, starting as microscopic organisms thought to have inhabited ancient seas.

With the passage of time, their remains, covered with layers of mud and sand, underwent chemical changes leading to the fluid fuels that we extract today. (See also 'Reserves and Resources' in Chapter 12.)

Oil and natural gas have been called the 'noble fuels'. This is by analogy with the noble metals (silver and gold, etc.) and whilst we may have reservations about the results of using them, there is justification for the name. They are amongst the most concentrated natural stores of energy, and being fluids, are not difficult to store, are relatively easy to move from place to place, and are very convenient to use. We don't need a detailed technical analysis to see why most people who had the opportunity changed from coal to gas for household heating and hot water; or why we are reluctant to adopt the electric car when we have a system that can load a thousand megajoules of energy in a matter of seconds, store it within the volume of a small petrol tank, and deliver power at a rate of tens of kilowatts. (It should be added that the nucleus of an atom is a very much more concentrated energy store than any fossil fuel; but perhaps not quite as convenient for everyday use.)

Natural Gas

Natural gas is the simplest of the naturally occurring fuels, and is therefore a nice example for our first detailed look at combustion. It is simple because, apart from minor impurities, it consists of one well-defined material, the gas called **methane**. This is a compound of two elements: carbon and hydrogen, each methane molecule consisting of one carbon atom surrounded by four hydrogen atoms: CH_4. Burning, as we've seen, requires oxygen, and an oxygen molecule consists of two oxygen atoms: O_2. The result is that one methane molecule reacts with two oxygen molecules, as follows:

$$CH_4 + 2O_2 \rightarrow CO_2 + 2H_2O + energy$$

The combustion products are easy to identify: carbon dioxide and water, the latter usually in the form of water vapour or steam.

(Note that the numbers of atoms are unchanged: one C, four Hs, and four Os.)

We still have to see why energy becomes available from this re-assembling of atoms. The essential starting-point for an explanation is that an input of energy is needed to separate any molecule into its component atoms. (If this were not so, the world about us would spontaneously fall to pieces all the time, with wooden chairs turning into gases and a little soot, and table salt into a rather nasty metal and a poisonous vapour.) There are four different molecules in the equation above, and the important feature—not of course evident from the equation—is that the energy input needed to take apart the methane and oxygen is appreciably less than the energy released when the same atoms come together as carbon dioxide and water. It is this ease with which they 'come apart' and the eagerness of their elements to react with oxygen that makes the compounds of carbon and hydrogen such good fuels. Once the process starts—once you light the flame—it continues as long as the supplies of fuel and oxygen are maintained. The spare energy, having nowhere else to go, increases the speeds of all the molecules. In other words, the burning gases become hot—reaching thousands of degrees Celsius in a fierce gas flame.

With a little more information, we can make useful deductions from the chemical equation above. If we know how the masses of the different atoms are related, we can easily find how much carbon dioxide is produced for each kilogram of gas we burn. Table 4.1 shows the reasoning and the result: we release just under three kilograms of CO_2 per kilogram of gas. Consider the following. The average person in Britain uses about 1300 kWh of heat energy a year just for hot water. Burning natural gas releases about 14 kg of CO_2 per 100 kWh of heat energy produced (Table 4.2), so each person's baths, showers, clothes washing, etc. contribute about a fifth of a tonne a year of carbon dioxide to the atmosphere. (The reality will be a lot worse, as domestic boilers are not usually very efficient; and using electricity instead won't help, because the power-station will have released about a tonne and a half of CO_2 in producing it!)

Table 4.1. *Calculating the CO_2 released in combustion*

Data

The mass of one carbon atom is 12 times the mass of a hydrogen atom.
The mass of one oxygen atom is 16 times the mass of a hydrogen atom.

Calculation

We can use these masses in the equation for natural gas combustion:

$$CH_4 + 2O_2 \rightarrow CO_2 + 2H_2O$$
$$12 + 4 \times 1 + 2 \times (2 \times 16) \rightarrow 12 + 2 \times 16 + 2 \times (2 \times 1 + 16)$$
$$16 + 64 \rightarrow 44 + 36$$

Showing that burning 16 kg of natural gas (methane) requires 64 kg of oxygen and releases 44 kg of CO_2 and 36 kg of steam.

Burning 1 kg of natural gas produces 55 MJ of heat, so 16 kg produce 880 MJ. We can therefore say that 1 kg of carbon dioxide is released for every 20 MJ of heat produced (or 1 tonne for every 20 GJ).

Table 4.2. *Heat and CO_2 from fuels*

Fuel	Heat produced by combustion			CO_2 released (kg)	
	kWh per kilogram	GJ per tonne[a]	GJ per cu m	per 100 kWh of heat	per GJ of heat
Coal (UK average)	7.2	26	50	35	120
Oil	12	42	34	20	75
Natural gas (methane)	15	55	0.04[b]	14	50
Hydrogen	37	130	0.012[b]	none	none
Wood (air-dry)	4.2	15	10	~20	~80
Straw (baled)	3.9	14	1.4	~25	~100
Dung (dried)	4.4	16	4	—	—
Domestic refuse	2.5	9	1.5	—	—

Note: The data for the biofuels are very variable. Note also that if they are grown sustainably the net CO_2 production can be close to zero.

[a] 1 GJ per tonne is the same as 1 MJ per kilogram.

[b] Gases at normal pressure.

Oil

Oil is a more complex material than natural gas, but not unrelated. Methane is the simplest of a range of compounds of carbon and hydrogen called the **hydrocarbons**, and crude oil is a mixture of many of these. We find that in general crude oils contain 80–90 per cent (by mass) of carbon and 10–15 per cent of hydrogen, with up to 4 per cent sulphur, some oxygen and nitrogen, and traces of other elements. Remembering that a carbon atom has 12 times the mass of a hydrogen atom, we can deduce that the average ratio of carbon to hydrogen atoms must be about 7:12, or very roughly one to two.

What then are the 'oil molecules'? A molecule of any specific hydrocarbon has not only a particular carbon–hydrogen ratio but also a characteristic arrangement of its atoms. One series that plays a major role in many oil products is the family of **paraffins**. Figure 4.1(*a*) shows a few of these: strings of carbon atoms with hydrogen atoms attached. The first four members of the series are gases at normal temperatures. Bubbling off as the oil flows from the well, these were for many years allowed to escape or burned on site, but this waste of valuable fuel is changing and the gases are now collected where economically feasible.

A very important feature for the processing of crude oil is the fact that as you progress up the series the temperature at which each hydrocarbon becomes a gas (the boiling-point) rises. Pentane is just still a liquid at normal temperatures, octane can be heated above the boiling point of water before it vaporizes, and so on. This progression is the basis for separation by distillation: if the crude oil is heated to about 200°C everything whose boiling-point is lower than this will boil off and can be collected and condensed. At this particular temperature just under a fifth of the contents of the crude are distilled and the result, 'straight-run gasoline', contains all the paraffins from pentane to octane. There are other hydrocarbons present, too, and a couple of the 200 or so in petrol (gasoline) are also shown in Fig. 4.1(*b*). The need to increase the proportion of petrol obtained from crude oil led many years ago to the development of 'cracking', breaking down heavier hydrocarbons into lighter molecules. This process, and others such as reforming and purifying the products, can consume up to 5 per cent of the energy of the oil entering a refinery.

The combustion of any hydrocarbon is similar to that of methane. Consider for instance pentane, one constituent of petrol. To

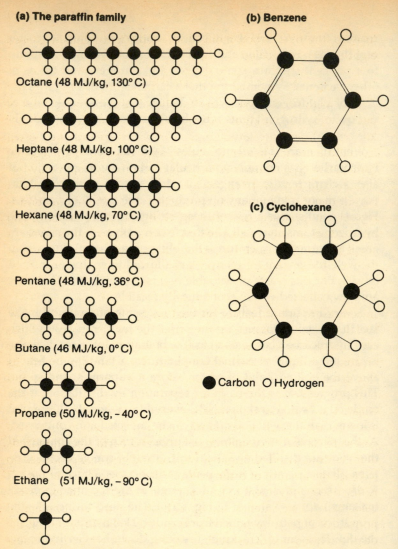

(a) The paraffin family

Octane (48 MJ/kg, 130° C)

Heptane (48 MJ/kg, 100° C)

Hexane (48 MJ/kg, 70° C)

Pentane (48 MJ/kg, 36° C)

Butane (46 MJ/kg, 0° C)

Propane (50 MJ/kg, – 40° C)

Ethane (51 MJ/kg, – 90° C)

Methane (55 MJ/kg, –160° C)

(b) Benzene

(c) Cyclohexane

● Carbon ○ Hydrogen

Fig. 4.1 Hydrocarbons

The figures in brackets show the heats of combustion and the normal boiling temperatures of the paraffins.

Molecules are, of course, three-dimensional entities, so these diagrams must be regarded as schematic versions of the arrangements of the atoms. Some of the paraffins also occur in other patterns, with side-branches.

'use up' the five carbon atoms and twelve hydrogens, we need eight oxygen molecules:

$$C_5H_{12} + 8O_2 \rightarrow 5CO_2 + 6H_2O + \text{energy}$$

A little arithmetic leads to the conclusion that burning 72 kg of pentane releases 220 kg of carbon dioxide—about 3 kg of CO_2 per kilogram of pentane. Although the conditions are rather different from those in a gas heater, the combustion of petrol in an internal combustion engine involves just this reaction between the hydrocarbons and oxygen from the air. One litre of pentane is about two-thirds of a kilogram, so we see that if the above equation is typical, you produce some 2 kg of CO_2 for each litre of petrol you burn. At an average of 10 miles per litre, and 5000 miles a year, a small car can therefore be responsible for adding one tonne of carbon dioxide a year to the atmosphere.

Coal

In contrast to natural gas or oil, coal might be called the 'ignoble' fuel. It is indeed a particularly unattractive energy source. A large coal-fired power-station can produce enough ash in a year to cover an acre of ground to the height of a six-storey building, while its flue gases may carry several tonnes a day of sulphur dioxide and nitrogen oxides into the atmosphere. The ash, if not carefully isolated, will pollute the ground-water with a variety of unpleasant substances such as sulphuric acid and arsenic, and the flue gases are claimed to contaminate lakes and harm trees hundreds of miles downwind. Compared with oil and gas, coal produces up to twice the amount of carbon dioxide for the same useful heat. It is much less convenient to transport, store, and use. Its extraction leads to land subsidence and spoil heaps, or the environmental horrors of strip mining, and is responsible world-wide for the deaths of hundreds of miners in an average year. There is obviously no difficulty in explaining why coal consumption has risen much less rapidly than total energy consumption throughout most of the present century, especially in those countries wealthy enough to afford the more attractive alternatives.

The oil crises of the 1970s did slightly reduce the relative decline. In the USA in particular, with the growing awareness of the uncertainties of imported oil supplies, attention suddenly focused on one overriding advantage of coal: *there is a very great deal of it.* The world's known reserves are sufficient to last for several centuries at current extraction rates. Moreover, the USA has about quarter of the total. So, as Fig. 4.2 shows, coal began to come back into favour. After the brief pause in all energy consumption during the recession of the early 1980s, the growth in demand for coal continued at its increased rate for nearly another decade. But the first half of the 1990s have seen a slight decline, against an overall energy consumption which remained steady or even rose slightly. A sign perhaps that memories are short?

Many of the unattractive features listed above are due to the

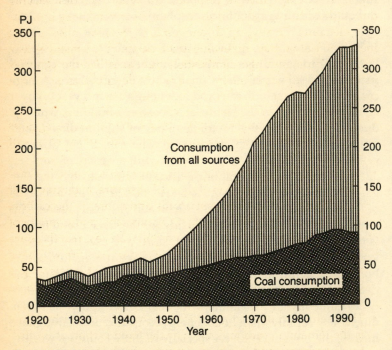

Fig. 4.2 World coal consumption and total consumption, 1920–1994
Commercially traded sources only.

extremely complex composition of coal. At the molecular level its structure cannot be analysed into relatively straightforward compounds as with natural gas or even crude oil. Rings of six carbon atoms play an important role, forming layered arrangements that incorporate not only hydrogen but significant amounts of oxygen and nitrogen. As we'll see later, compounds consisting mainly of carbon, hydrogen, and oxygen are characteristic of living materials, and in this sense coal is closer to its origins than are oil and gas. Indeed, the different types or **ranks** of coal, from anthracite at one extreme to 'brown coal' and lignite at the other, can be regarded as members of a sequence which also includes peat and wood (Fig. 4.3). The ratio of carbon to hydrogen atoms is roughly 1:1, which means an increased proportion of CO_2 in the combustion products (Table 4.2). The structure also unfortunately includes varying quantities of sulphur and traces of other environmentally undesirable elements. Finally, up to one-tenth of the total mass can be inert material with no fuel value at all, destined to remain as ash.

Not surprisingly, the combustion of coal is a more complex process than for gas or oil. In fact, it is best described as a series of processes:

- All coal contains some moisture, and during the early stages, as the coal heats up, this evaporates, using a little of the energy of the coal in doing so.
- As the temperature rises, a range of gases is evolved. These come from the dissociation of the coal structure, and carry most of the hydrogen and oxygen atoms and some of the carbon. They include carbon monoxide (CO), methane, and a variety of other hydrocarbons, and their important feature is that these are fuels. (Anyone who has watched a wood or coal fire will have noticed the spurts of intense flame as these little jets of gas burn.) As much as half the energy of the coal is carried in these gases, the **volatile matter**.
- The useful part of what is left after the volatile matter has gone is the remaining carbon, known as the **fixed carbon**. It is effectively charcoal, and burns in oxygen from the air:

$$C + O_2 \rightarrow CO_2$$

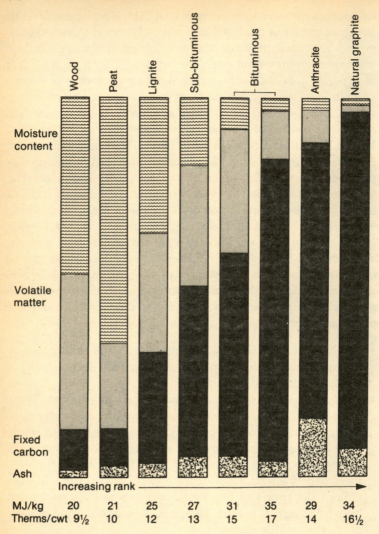

Fig. 4.3 Proximate analysis of fuels

- Finally, with all the fuel burnt, any inert material remains as ash.

This analysis carries a number of lessons for the designer of any furnace burning solid fuels, a subject to which we return shortly. First, however, we must look at the remaining important class of fuels: those which come from materials that were alive much more recently.

The Biofuels

The common feature of the fossil fuels and the biofuels is that both were originally living matter. The very important difference between them is the time-scale. The living material that became the fossil fuels died many millions of years ago, but the biofuels derive from matter that was alive within the past few years—or even last week. The term has come to cover an extraordinarily broad range of materials. Those already widely used in different parts of the world include not only wood, but plant wastes such as straw, sugar-cane residues or rice husks, and animal wastes such as human sewage and dried dung, both valuable sources of energy. Ordinary domestic rubbish is also proving a useful resource as a fuel for power-stations, or in landfills, where it generates a gas that can be burned. Then there is increasing interest in 'energy crops', not only wood but other, faster-growing plants which can be cut regularly to serve as fuel. As we saw in Chapter 2, it is estimated that these various sources already contribute at least one-seventh of the world's primary energy.

Carbohydrates

Even a simple plant is a much more complex system than a piece of coal, and there aren't any tiny particles that we can simply identify as 'wood molecules' or 'straw molecules'. But this doesn't mean that we can't say anything about the combustion of biofuels. Biomass, living matter, is a fuel because, like the fossil fuels, it contains suitable compounds of carbon and hydrogen; but the sugars, starches, cellulose, etc. which make up 'vegetable matter' differ from the fossil fuels in that their molecules also contain appreciable quantities of oxygen. We'll use the **carbohydrates** as an example. These are large molecules with a ratio of approximately one oxygen atom and two hydrogen atoms to each carbon atom, and we can represent a typical sub-unit of a carbohydrate molecule as $[CH_2O]$. In combustion, one such unit reacts with one molecule of oxygen:

$$[CH_2O] + O_2 \rightarrow CO_2 + H_2O + energy$$

The source of energy, as before, lies in the rearrangement of the atoms to form new molecules, but because the biomass already contains some oxygen, the energy produced per kilogram of fuel is rather less than from the fossil fuels (Table 4.2). One consequence of this is that the amount of carbon dioxide released per unit of heat output lies in the same range as for the fossil fuels.

Less energy and the same CO_2 with it would suggest that the biofuels are not very attractive; but that is to ignore the essential point: *these are renewable energy sources*. A stick or a bundle of straw, unlike a piece of coal, can be replaced in a relatively short span of time, and if we take care to grow our biofuels in a sustainable way, we can continuously replace everything: the fuel, the oxygen, and even the energy we've released. Or to be more precise, the sun, a very sustainable source indeed, will replace them for us. How does it do this?

Photosynthesis

How does a plant grow? The answer can be very complicated, because most living things are complicated systems. But, as with combustion, we'll take a simplified view, starting with the name of the process. **Photosynthesis** comes from two Greek words, *photo*: to do with light and *synthesis*: putting together. Plants are put together by light.

To be more specific, a growing plant takes in carbon dioxide and water from its surroundings and uses energy from sunlight to convert these into the 'vegetable matter'. I'll use the carbohydrate unit again as an example, but looking now at its synthesis rather than its combustion. The inputs are one molecule each of carbon dioxide and water, and of course some energy from the sun:

$$CO_2 + H_2O + energy \rightarrow [CH_2O] + O_2$$

It doesn't take much research to see that this is precisely the combustion process above, run backwards. As far as the materials are concerned, the solar energy has used all the combustion products and made them into new fuel.

It is an important feature of the natural world, that both the above processes occur continuously. The process described earlier as combustion also occurs in the much slower natural decomposition of the plant material using oxygen from the air. So when we burn biofuels, we do no more than would happen naturally, provided we take care not to use the biomass more rapidly than it regenerates. The critical issue is of course the proviso. If we are careful, we have a truly sustainable energy source, but if we chop down forests or otherwise reduce the Earth's plant resources faster than they can regenerate, the results could be much more serious than just a bare landscape. (Chapter 13 discusses this further.)

Furnaces and Boilers

The design of furnaces may not seem the most glamorous topic in the world, but it is certainly an important one in the world of energy. As we have seen, all but a tiny fraction of our primary energy comes from fuels—fossil or biofuel—and the first destination of three-quarters of these fuels is a furnace. (The destination of the remainder is the internal combustion engine, to which we return in the next chapter.) So the efficiency with which a furnace extracts energy from the fuel is a critical factor in determining how much gas we burn in heating our houses or how much coal is used to produce our electricity. The better the furnace, the lower the fuel requirement, and correspondingly, the less carbon dioxide and other undesirable materials we produce. Or in another context, the more efficient the stove, the less wood is needed to cook our meals and the less of our valuable vegetation we need to destroy.

This last example can serve to illustrate the situation facing anyone trying to design a really efficient system. How much wood do you think you would need to boil one litre of water on a fire? Common experience will give a rough answer, but we'll use easily available data to calculate it. Table 4.3 shows the reasoning, and the conclusion that we need about 34 cubic cm of wood: say, one thin stick about a foot long—to bring a whole litre of water to the boil! The obvious absurdity of the answer shows, not that our calculations are wrong, but that open fires are extremely inefficient.

Many interesting ideas have gone into the design of household boilers, and of cooking stoves using biofuels; but space doesn't allow discussion of all these systems, and we'll concentrate instead on one major consumer of fuels: the large 'boilers' used to produce steam in power-stations. They provide a useful study for several reasons:

- Their range of fuels includes almost everything discussed earlier in this chapter.
- At their best, they are amongst the most efficient fuel-burning systems we have.

TABLE 4.3. *How much wood to boil a litre of water?*

Data

Heat energy needed to raise the temperature of 1 litre of water by $1°C$	$= 4200\,J$
Heat energy released in burning 1 cubic metre of wood (Table 4.2)	$= 10\,GJ$
1 cubic metre is 1 million cubic centimetres	
10 gigajoules is 10 million kilojoules (kJ)	

Calculation

Heat energy needed to heat 1 litre of water from $20°C$ to $100°C$	$= 80 \times 4200\,J$
	$= 336\,kJ$
Heat energy released in burning 1 cubic centimetre of wood	$= 10\,kJ$
It follows that the amount of wood required is 33.6 cubic centimetres	

- Their waste products create some of the world's major pollution problems.
- There are interesting technologies that might overcome many of the problems, but these are not yet widely used.

We'll concentrate here on furnaces which burn solid fuels, the major input for power generation world-wide. (For accounts of the other components of a power-station, see 'Turbines' in Chapter 5 and 'Generators' in Chapter 7.)

The starting-point for the furnace designer must be the sequence of events described in the above section on coal. To extract the maximum energy from the solid fuel, both the fixed carbon and the volatile matter must be fully burnt. As one part is solid material and the other a stream of gases rising rapidly towards the flue, this is not simple. Modern plants have of course long abandoned the person with a shovel, and operate continuously, so the solids and gases must burn completely at about the same rate. The air supply is also critical. It must provide sufficient oxygen for complete combustion, but excess air is wasteful, carrying heat away up the chimney. As we are talking about a plant to produce steam, another requirement is for the best possible heat transfer from the burning fuel into the circulating water. Then there must be a method for dealing with the wastes, both solids and gases. This is such an important topic that we'll deal with it separately.

Figure 4.4 shows in schematic form three types of solid-fuel boiler. None of these, it should be noted, is fed with logs or large lumps of coal. In (*a*), the fuel is chopped or otherwise processed into pieces an inch or less in size. Fed in from a hopper or perhaps a conveyor belt, the fuel moves across the grate in an upward flow of air. With this arrangement, the fixed carbon burns on the grate and the volatile matter in the space above. Radiant heat from both reaches an array of tubes through which the water circulates, while the hot gases from the combustion pass between another set of tubes. Note that the few tubes shown in the diagram represent the large, much more complex array used in the actual system. Boilers of essentially this type are used for some smaller coal-fired

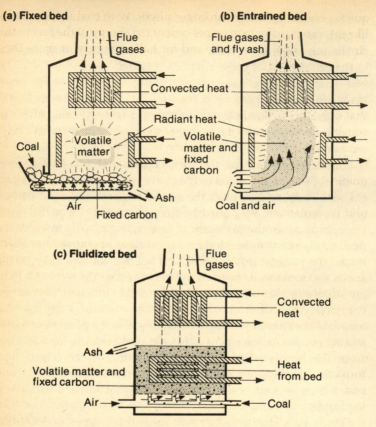

Fig. 4.4 Three types of coal-fired boiler

plant and for biofuels such as wood chips, suitably processed domestic wastes, and other materials which are not suitable for the more efficient type of boiler shown in (b).

The essential difference between (a) and (b) in Fig. 4.4 is that the fuel for the latter is pulverized into particles about a thousandth of an inch across, forming a dust so fine that it floats. This dust enters the boiler in the air stream, and the fixed carbon and the volatiles burn together. Not only is all the heat then produced in roughly the same part of the furnace, but the tiny particles burn more quickly and completely than larger pieces. With coal as fuel, plants like this can transfer over 90 per cent of the energy of the fuel to the circulating water (or steam), and for half a century or more they have been used in large coal-fired power-stations. The fact that the fuel is finely powdered has the further advantage that the same plant can burn different types of coal; but the converse of this is that only those fuels which can be pulverized into dry dust are suitable, and this limits its use with biofuels. Even for coal, there is one serious disadvantage. If the fuel is so fine that it floats, then so will the ash—straight up the chimney and into the atmosphere, unless it is collected.

The third type of plant in Fig. 4.4 uses a rather different principle. To appreciate why many people think that these **fluidized beds** could solve the problems of coal combustion and offer opportunities for burning many other fuels, we need to see how they work. The starting-point is a thick layer of inert material—sand, gravel, or even ash. This lies on a base with many small holes in it. Jets of air are blown up through these, and at a certain air speed the whole mass of material expands and starts to behave like a liquid. Objects in it will float or sink, it will flow and—very important for combustion and heat transfer—the inert particles bounce around as if they were indeed particles of a boiling liquid. In a furnace or power-station boiler, particles of fuel are fed into the bed, where, because of the constant motion and the air flow, both the fixed carbon and the volatile matter will burn quickly, heating the entire bed. The tubes carrying the water to be heated are also buried in the bed, and the excellent thermal contact with the constantly moving material means that good heat transfer can take place without the very high temperatures needed in an 'open' furnace. The whole system is much smaller than the corresponding conventional plant, and, as we'll see, can greatly reduce the output of pollutants. Fluidized bed systems have been used for some time in various industrial processes, but investment in the development of coal-burning plants was at a relatively low level until the 1970s. Work then accelerated, in the USA in particular, and the first plants came on stream in the 1980s, generating a few hundred megawatts in total.

Flue Gases

In the absence of any pollution reduction system, a modern 600 MW coal-fired power-station would release into the atmosphere in one hour:

- 2500 tonnes of nitrogen. This is four-fifths of the air drawn in for combustion and has passed largely unchanged through the whole system, except that heating it accounts for about half the energy loss in the boiler. Four-fifths of the air we breathe is in any case nitrogen, so it presumably remains harmless.

- 700 tonnes of carbon dioxide produced in combustion. CO_2 is a minor constituent of normal air and is not thought to be harmful to life in the concentrations produced by power-stations. (The cumulative effect of the CO_2 from all the world's power-stations on the climate is a question to which we return in Chapter 13.)

- 150 tonnes or more of steam. This is the other combustion product, and some also comes from moisture originally in the coal. Not condensing this accounts for the other half of the lost energy, but the flue gases need to stay hot if they are to rise out of the chimney.

- A tonne or so of oxides of nitrogen. These compounds (N_2O, NO, NO_2, etc., known generically as NOXs) are produced mainly by the interaction of nitrogen from the coal with excess oxygen, but also from nitrogen in the air. The higher the furnace temperature, the greater the production. NOXs contribute to acid rain and are damaging to health, but at present the worldwide contribution from power-stations is considerably less than that from internal combustion engines.

- From one to twenty tonnes of sulphur dioxide (SO_2). Sulphur is present in varying amounts in most fossil fuels, and cannot be removed entirely from coal because some of it lies within the molecular structure. The sulphur content of different coals varies from 1 to 5 per cent by weight and the power-station of this example would produce about four tonnes of SO_2 an hour from coal with 1 per cent sulphur. It is this sulphur compound which is held largely responsible for acid rain.

- 10–20 tonnes of fly ash. Otherwise known as 'particulates', this is the fine ash resulting from burning pulverized coal. Its main visible feature is that it is very dirty, but the tiny particles can damage the lungs, and may also contain poisonous impurities.

There are two ways of dealing with these pollutants: remove them, or don't produce them in the first place. The second is technically the more elegant solution, and is also at present the only way to deal with the NOXs. Adoption of the fluidized-bed boiler discussed above, operating at under $1000°C$ instead of the $2000°C$ in the hot gases of conventional plant, could go some way towards reducing NOX production. It is also possible to remove the sulphur compounds by introducing limestone particles into the bed. The SO_2 will react with this to produce calcium sulphate, a solid material that can be removed with the ash. Finally, as the fuel does not need to be pulverized for use in a fluidized bed, the ash from it is in the form of relatively large particles—not fly ash.

With existing power-station boilers, the only practicable option is to remove the fly ash and SO_2 from the flue gases. Although there are several techniques for doing this, relatively few coal-fired plants world-wide yet reach the best achievable levels of reduction of both pollutants. Before we criticize 'them' for failing to do this, we should perhaps place the problem in context. Three thousand tonnes an hour of gases leave the boiler. They are hotter than the hottest domestic oven, with a particulate level greater than in the worst ever London smog, a concentration of SO_2 a thousand times worse than downtown Los Angeles on a bad day, and enough moisture to cause it to start raining in the gas stream if the temperature falls below that of a moderate oven. Any cleaning system must be able to handle this hot, dirty corrosive mass on a continuous basis. It should remove most of the pollutants (about 90 per cent of the SO_2 and 99 per cent of particulates are current aims),

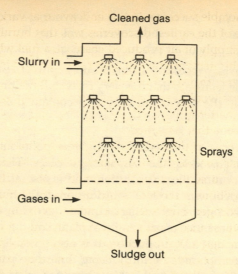

Fig. 4.5 Flue gas desulphurization: wet scrubber

use as little energy as possible, leave environmentally acceptable residues—and be cheap. There is of course no such system.

In Britain, most effort has gone into reducing the particulates in the flue gases, and it is claimed that the target of 99 per cent removal has been achieved. **Flue gas desulphurization** (FGD) to remove the sulphur compounds usually involves reacting the SO_2 with finely divided limestone (calcium carbonate, $CaCO_3$). This can be a dry process, but more usually a slurry or spray or jets of water are used to bring the limestone into contact with the flue gases, so that the resulting insoluble calcium sulphate precipitates and can be removed (Fig. 4.5). The extent to which FGD systems have been installed in coal-fired power-stations varies greatly from country to country. (See also Chapter 13, 'Acid Rain.')

Secondary Fuels

With enough effort, energy, and expense, it is in principle possible to convert any fuel into any other: coal or wood into gas or petrol, domestic rubbish into gas for cooking, etc. There have been a number of notable successes in this endeavour at various times in history. One of the earliest discoveries was that burning wood in a restricted supply of air produced charcoal, a fuel which burned at much higher temperatures and therefore greatly increased the range of metals that could be extracted and worked. In present-day terms, we would say that the charcoal-burner was allowing the volatile matter to burn off, and the metallurgists were using the fixed carbon that remained.

More recently, at the end of the eighteenth century, came the discovery that a useful gas could be produced by heating coal. The 'gas' was of course the volatile matter from the coal, and under suitable conditions a mixture could be produced that consisted mainly of hydrogen, methane, and carbon monoxide—three fuels. (The last of these made coal gas lethal if inhaled.) In this case the fixed carbon that remained, known as coke, was also sold as fuel. Coal gas or 'town gas' provided lighting throughout the nineteenth century and well into the twentieth, and had been an important fuel for cooking and heating for many years when 'natural gas' took its place—as recently as the 1960s in much of Europe.

The present century has seen intermittent attempts to produce liquid fuel from coal. Both Britain and Germany operated plants in the 1930s and the first production on an appreciable scale was in Germany during World War II. Cheap oil in the post-war period made further development uneconomic, and production ceased almost everywhere. South Africa, however, with relatively cheap coal and a sensitive reliance on imported oil, continued to develop its SASOL plant, which now uses some thirty million tonnes of coal a year to produce enough liquid fuel to replace five million tonnes of imported oil.

In the most recent decades, wider interest in the conversion of one fuel into another has come from two very different directions. The first, as with so many recent developments in the world of energy, was the series of oil crises in the 1970s. In the USA, the sudden realization that half the nation's oil supply depended on the goodwill of foreign producers led to a burst of new research into processes for the conversion of coal to motor fuel. Another, even more recent, period of development has come from the growing interest in the use of renewable energy resources, which has led to research into ways of converting biomass into more convenient fuels. (See for instance 'Gas Turbines' in Chapter 5.) The methods used for converting one fuel into another are as varied as the fuels themselves, but there are some common principles underlying many of them. So we'll look at these by considering just a few examples.

Means and Ends

Essentially, all the changes mentioned above are rearrangements of the Cs, Hs, Os, etc. of one fuel to make the different molecules or structures of another; simple enough to state, but not necessarily an easy process in practice. To bring out some of the problems, and a little of the science behind them, we'll consider one simple case. Suppose some far-sighted government, aware that the known natural gas reserves of the country it governs will last for no more than a few decades and that gas is a very popular fuel, has asked its chemical engineers to look at the possibilities for the production of methane.

Any sensible technologist will start with the cheapest raw materials, all other things being equal. But of course they never are; consider for instance the following splendid scheme. The desired product is methane: CH_4, so why not start with two very cheap materials, carbon dioxide and water?

$$CO_2 + 2H_2O \rightarrow CH_4 + 2O_2$$

There is just one flaw in this. A look at the earlier part of this chapter will show that it is simply the combustion of methane run backwards, and it follows that we would need to supply at least as much energy to produce the methane as would be obtained in burning it. Not a very useful source of fuel. Back to the drawing board then, with a change of raw materials. The country has large coal reserves, so how about coal and water? The reaction with the carbon of the coal might be:

$$C + H_2O \rightleftharpoons CO + H_2$$

No methane, but, as we'll see, the mixture of CO and H_2 would be useful. Common experience tells us, however, that putting a piece of coal in a bucket of water produces nothing more useful than a piece of wet coal. The process needs heat: not cold water but hot steam. If we use some of the energy of the coal to produce the steam, we do indeed find that the reaction takes place and the gases are produced. That double arrow then becomes the question, because, like any chemical process, this one can go either way. As soon as some carbon monoxide and hydrogen are produced, they will start reacting to give carbon and steam, and there will always be competition between the opposing processes. How can we ensure that the end result is what we want: more product than raw material? The answer is that without further data we can't; but there is one simple rule that might be useful:

- If a process is one that *uses* heat, it is favoured by higher temperatures, and conversely, processes that *produce* heat are favoured by lower temperatures

The rule is an example of a well-known physical law expressed politely as 'Nature is cussed'. (It is a version of the Second Law of Thermodynamics, which we'll meet in Chapter 5.) The 'carbon-steam reaction' above is one that needs heat, and increasing the temperature from, say, 700°C to 800°C can change the balance tenfold in favour of CO and H_2. The gasifiers used to produce gaseous fuel from solids, such as coal or various biofuels, run at these sorts of temperatures, and often at high pressures too. (For some of their uses, see 'Gas turbines' in the next chapter.) The mixture of carbon monoxide and hydrogen, known as **synthesis gas**, is also a useful starting-point for the production of **methanol**, a form of alcohol with the chemical formula CH_3OH. The point of this is that methanol is a liquid fuel, and we therefore have one possibility for motor fuel from coal or biomass (see below). Returning to the attempt to produce methane, suppose that the hydrogen now reacts with more carbon:

$$C + 2H_2 \rightleftharpoons CH_4$$

This reaction actually produces heat, so it looks an excellent prospect. But we must be careful. We have considered the final balance in a reaction, but not how long it takes to reach it. Cold hydrogen flowing over cold carbon may produce methane, but this won't help the nation's coming gas shortage if it takes centuries to happen. Again there is a general rule:

> The higher the temperature the more rapid the reaction: 'Hotter means faster'.

But according to the first rule, cooler conditions will favour the methane side of the equation, so in this case a compromise is necessary, between the final amount of methane and the rate at which it is produced.

The moral of all this is that any commercially useful process for producing a fuel must satisfy the following conditions:

- All its reactions must go in the right directions at accessible temperatures.
- They must do so at reasonable speeds.
- Overall, the process should be a net producer of useful energy.

To these we might add the requirement that the total cost of the product, including raw materials and processing, must be no more than consumers are willing to pay.

Motor Fuel from Solid Fuels

As mentioned above, the South African SASOL plant is the only large-scale coal-to-oil processing system in operation. Figure 4.6 shows the system in outline. The first item is the gasifier, in which coal reacts with steam and oxygen (see 'Gasification', below). The resulting synthesis gas is cleaned and then reacted with more steam, in the 'water-gas shift reaction'. Here some of the CO reacts with the steam to produce carbon dioxide and hydrogen, thus increasing the proportion of hydrogen in the mixture, an important step in going from coal, with its carbon-to-hydrogen ratio of about 1:1, to oil where as we've seen the ratio is more nearly 1:2. The CO_2 is removed in the scrubber and the CO and H_2 pass to the synthesizer, where they react and produce a sort of synthetic crude oil consisting of a range of hydrocarbons from methane to heavy oils (see Fig. 4.1 for some examples). This is then separated into the required components.

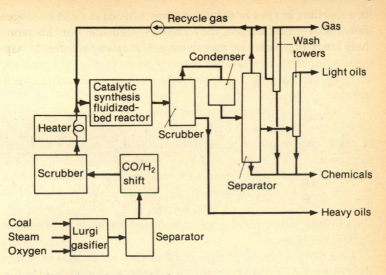

Fig. 4.6 Sasol liquid fuels synthesis

In terms of its production of motor fuel, the SASOL process is not very efficient. Each tonne of coal produces about an eighth of a tonne (160 litres) of petrol: an energy output of less than 6 GJ from an input of 25 GJ or more. If the other oil products are included, the conversion efficiency is technically greater, but the economics will depend on the demand for these. With world prices of some $50 a tonne for coal and $150 a tonne for gasoline at the time of writing, the output might just cover the cost of the input—leaving nothing to pay for the expensive plant or its running costs. It is not surprising, then, that only in times of oil crisis have most countries shown serious interest in investing in this particular technology.

An entirely different approach starts not with coal but with biomass, and leads to another alcohol that can be used as motor fuel: **ethanol** (C_2H_5OH). This is produced by the biological process called fermentation (a technology developed during the past few thousand years with entirely different purposes in mind!). Probably the best-known example of this method has been

Brazil's attempt to reduce oil imports by using a local solid fuel. The 'local solid fuel' in this case is sugar-cane—or the residues remaining after the cane juice has been extracted—and the resulting ethanol can be used 'neat' in suitably adapted engines, or in normal car engines as a 20:80 mixture with petrol called 'gasohol'.

As brewers, vintners, countrywomen, and moonshiners know, alcohol can be produced by fermentation of many different types of plant: apples, potatoes, corn, even wood. A number of European countries are looking at the possibilities for producing motor fuel from plants which grow well in temperate climates, and as concern about CO_2 emissions increases, we may yet see 'petrol fields' as part of the landscape. Switzerland even has an experimental installation producing motor fuel from suitably sorted domestic rubbish.

(Note that the idea of using natural oils from the seeds of plants such as rape as a diesel substitute is yet a third approach, quite different from the two described here.)

Gasification

The processes by which gas is produced from solids are if anything even more varied than those for liquids. At one extreme are large chemical plants, processing the raw material at high temperatures and pressures. At the other we have the local rubbish dump or pig farm. We'll look at each of these in turn, starting with the sophisticated technology.

A **gasifier** is a plant designed to enable the processes described above in the 'Means and Ends' section to take place—or at least those which are of interest. The end product is some mixture of hydrogen, carbon monoxide, and possibly other gases, and the input is the solid fuel accompanied by steam and either air or oxygen. The design has much in common with the furnaces described earlier in this chapter, because the aim is similar: to promote a reaction between the solid fuel and a gas or gases. In different types of gasifier the solid can be on a moving grate, or in the form of a fine dust, or fed into a fluidized bed (see Fig. 4.4 above). Heat to produce the reactions comes from the burning of some of the solid fuel, and operating temperatures vary from several hundred to over a thousand degrees Celsius.

The exact product depends on the gasifier conditions, of course, but the resulting gas is usually mainly hydrogen (40–50 per cent) and carbon monoxide (20–30 per cent), with some methane (another fuel of course), some CO_2 (of no use as a fuel) and about 50 per cent nitrogen if the plant uses air (little or none if oxygen is the input). If the aim is simply to use some locally available solid fuel, vegetable matter perhaps, and to burn the resulting gas locally, a simple gasifier will produce a mixture which is a rather poor fuel but might nevertheless be worth having because it burns more cleanly than the original solid. At other extremes, a high-temperature oxygen-fed gasifier can produce a gas which is 90 per cent H_2 and CO, a mixture of two highly reactive gases which can be used to run a gas turbine.

Biogas and Landfill Gas

The production of gas from animal or vegetable wastes needs no high temperatures, high pressures, or high technology. It occurs entirely naturally, and has presumably been generating gas for as long as plants have been rotting in ponds. It just took us a few millennia to realize that this could be a useful source of energy.

The process is called **anaerobic digestion**: the decomposition of living material in the absence of air. Like fermentation, it is caused by bacteria, and is favoured by warm, wet conditions. No air means no oxygen, so it shouldn't surprise us that, unlike the decomposition discussed earlier in the chapter, fully anaerobic digestion doesn't produce H_2O and CO_2. Its product is that far more useful gas, methane (CH_4). In the form of 'marsh gas', bubbling up from decaying vegetation at the bottom of ponds, it has been known for centuries. In days when natural ponds were more common and there were fewer lights to dispel the darkness, spontaneous ignition of the gas gave rise to stories of the 'Will o' the wisp'. More recently and less romantically, the methane generated in large landfills containing domestic waste was a known 'problem', and measures were taken to burn off this dangerous product—until people began to realize that it might be worth collecting.

The systems developed in the past twenty or thirty years fall into two distinct categories: **biogas** and **landfill gas**. Biogas is the product of wet wastes, often animal dung or human sewage. Held in a closed 'digester' (Fig. 4.7) and maintained at 30–40°C, preferably using its own generated heat, each batch of material will be digested over a period of a few weeks. The process is never totally anaerobic, and from a quarter to half the resulting gas is CO_2, but nevertheless it can be a useful fuel, and the residual solid is considered a better fertilizer than the original waste material. However, despite its apparent simplicity, running a digester successfully requires rather careful control of conditions; and this, together with the capital cost, made some earlier attempts at widespread introduction less than entirely successful. Nevertheless, there are

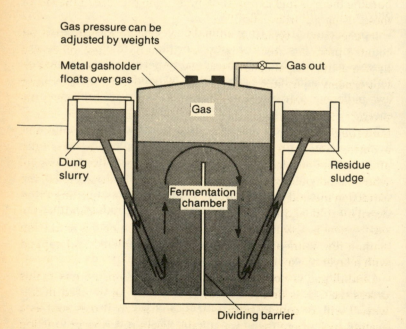

Gas pressure can be
adjusted by weights

Metal gasholder
floats over gas

Gas out

Gas

Dung
slurry

Residue
sludge

Fermentation
chamber

Dividing barrier

Fig. 4.7 A biogas digester

now estimated to be several million small plants operating in India and China, whilst some European countries, notably Denmark, have developed large-scale systems serving groups of farmers and producing over a thousand cubic metres of gas a day.

The gas can be used on site for heating or to run internal combustion engines, and an increasing use couples these engines to generators. A large farm digester can produce enough gas for 100 kW or so of power, and many sewage plants in Britain now generate in excess of a megawatt, selling the power to the national electricity grid. Other types of waste can also be treated in digesters (for instance the 'biological' fraction of ordinary domestic rubbish), but systems to separate out and treat such materials are still at an early stage. Obtaining useful energy from commercial, industrial, and domestic wastes is at present more likely to mean burning them as fuel in power-stations, or in the case of the last of these, using gas from landfills.

In one year, a typical household in a modern industrialized country produces about a tonne of domestic wastes, otherwise known as municipal solid wastes (MSW). Disposal is a problem which many of us still 'solve' as our ancestors did, by throwing our collective rubbish into the nearest pit to rot. Landfill gas is the product of this 'rotting'. Like the biogas discussed above, it contains roughly 50 per cent methane; but unlike the gas produced in a warm, wet digester, it takes ten years or more to develop fully after the site is filled and covered. Twenty or thirty years ago, when the potential value of this fuel began to be appreciated, the extraction method was effectively 'mining for gas'—putting pipes down into old landfills in order to collect it. With new landfills, the pipe system is now installed as the site is filled, and gas extraction starts a few years after the fill has been completed and capped with a layer of clay or soil.

Landfill gas is not suitable for distribution in the gas mains unless the CO_2 is first removed, so it is only rarely used in this way. It will, of course, burn as it is, and is sometimes sold as a heating fuel where there are suitable users near the production site. By far the most common use, however, is for the generation of electric power. Peak production from a typical landfill might be up to 2000 cubic metres of gas an hour, representing over 40 GJ an hour of useful energy. Used in large internal combustion engines driving generators, this can give a power output of 2–3 megawatts. The world's largest site, in California, generates 46 MW, enough power for a small town. Britain, with nine-tenths of MSW disposed of in landfills, has at the time of writing nearly 100 plants with a total output of over 150 MW. The potential is even greater, and if all suitable existing landfill sites in the UK were used, the 'power from rubbish' could be sufficient to replace one large coal-fired or nuclear power-station.

5

Energy Conversion

___

Energy Systems

We use the term 'energy system' for the sequence of processes which leads from primary resource to end use, starting when we acquire a certain number of joules and finishing when we have, literally, no further use for them. All energy systems, past, present, or in the foreseeable future, have certain common features. Every system involves processes of energy conversion and of transportation or distribution, and these processes share the important characteristic of producing wastes; waste energy in particular. This is an unavoidable consequence of basic physical laws, and our main concern in this chapter is to discuss these laws and find out what they say about the limits to efficiency. In this way we can develop some criteria for later use when we come to assessing processes and technologies.

Of course the details will be very different for different energy systems. One with which we are all familiar leads from the oil well to the petrol tank of a car. Here the energy enjoys a rather uneventful life. Apart from a fairly exciting episode in the refinery, the fuel remains a liquid throughout, with the energy stored chemically in its molecules from primary resource to end use. This is by no means always the case. In a nuclear power plant several major conversions take place: from changes in the very atoms themselves, releasing nuclear energy; to the thermal energy of a hot fluid; then via a spinning turbo-generator to the final electrical energy. In contrast, chopping down a tree and burning the wood

Table 5.1. *How to make a pot of tea using 50 grams of best coal*

1. Heat content of the coal, 50 g at 29 MJ per kilogram	1450 kJ
2. Subtract about 7% used in mining and transporting the coal	100 kJ
3. Energy of coal delivered to power-station	1350 kJ
4. Energy of electricity generated from coal, at 33% efficiency	450 kJ
5. Subtract 20% 'losses' in electricity distribution to consumer	90 kJ
6. Energy delivered	360 kJ
7. Energy needed to run a 2 kW electric kettle for 3 minutes or	360 kJ
energy to heat 1 litre of water to boiling point (Leaving a few kilojoules for warming the pot)	336 kJ

involves very few processes—although, as we've seen, this doesn't necessarily make it efficient.

Another everyday sequence starts in the coal mine and leads to the teapot. In this case Table 5.1 provides some data. An important fact (one that is no surprise by now) is that about three-quarters of the original energy is lost between primary resource and end use; and looking carefully at the loss processes we find that in every case the missing energy has become heat.

The inevitability with which waste heat occurs is closely related to another feature of all energy technologies: they use once-through processes. None of them is cyclic. In no case do we replace all the energy in the form in which we found it. This is just as true for the 'renewable' resources (solar, wind and wave power, etc.) as for the fossil fuels. We never renew our energy resources. The sun may do it for us, and the chief difference between 'renewable' and 'non-renewable' sources is the rate at which this happens. Plants grow and reservoirs refill in months or years, but the formation of coal or oil took millions of centuries.

Inevitable Heat

The question is, why must there be heat losses in every process? The answer, unfortunately, is more in our stars than in ourselves. There may be (undoubtedly are) losses which are due to our incompetence or carelessness, but it is important to understand that there is always a necessary inefficiency. Necessary in the sense that the laws of physics tell us that it is bound to occur.

We start with four observations:

- All energy tends to become heat energy.
- All energy processes are once-through. None is completely reversible.
- A generator whose input is mechanical energy (hydroelectric power-station, wind turbine, car alternator, bicycle dynamo, etc.) can convert its input into electrical energy with almost no losses; and the same is true for the reverse process in an electric motor.
- Any system whose input is heat energy (fossil fuel or nuclear power-station, internal combustion engine, gas turbine) converts much less than 100 per cent of its input into useful energy.

These statements obviously lack precision, but they are sufficiently definite to allow us to add two comments: that the word 'almost' is essential in the third, for otherwise it would contradict the second; and that the first observation tells us the fate of the 'missing' energy in all processes. Putting all these thoughts together we notice that they have a 'one-way' aspect in common, and that this arises in connection with heat energy. It seems that it is only too easy to go from any other form of energy to heat but that there are severe constraints on the reverse process.

We are of course surrounded by examples of this truth. Heat is produced whenever an electric current flows, but putting hot water into the kettle does not generate useful electric power to feed back to the mains. We bring the car to a skidding halt, producing quantities of heat in brakes and tyres, but making use of this warmth to set the vehicle in motion again is unfortunately not possible.

We have seen ('Heating Things', Chapter 4) that the temperature of anything is a measure of the speed of its constantly moving atoms and molecules, and that heat is the energy we add or remove to change the average speeds in this thermal motion. With this in mind, we can see what it is that distinguishes heat from all other forms of energy: the characteristic quality of thermal motion is that it is disorganized motion. The gnats in the analogy of Chapter 4 may or may not be moving at random but the molecules of the air certainly are. They move with a variety of speeds in all directions, bouncing off each other and the walls, changing both speed and direction all the time.* The same picture of random motion holds for the vibrating atoms or molecules of a solid material.

If this is heat, then the principle that all energy tends to become heat is no more than a law that we all know: *things tend to become disorganized*. Which is one, rather informal, way of expressing the Second Law of Thermodynamics. (We already know the First Law of Thermodynamics: it is the Law of Conservation of Energy.)

The above 'statement' of the Second Law is hardly going to tell us how much waste heat to expect from a power-station. It is far too imprecise to lead to quantitative results. It does however throw light on some of the processes we have discussed. Consider, for instance, a stationary car as an assembly of atoms moving at random. In a similar car moving north-east at 30 mph all the atoms have a directed motion superimposed on their random movement, and this gives the extra energy of the moving vehicle. As this car stops, the extra energy must go somewhere. It becomes heat—further disordered motion of the atoms. We now have a warmer, stationary vehicle. To reverse the process and recoup the heat energy requires part of the random motion to become ordered again, something which is very, very unlikely to happen spontaneously. It is easy to produce chaos. Order presents more of a problem.

Refrigerators, Heat Pumps, and a Very Important Rule

A one-way process that we meet every day is the flow of heat from a hot object to a cooler one. You pour hot coffee into a cold cup and the almost instantaneous result is slightly cooler coffee and a

---

* The pressure that a gas exerts on any surface is the result of these collisions and therefore depends on the number of gas molecules present. This is why atmospheric pressure is greatest at sea-level and less on mountain tops, where the atmosphere is less dense.

much hotter cup—assuming of course that there is much more coffee than cup. A little hot coffee in a large cold mug leads to a slightly different result, but in both cases there is a flow of heat energy from hot coffee to cold container. We would be very surprised indeed if the reverse were to occur, with the coffee becoming even hotter and the cup ice-cold. Yet, provided the heat energy gained by the coffee is the same as that lost by the cup, energy is still conserved in this bizarre case. Once again we must look to the Second Law of Thermodynamics rather than the first to tell us the direction in which things happen.

'Hotter means faster'. The atoms of a hot object have higher average speed than those of a cold object. To take another domestic example, suppose you were to observe with astonishment one day that the handle of a metal fork lying on the table was becoming red-hot while ice crystals appeared at the other end. This would mean that, starting with the same average speed everywhere, the faster atoms were now on the whole at the handle end and the slower ones at the other end. Rather as though a large number of people entered a theatre, sat down at random and then found that all the people on the left wore spectacles while no-one on the right did. A very improbable occurrence, with long odds against its happening, and longer the greater the number of people. Now the fork contains a very large number of atoms indeed (about 10^{24}, which is 1 000 000 000 000 000 000 000 000) so your astonishment would be entirely justified. We see that the Second Law has something to do with all this when we reflect that once again the issue is order versus chaos. The people in the theatre and the atoms in the fork won't spontaneously adopt the more ordered arrangement:

Heat will not of itself flow from a colder to a hotter body.

The natural way is the reverse, the direction of increasing chaos.

Yet heat *can* be transferred from a colder to a hotter body. Every ordinary refrigerator or air conditioner does it. Take a jug of milk at room temperature and put it in the refrigerator. It will cool spontaneously because heat flows from it to the (colder) interior of the refrigerator. This heat must now be removed if the interior is not to warm up, so the refrigeration unit switches on and 'pumps' heat out into the (warmer) room. The refrigeration unit uses energy (usually from the electricity supply), so the situation is as shown in Fig. 5.1(*a*). Notice that the electrical energy, which has to go somewhere, also eventually becomes heat and contributes to the total heat entering the room.

Suppose now that we want to compare the performances of two refrigeration units. We will presumably regard the one that uses less electricity in order to pump out a certain quantity of heat as the better one. Figure 5.1 includes data for a refrigerator of modest size. Using 250 W of electric power, the unit removes 2.2 MJ of heat energy from the interior in an hour. Is this a good or bad performance? As a start, let's convert both amounts of energy into joules (Fig. 5.1(*b*)). We can now see that the heat removed is a little under two and a half times the electrical energy supplied. The **coefficient of performance**, or COP, is just under 2.5. Is this good? How do we know what should be possible?

The answer comes from the Second Law of Thermodynamics. With its aid we can calculate a value for the possible COP even if we know nothing about types of refrigeration unit or how they work. The inside and outside temperatures are all we need to know. The value obtained is of course for an 'ideal' refrigerator, representing a best possible performance that could never quite be reached in practice. Nevertheless the result is very important, because we learn that no designer, however brilliant, could increase the COP above this value, given the two temperatures. The input energy needed to pump a certain amount of heat can never be lower. We can see that the Second Law might impose a limit of this sort, because it says that the heat will not flow out by itself. So some input is needed—but now the claim is that we can tell how much. To substantiate this claim in detail is unfortunately beyond our present scope. The result, however, is straightforward:

- The 'ideal' coefficient of performance is equal to the temperature of the interior divided by the temperature difference between the interior and the surroundings.

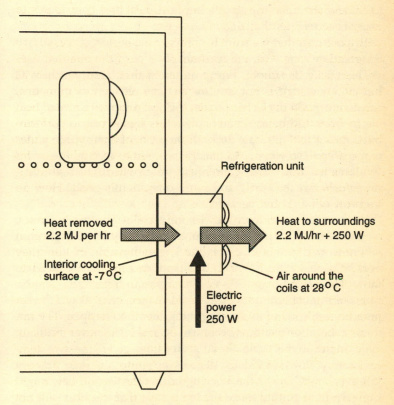

Heat removed
2.2 MJ per hr

Interior cooling
surface at -7°C

Refrigeration unit

Heat to surroundings
2.2 MJ/hr + 250 W

Electric
power
250 W

Air around the
coils at 28°C

Fig. 5.1 Refrigerator performance

This is a very important result, with much wider implications than just keeping the milk cold. What does it say, then, that is so significant? It is hardly surprising that the performance gets worse if the temperature difference between inside and outside is increased—one reason why your refrigerator runs for more hours on a hot day. The significant point is that the performance gets worse as the actual inside temperature is reduced, even if you take care to keep the same temperature difference between inside and outside. Now this ought to be a surprise. For one thing, the rule implies that if the temperature inside becomes zero, so does the COP, and the unit stops pumping heat out altogether. Common experience tells us that this is nonsense—every freezer working with a sub-zero temperature inside is an example to the contrary. So what is wrong with the reasoning?

The answer is simple. We've assumed that 'zero' means $0°C$, but the above rule is not true for just any old way of measuring temperature. On the Celsius scale, $0°C$ and $100°C$ are respectively the freezing and boiling points of water. This is very convenient, but it means that the scale depends on the behaviour of one particular material, so we would hardly expect it to feature in a really fundamental law. (The Fahrenheit scale, with $0°F$ based on a rather cold day in Danzig and $100°F$ on a slightly mistaken measurement of blood temperature, is an even less likely candidate.) What we need is a zero point with universal significance. There is one, and it's called **absolute zero**, an extremely low temperature whose importance is that it is the lowest possible. Nothing can ever be cooled right down to this absolute zero (that's the Third Law of Thermodynamics). Very complex refrigeration systems can cool minute amounts of material to near zero, at which temperatures all sorts of interesting things begin to happen. The random heat motion of atoms becomes less and less. Things freeze up, even on the atomic scale. So no more chaos.

Counting down in Celsius degrees, absolute zero is found to be just over $273°C$ below the freezing point of water, i.e. below $0°C$. Conversely, if you measure the temperature of freezing water by counting upwards from absolute zero, it is 273 Celsius-sized degrees up. The temperature of anything measured up from absolute zero in this way is called its absolute temperature, and it is this that we must use in the above rule. If we count in Celsius-sized degrees, the absolute temperature of anything is called its Kelvin temperature. For instance, water freezes at 273 degrees on the Kelvin scale, written $273K$, and boils at $373K$. (Absolute zero on the Kelvin scale is of course $0K$!)

The above rule tells us, then, that the COP, the heat pumping performance, of even an ideal refrigerator becomes smaller and smaller as the inside temperature approaches absolute zero. In other words, the cooling process gradually stops, and you can't go any lower.

Returning to the more mundane refrigerator of Fig. 5.1, we see that the temperature of the warm air around the coils is $273 + 28 = 301\,K$. On the cold surface inside, it is well below freezing: only $266\,K$. Using the rule, we can find the 'ideal' COP:

$$266 \div (301 - 266) = 7.6$$

So the actual performance achieved in practice, a COP of 2.5, is about a third of the ideal. This is not unusual, and a system that reached half the ideal value would be considered very good.

Another device which functions in essentially the same way as a refrigeration unit is the one that is actually called a heat pump. Here (Fig. 5.2) the surrounding air or ground is the colder region, and heat is 'pumped' from this into the house. As with the refrigerator, the electrical energy input to the pump also becomes heat, so if the pumped heat energy is, say, three times the electrical input, the total heat entering the house will be four times as much as it would be using conventional electric heating. In principle, then, this should be an economical way of heating a building with electricity; but unfortunately the initial cost of the plant, together

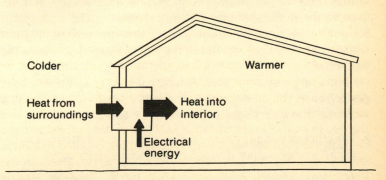

Fig. 5.2 Heat pump for a house

with the relatively high cost of electricity in many countries, and perhaps the unreliability of some early systems, seem to have limited its attractiveness. There is also the fact that the heat gain decreases as the temperature outside falls—a result of the rule discussed above; and at very low outdoor temperatures the heat pump may be no better than direct electrical heating.

On the other hand, if a slightly warm external source is available, so that the heat pump takes in energy from this and boosts it to the required indoor temperature, the value of the COP will be much higher. This idea has been adopted as a way of using underground geothermal heat—in Switzerland, for instance. Another idea is to use warm water from solar panels (see Chapter 11), but this would of course depend on the availability of sunlight, and wouldn't be very useful on a cold night.

Heat Engines—and Another Rule

Now that we've solved the case of the domestic refrigerator, the turbo-generator of a modern power-station should present no problem: it is a heat engine, and a heat engine is a heat pump run backwards. Consider Fig. 5.3. In (*a*) we have the refrigerator or heat pump, removing heat from the cold region, using electrical energy, and delivering the total of these two amounts of energy to the warmer region. In (*b*) there's the turbo-generator, taking in heat from the hot steam, producing electrical energy, and delivering the remainder into the cooling water. The heat pump becomes a heat engine if you just reverse the arrows. It's not surprising, then, that once more the Second Law determines the performance.

In comparing systems such as heat engines, or specifying their performance, the quantity that interests us is their **efficiency**, a word that has a very specific meaning for energy systems:

- The efficiency of any energy conversion system is defined as the useful energy output divided by the total energy input.

In practice it is very common to multiply by 100, giving the output as a percentage of the input. Because of the similarity between a

(a) Refrigerator (heat pump)

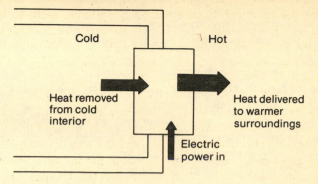

(b) Power-station (heat engine)

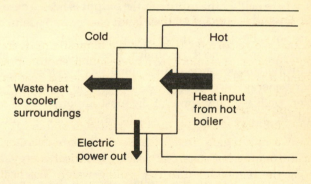

Fig. 5.3 Refrigerator into power-station?

heat pump and a heat engine, it is quite easy to go from the rule for the COP of an ideal heat pump to the rule for the efficiency of an ideal heat engine. Again, the detailed reasoning is a little beyond the scope of this book, but the result is simple:

• The maximum possible efficiency of a heat engine is equal to one minus the output temperature divided by the input temperature:

$$\text{eff}_{max} = 1 - \left(T_{out}/T_{in}\right)$$

We must, of course, remember to use Kelvin temperatures, and to multiply the final result by 100 if we want the efficiency as a percentage.

This is an enormously important result in the world of energy, because the term 'heat engine' includes any machine whose input is heat and whose output is in some useful form such as electrical or mechanical power. It includes not only all the steam turbines and gas turbines in the world but all the internal combustion engines as well—everything that uses heat, usually from a burning fuel, to produce some form of energy that is not heat. There are only two exceptions: the systems where heat is the required output, such as a central heating boiler, gas furnace, or electric heater, and machines such as water turbines or electric motors and generators, where neither the input nor the output is heat. These can, in principle at least, convert all their input energy into useful output, and are not subject to the above limitation on their efficiency (often known as the 'Second Law limit'). Everything else is, and the world-wide consequence is that some three-quarters of all our primary energy becomes waste heat. In the remainder of this chapter, we'll see how some of the most important heat engines behave in practice, and ask whether this behaviour might be improved.

Steam Turbines

We concentrate here on the turbines because these are the heat engines in power-stations. (The furnaces producing the heat in fossil-fuel plants were discussed in Chapter 4, the 'furnaces' of nuclear plants are the subject of Chapter 8, systems using warm ocean water appear in Chapter 9, and solar thermal plants in Chapter 11. The generators and other parts making up the complete power-station are described in Chapter 7.)

If you look in a dictionary, you might find something along the following lines:

> *Turbine* (noun): Any motor in which a shaft is steadily rotated by the impact or reaction of a current of steam, air, water, or other fluid upon the blades of a wheel.

In other words, anything from an ancient windmill to a modern gas turbine. The name comes from the Latin word *turbo*, meaning something that spins, and was coined just over 100 years ago to describe the first modern water turbine. Our subjects here, however, are the large steam turbines of present-day thermal power-stations (Fig. 5.4). As the name suggests, a 'thermal' plant is any type where the fuel is used initially to produce heat. A turbine doesn't mind where its steam comes from: fossil fuel, biofuel, nuclear fuel, or even sunlight. And it doesn't even have to use steam; any turbine driven by a vapour or gas that enters hotter and exits cooler comes under this heading.

An old-fashioned steam engine is a useful starting-point. In this, hot steam pushes pistons, expanding and cooling as it does so. With steam entering at its normal temperature of 100°C and being condensed to about 55°C (rather below household hot water temperature) the above rule tells us that the maximum possible efficiency is

$$1 - (328/373) = 0.12 \qquad \text{(Note the Kelvin temperatures)}$$

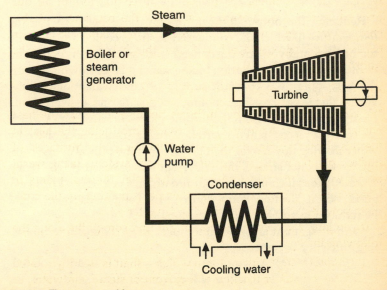

Fig. 5.4 The steam turbine

In percentage terms, this means that 12 per cent of the energy of the steam becomes useful output, the remaining 88 per cent being carried away as waste heat. Pretty poor, and the actual efficiency of those lovely old engines was unfortunately even worse, often no more than a miserable 5 per cent or so.

How can this be improved? Part of the answer we know already. A great deal of heat was lost in the boilers of early steam engines, whereas modern power-station boilers, as we saw in the last chapter, can convert nearly all the energy of the fuel into useful heat. Another part of the answer comes from looking at the efficiency rule: the efficiency will be greater the higher the input temperature and the lower the output temperature. So what can the turbine designer do about these?

Increasing the input temperature above 100°C means using superheated steam. You can raise the temperature of steam above 100°C by heating it, provided you don't let it expand and cool down. So superheated steam means high-pressure steam: a pressure of some 200 atmospheres (i.e. 200 times normal atmospheric pressure) and a temperature up to 540°C in a large modern steam turbine.

Reducing the output temperature can also help. This is the temperature to which the condensed steam is cooled after leaving the turbine, and you obviously need some good means of cooling it. Building the power-station by the sea or a large flowing river is the best, offering a constant supply of cold water for cooling. Where this is not possible, cooling towers are one answer. Inside the tower, the steam from the turbine passes through pipes which are cooled by a constant upward flow of air, sometimes assisted by water flowing down over them. (Note that the plume over a cooling tower is not smoke, but water vapour released by the rising warmed air as it cools—like your breath on a cold day.) With very good cooling, the final temperature of the condensed steam might be reduced to 30°C.

With these input and output temperatures, the maximum possible efficiency becomes

$$1 - (303/813) = 0.63$$

An efficiency of 63 per cent certainly looks a lot better, but how closely can a real turbine approach this? Details of the design now become important. A modern steam turbine consists of a complex array of blades, closely interleaved so that as much as possible of the energy of the steam is transmitted to the rotating shaft. Using not one but a series of turbines at decreasing steam temperatures and pressures, and extracting some steam along the way to pre-heat the water entering the boiler, are amongst the many design features that help to increase the efficiency. There are limits to these measures however (including cost), and even under the very best conditions, present-day steam turbines can convert only 45 per cent of the energy of the steam into useful output—about two-thirds of the above 'ideal' maximum. This is a ten-fold improvement on the early steam engine, but nevertheless still means that over half the energy entering the turbine becomes waste heat.

When all the other energy 'losses' in the electricity supply system are taken into account, the energy reaching the final users is, as we've seen in Chapter 3, unlikely to reach even one-third of the energy of the original fuel.

You might wonder why the turbine designer drew the line at 540°C for the hot steam. It is possible to make it hotter, but the limit here is set by cost and the nature of materials. Steam at higher temperatures and pressures attacks the steel, and whilst special alloys could overcome this problem, the return in efficiency is not generally considered worth the cost. The search for higher temperatures therefore means finding an alternative to steam.

Gas Turbines

One option for increasing the input temperature of the turbine becomes obvious when you consider that although the steam temperature is limited to 540°C, the burning materials in the furnace are at a far higher temperature—up to 2000°C. Why not use this mass of hot gases to drive the turbine directly? A little arithmetic shows that the 'ideal' efficiency of a heat engine with its input at 2000°C and final cooling to 30°C would be a remarkable 87 per cent. Reducing the wasted energy of all our power-stations from half their input to not much over one-eighth would be wonderful. A little too wonderful to be true, needless to say; but any potential improvement is worth investigating.

Gas turbines have much in common with aircraft jet engines. Figure 5.5(a) shows the idea. A compressor uses some of the power from the turbine to raise the pressure of the incoming air to 10–20 atmospheres before it enters the 'furnace'—now called the combustion chamber. The resulting hot, high-pressure gases then drive the turbine. Unfortunately, however, the figures are not quite those quoted above. The best input temperature is about 1300°C, but more importantly, the gases leaving the turbine are still at some 500°C. This means that the 'ideal' efficiency is not all that high:

$$1 - (773/1573) = 0.51$$

Far from being an improvement, this is actually less than the 63 per cent of the 'ideal' conventional steam turbine, and the overall fuel-to-electricity efficiency of simple-cycle gas turbines like this is in practice no more than about 33 per cent. Very disappointing; and it's easy to see from the calculation that the chief cause is the very high output temperature. But let's take a second look at this temperature: 500°C is within the range of input temperatures for steam turbines. So why not use these gases to raise steam? There are then two routes available. In one, the steam joins the flow of gases at some stage, often in the combustion chamber, and enhances the efficiency of the turbine. The system is then a steam-injected gas turbine (STIG). The alternative, by far the most common at present, uses the steam to run a second turbine, adding its power to the first. This is the combined-cycle gas turbine (CCGT) shown in Fig. 5.5(b). Both methods really do lead to improvements, with overall plant efficiencies approaching 50 per cent.

The gains in efficiency are very significant for a number of reasons. A change from the 35 per cent of ordinary steam-turbine plants to 50 per cent would reduce the input needed for a million kWh of electricity by 3000 GJ, saving as much as a hundred tonnes of fuel. This brings important environmental gains, redu-

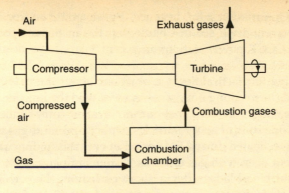

(a) Simple gas turbine

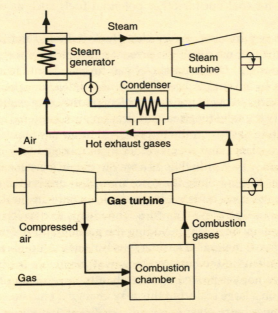

(b) Combined-cycle gas turbine

Fig. 5.5 Gas turbines

cing CO_2 emissions, for instance, by several hundred tonnes. (However, as we'll see in Chapter 14, the main reasons for the rise of CCGT power-stations in recent years have been rather different.)

Coming to practicalities, we must ask about the nature of the fuel and the resulting hot gases. As we saw in the last chapter, the gases leaving a modern coal-burning system carry tonnes of fly ash—a fine dust of sooty particles. Direct coal-fired gas turbines were investigated during the period of enthusiasm for coal in the 1970s, but even with gas-cleaning systems in place, photographs of the turbine blades after a short run show them looking as though they've been equipped with black fur coats. And the flue gases are likely to contain corrosive impurities as well, a problem not only for coal but for other potential fuels such as domestic wastes.

So one requirement is very clean fuel. It should not therefore surprise us that nearly all the present gas turbine power-stations use natural gas. Development of gas turbine plants using solid fuels has by no means been abandoned, however. The method now favoured to overcome the problem of dirty combustion gases is to gasify the solid fuel (see 'Gasification', in Chapter 4) and burn the resulting gas to run the turbine. Although this requires effectively two plants, and seems rather a complicated way of doing things, it may be worthwhile as a way to obtain a clean gas as fuel for the gas turbine. Since the 1970s many hundreds of millions of dollars have been invested in research, mainly in the USA but also in Japan and other countries. The idea is to develop an integrated system: one plant including the gasifier and the turbine— known as coal integrated gasifier/gas turbines. A number of such CIG/GT plants in the hundred-megawatt range are in operation. They have not yet proved sufficiently attractive financially to be adopted on a large scale, but this may change if emissions legislation becomes more severe.

Even more interesting possibilities are the family of systems coming under the heading BIG/GT: integrated plants using gas from biomass in steam-injected or combined-cycle gas turbines. If it becomes essential in the near future to replace fossil fuels by alternatives which don't further increase atmospheric CO_2, these may become the backbone of our power systems.

Internal Combustion Engines

About a sixth of all primary energy goes into internal combustion engines, which makes them collectively the world's second-largest consumer. We have seen that the leaders, the thermal power-stations, convert perhaps a third of the energy of their fuel into useful power. Now we'll find the runners-up gasping along at little more than half this level of performance. An internal combustion engine is, of course, a heat engine and its efficiency is therefore subject to the 'Second Law limit'; but surely all the design effort that goes into the motor car should be leading to something better than efficiencies that don't even reach 20 per cent? Vehicle design and engines have indeed been gradually improving for several decades now, with correspondingly better miles-per-gallon figures; but unfortunately the demand from drivers for ever more energy-consuming systems in cars makes this an uphill task.

Everyone probably has a rough idea of how a car engine works (Fig. 5.6). A little fuel and some air are drawn into the cylinder and compressed, an explosion (high-speed combustion) produces hot gases at high pressure, and these push down the piston, forcing the shaft to rotate. From the energy viewpoint, each cylinder is a small heat engine, converting part of the energy of the combustion products into mechanical energy and rejecting the remainder as heat. So, as with all heat engines, we can ask how much of the heat energy produced is converted into useful mechanical energy on each piston stroke. We can't use the heat engine rule directly because the temperatures are not at all well-defined. Explosions are complex events, difficult to analyse using simple science (or advanced science either, for that matter). However, if we assume that all the heat becomes available instantaneously, before the piston starts to move, and that there are no heat losses through the cylinder walls, and one or two further unlikely simplifications, we can use the Second Law to predict the efficiency. The result is rather surprising, because it claims that the efficiency of the result-

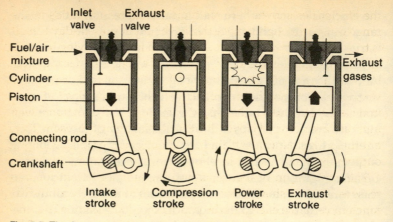

Fig. 5.6 The four-stroke internal combustion engine

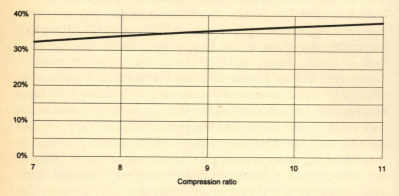
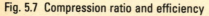

Fig. 5.7 Compression ratio and efficiency

The curve shows how the efficiency of an idealized internal combustion engine depends on the compression ratio.

ing idealized engine depends almost entirely on its **compression ratio**: the ratio of the largest volume in the cylinder (when the piston is at its lowest point in our diagram) to the smallest volume (when the piston is at the top). Fig. 5.7 shows the theoretical results for a wide range of compression ratios.

Now we don't expect real engines to behave like ideal ones, but the efficiencies shown here for typical compression ratios in the range 9–9.5 are roughly twice those we find in present-day cars. It is true that the 17–18 per cent achieved in normal driving today is an improvement on the 14–15 per cent of a couple of decades ago; but why are we still getting only half the energy that theory says we should? Some of the answer lies in heat losses cooling the gases in the cylinder, and a rather larger part is due to the friction which must always occur when you have surfaces rubbing on each other, but these together can explain only about half the missing engine output.

The explanation of the remaining losses is important for two reasons. First, it shows how our demands as drivers ensure that much more of the energy of the petrol is wasted than need be, and secondly, it is an aspect which is seeing real improvement. The 'lost' energy is the result of 'pumping friction', the force needed to draw in and later push out the vapours and gases; and the important point is that this loss depends critically on the throttle valve that controls air intake and on the opening and closing sequence of the inlet and outlet valves. The engine is at its most efficient, with minimum pumping losses, when the throttle is wide open—but most of us drive most of the time with it half closed. In level driving at a steady 60 mph, for instance, you are probably using only a fifth of the power that the engine could develop with an open throttle. And this is where our demands come in, because we want the extra power in order to accelerate 'if necessary'. (Some of the strange vehicles that achieve miles-per-gallon records don't even have a throttle; the engine is either on or off.) However, the improvement mentioned above has come, not from any change in our habits, but from an entirely different direction. Electronic control of the valve sequences, reducing pumping losses by optimizing the flow of intake and exhaust gases and vapours, is becoming increasingly widely available, with a noticeably beneficial effect on petrol consumption.

The overall petrol consumption of a vehicle depends, of course, not only on the efficiency of the engine but on the output it has to produce in order to move the vehicle along the road, accelerate, climb hills, run fans etc., and provide power for the electric windows, stereo, air conditioning, and other luxuries we increasingly demand. In the next chapter we'll look at a typical journey in a present-day car to see where all the energy goes, and how a few changes might make a real difference to petrol consumption. First, however, let's ask if we can't do something about all that waste heat.

Waste Heat

Every year we—the population of the world—convert some 300 exajoules of chemical and nuclear energy into heat. We do this for two reasons: because we want the heat itself, or because this is the first step in producing mechanical or electrical energy. Roughly half the world's total primary energy is used for the second of these purposes, driving machines of some sort, and we've now seen that the average efficiency of these 'heat engines' is rarely above 30 per cent, with the consequence that about one-third of all primary energy is almost immediately thrown away as waste heat. This seems a rather poor way to deal with a valuable resource, and considerable effort has gone into attempts to increase the useful fraction of the heat. If nothing else, it makes good economic sense for the energy producers ('converters' might be a better name) to do this. We have seen above how the efficiencies of the main heat engines—turbines in power stations and internal combustion engines in vehicles—have increased over the years. But we have also seen that the Second Law of Thermodynamics imposes a fundamental limit, and there is little immediate prospect of reducing the waste heat to less than about half the input.

If we want to improve the situation we are left with three possibilities:

- Reduce our use of machines.
- Find ways to run machines which don't involve burning fuels.
- Find ways to use the waste heat.

The first of these is probably unacceptable and the second is not at present possible on a large scale (but see 'The all-electric economy' in Chapter 15). We are left therefore with the third. No one has yet found a way to use the waste heat produced by vehicle engines—except for keeping the occupants warm—so we'll confine ourselves to power-stations. If we can use only half the waste heat from the average steam plant, the conversion efficiency rises at once from about 35 to over 65 per cent, which must surely be a desirable change. So why don't we do it?

Combined Heat and Power

For sale: Half a billion gallons a day of luke-warm water.
Purchaser to pay delivery charges.
Bids to UK power generators incorporated.

The trouble with waste heat from power-stations is that it is both too cold and too distant. This is a pity, because the total quantity of energy is enough to be very useful indeed. In Britain, it would provide central heating for every house in the land, and world-wide it accounts for about 70 EJ of energy a year—roughly the total energy consumption of the USA. The above 'offer' gives some idea why we don't in fact use this form of free heat to warm our houses. To understand in more detail why all our power-stations are not yet combined heat and power (CHP) plants, we need to look at the situation from two directions. How does it appear to the potential user and to the power-station engineer?

A typical centrally-heated British house is likely to have a boiler burning some form of fossil fuel, with water circulating through radiators to distribute the heat. (An inappropriate name, 'radiator': like all objects they do radiate, but unless they are glowing red-hot, most of their heat is being transferred by convection.) The water probably leaves the boiler at between 55°C and 80°C and returns 10–15°C cooler. Whether the desired indoor temperature is reached by circulating very hot water for short periods or cooler water for longer periods is a matter of choice, but there will always be a limit. If the water is too cool it won't be able to supply enough heat to make up the losses from the house, even if it circulates continuously.

Now any alternative will be cheapest, and therefore most attractive, if it involves the minimum amount of change to existing systems. So from the consumer's point of view, any centralized heat-distribution system should provide water at roughly the above temperatures. Huge quantities of water at 40°C could heat our houses, but only with enormous radiator areas. Hot air might use lower temperatures, but that would involve all the cost of installing ducting. To summarize, waste heat is most likely to be useful if it arrives in controllable quantities of water (up to several gallons a minute) at a temperature of at least 65°C.

Back to the power-station, where skilful engineering and 100 years' experience have brought steam turbines to an efficiency of 45 per cent. One essential for this is that the steam leaving the turbine is cooled to the lowest temperature possible. And now comes along some bright CHP enthusiast asking for waste heat at, let's say, to be on the safe side, and allowing for losses, 90°C. Put this figure instead of the 30°C in the calculation for the modern steam turbine above, and the efficiency falls with a thud, undoing the effect of about a century of research and development. You can understand why the devoted power engineer is rarely a fan of CHP.

There are a few other problems too. What happens in the summer when we don't want the heat? Does the engineer re-design the power plant or just throw away millions of gallons of hot water? Waste heat with a vengeance. And how about the distances of power-stations from people? The electricity utilities in most countries build large plants because they consider them most efficient, and locate them near either their fuel sources or good sources of cooling water for similar reasons. Do we even want them back in the middle of residential areas? Nuclear power-stations?

What about the positive points, then? The above problems need a little lateral thinking. If you want a flexible system, then design it to be flexible from the start. About 4 per cent of all electricity generated in the UK already comes from CHP plant, but most of it is not heating houses and most doesn't involve huge power-stations. Nearly 90 per cent is in the form of 'cogeneration' plants with typical outputs of a few megawatts, used by industries that require heat in any case, and designed so that the amounts of steam used for heating and for power generation are adapted to the particular requirements. These systems can be looked at in either of two ways: as using waste heat from power generation or as producing power from surplus steam not needed for heat. Either way, they manage to convert about three-quarters of their input into useful output, certainly a great improvement on one-third. The privatization of the electricity industry in Britain, with new regulations allowing small generators to sell power, has meant that owners of CHP plants like this can also sell their surplus or buy extra power from the grid. The major generating and distribution companies are taking an interest too, offering CHP 'packages' to industrial users. The result has been a rapid growth in such systems during the early 1990s.

Britain's large power-stations are still there, of course; but even for them there is a partial answer. If there are no suitable houses to be heated, find something else that could use all that warm water: greenhouses, for instance, or fish farms. This has indeed been done, although naturally it doesn't absorb all of those millions of megajoules. More lateral thinking in the other direction has led to much smaller local power-stations within cities, with a dual role of generating power and providing heat for commercial buildings and occasionally blocks of flats. In other European countries where district heating is more common, plants like this are much more usual, sometimes combining the combustion of municipal wastes with their CHP function. Many years ago a review of the situation in the UK concluded that as much as a third of the total heating and hot water needs could be met in this way, and that the heat could be sold at a price which would make it attractive to householders whilst bringing a reasonable return to the utility company. Unfortunately there is little sign that this view has been accepted in the private housing market. A pity, because if half of Britain's generating capacity could be converted to CHP, the saving in fuel would reduce the nation's carbon dioxide emissions by over 10 per cent.

In Conclusion

To conclude, the message of this chapter is that there are rules that govern the performance of any system which comes under the heading 'heat pump' and any system which comes under the heading 'heat engine'. These rules are universal. They are not consequences of our choice of materials or the particular design, but apply whenever we transfer heat from a lower to a higher temperature, or produce useful work from heat energy. Of course, the whole of current physics can at some future time be proved false, but as far as our present understanding goes the message is clear: *you cannot beat the Second Law.*

This doesn't of course mean that we can only shrug our shoulders and do nothing about reducing energy consumption, and consumption of fossil fuels in particular. A very large number of measures are open to us. We have just looked at possibilities for using the waste heat. We could improve not only our vehicles but the way we use energy at home (the next chapter looks at both of these). Or we could change to other sources of energy, the renewables which are introduced in Chapters 9–11. We might even change our habits.

Footnote

In case anyone reading this chapter has been listening to scientific gossip and is wondering where that ineffable thing called 'entropy' comes in, the answer is simple: we've been talking about it throughout the chapter. Entropy is the physical scientists' way of quantifying chaos.

6

Using the Energy

Introduction

In the early part of the book we looked at the broad picture of the ways people use energy. This chapter fills in a few details and asks how we might reduce our consumption. It concentrates on two topics that concern us all fairly directly: the use of motor fuel, and energy in the household. The annual consumption of motor fuel in western Europe is equivalent to over 1000 litres a year for every man, woman, and child. Each year the average UK household uses some 26 000 kilowatt-hours of energy, at a cost of nearly £600. Where does it all go, and could we—or should we—be using less?

A Short Drive in the Country

On a sunny Sunday in June the Smiths decide to go to the seaside. They go by the scenic route over the moors—a round trip distance of 200 km (125 miles), mainly on minor roads. The total journey time is just over $2\frac{3}{4}$ hours and the car uses a little over 12 litres (not quite $2\frac{3}{4}$ gallons) of petrol, a fuel consumption of about 46 mpg at an average 45 mph. Our problem then is the following: the outing has used over four hundred megajoules of energy, but the Smiths (and their car) have gained none of it. They are all back where they started. Where has the energy gone, and could they have done the trip for less?

Kinetic Energy

To track the missing joules we'll consider the main energy-consuming processes in turn. First, we know that any energy used to accelerate the vehicle is not returned; the petrol doesn't flow back into the tank when you slow down again. How many joules are consumed each time the car needs to accelerate again after braking?

The energy which an object has by virtue of its motion—its **kinetic energy**—depends on its speed and how heavy it is. The dependence on the mass is simple: at any given speed, a two-tonne vehicle has twice the kinetic energy of a one-tonne one. Or to put it another way, an additional five kilograms of groceries in the back adds the same extra kinetic energy at 30 mph whether you are driving a very small car or a thirty-tonne truck. In other words, the kinetic energy is proportional to the mass of the moving object. Not so for the speed. If you double your speed, you increase your kinetic energy fourfold, with the consequence that an extra mile an hour needs twice as much extra energy at 60 mph as at 30 mph. (Note that this has nothing to do with factors like air resistance; it would be just the same if you were driving a rocket out in empty space.) A four-fold increase on doubling the speed, nine-fold at three times the speed, etc., means that the kinetic energy is proportional to the square of the speed. The kinetic energy your vehicle carries at 80 mph is sixteen times that at 20 mph—a fact with obvious consequences when the energy is dissipated as heat, light, and sound as you hit a brick wall.

To compute the kinetic energy of a moving vehicle in joules, we need to know its mass in kilograms and its speed in metres per second. The relationship is then

• kinetic energy = one half the mass × the square of the speed

Converting the familiar mph into metres per second is rather tedious, but not too complicated. One mile is very close to 1600 metres. So 1 mph is 1600 metres in 3600 seconds, or four-ninths of a metre per second. For example, 36 mph is 16 metres per second, 63 mph is 28 m/s, and so on.

Now we can return to the Smiths' car. We'll assume a medium-sized vehicle whose mass is 800 kg. A simple calculation shows that its kinetic energy at 36 mph is

$$\tfrac{1}{2} \times 800 \times (16 \times 16) = 102\,400 \text{ joules}$$

and at 63 mph it is

$$\tfrac{1}{2} \times 800 \times (28 \times 28) = 313\,600 \text{ joules}$$

So about one fifth of a megajoule of extra energy should be needed each time the car accelerates from 36 mph to 63 mph. As we are trying to account for over four hundred MJ, this doesn't take us very far. (Even the Smiths' teenage son is unlikely to change from 36 to 63 mph and back again over two thousand times in a 125-mile trip.) To simplify our accounting, we'll assume that all the accelerating during the entire trip is equivalent to doing this about 50 times, so the total energy needed becomes 10.5 MJ.

Climbing the Hills

The road across the moors climbs in and out of a few valleys, and the climbing parts will need extra energy. Suppose all the uphill sections together amount to climbing 400 metres (1300 feet) during each half of the journey. How much energy is needed? The reason that we need extra energy to move upwards is that the gravitational force of the Earth is always pulling us down. This force, technically the **weight** of any object, is numerically equal to about ten times its mass in kilograms.* It is also equal to *the energy in joules needed to rise by one metre*. So the 800 kg car climbing the 400 metres needs

$$10 \times 800 \times 400 = 3\,200\,000 \text{ joules}$$

Climbing the hills on the out and return journeys therefore needs 6.4 MJ. (We have ignored any gain on descending, as you don't usually free-fall downhill in a car.)

The energy accounted for so far is 16.9 MJ—still only about 4 per cent of the total, so it seems reasonable to conclude that most of the energy from the petrol goes in just keeping the car moving, even

* For further discussion of weight, see 'Pumped Storage' in Chapter 9.

when its speed isn't changing and there are no hills. This is of course common experience. Constantly starting and stopping does increase fuel consumption, and we do use more fuel in crossing the Alps than driving the same distance in Holland; but we know that any car steadily consumes petrol when driven at constant speed on a flat road. This seems to contradict a very fundamental law of physics, Newton's First Law of Motion, which tells us that a moving object will continue to move in a dead straight line with no change in its speed unless we do something to stop it. There's nothing wrong with the law, however; it's just that we haven't properly assessed the 'unless' part. All sorts of things are happening to slow down a moving car; it is subjected to many different forces. And fighting against forces uses energy.

Rolling Friction

We'll consider just a few of the energy-consuming processes in a moving vehicle. The first is called 'rolling friction', and the most obvious evidence for it is the temperature of the tyres after a long drive. As a wheel rotates, its tyre is compressed where it makes contact with the road. This compression uses energy, some of which becomes heat and is not therefore recovered as the tyre expands again. The amount of energy 'lost' in this way depends of course on the force pressing the wheels down—i.e. the weight of the vehicle. It also depends very much on the nature and condition of the tyres and the tyre pressure. High tyre pressure reduces it, and thin tyres lose less energy than thick ones. Rolling friction can account for half a car's petrol consumption at low speeds, so anything that reduces it is welcome. (To draw the obvious conclusion and drive on over-inflated worn-down tyres is not however recommended.)

The figure used to take into account all the factors is called the **coefficient of rolling friction** (C_R) of the tyres. It is equal to the energy loss per metre travelled, expressed as a percentage of the weight of the car. For normal tyres C_R varies between about 1 and 2 per cent. If we assume a fairly good 1.2 per cent for the Smiths' car, the total energy used in this way during the 200 km journey is . . .

1.2 per cent of 10 × 800 times 200 000 metres = 19 200 000 joules

This is 19.2 MJ, so we have now accounted for about 36 MJ.

(It is important to note that rolling friction, as the name suggests, is to do with *rolling*, not *skidding*. Although the C_R and the 'grip' both depend on the nature of the tyres, the energy loss we are talking about here has nothing to do with skidding to a stop or screeching round corners.)

Air Drag

A second major energy-consuming 'outside' force on the car is air drag. This results from the fact that in order to move, the car must push air out of the way. One way of looking at this is to imagine that all the air in front of a vehicle has to be accelerated to match the speed of the vehicle. Air has mass, so the energy needed is the kinetic energy gained by the air pushed ahead by the car. It is not difficult to calculate this using the kinetic energy relationship given above, but first we need to know the mass of air being moved. Suppose the frontal area of the car is 2 square metres. For each metre that it moves forward, 2 cubic metres of air would be pushed ahead. The mass of one cubic metre of air is 1.3 kg, so for each metre the car advances, 2.6 kg of air is accelerated. At the average speed of 45 mph (20 m/s), the kinetic energy going to the air for each metre is

$$\tfrac{1}{2} \times 2.6 \times (20 \times 20) = 520 \text{ J}$$

At this speed, therefore, it seems that the car needs to supply about half a megajoule for each kilometre it travels. The real figure, however, is less. Fortunately our vehicles don't just push all the air ahead of them. Instead, they are 'streamlined' so that they cut their way through it. How much this reduces the energy loss is indicated by the vehicle's **drag coefficient**, C_D. This is the percentage of the 'theoretical' energy that is actually required at any speed, so the lower the C_D the better the vehicle. Drag coefficients of normal cars have improved over recent years—one of the reasons for better petrol consumption figures, and the 30 per cent we shall assume for the Smiths' car is only about three-quarters of a typical value twenty years ago. With this figure, the energy consumed if the car travelled the whole 200 km at its average speed of 45 mph would be

$$30\% \text{ of } 520 \text{ joules per metre times } 200\,000 \text{ metres}$$
$$= 31\,200\,000 \text{ joules}$$

Which is 31.2 MJ, bringing the total to 67.3 MJ.

It is worth noting that there is one very important difference between rolling friction and drag. As we've seen, the rolling friction loss depends on the weight of the car and how far it travels, but the actual speed doesn't enter. (The rate at which the tyres are squashed and released does make a slight difference, but it isn't a major effect and we have ignored it here.) The drag loss is quite different: it depends on the size and design of the car and how far it travels, of course, but how *fast* it travels matters a great deal. The energy used is proportional to the *square* of the speed; so for instance the drag loss for each metre travelled at 63 mph is just about twice that at 45 mph. This explains why rolling friction tends to dominate at lower speeds and drag at anything above about 30 mph. (If the Smiths' car travelled 200 km at a steady 90 mph the drag loss would be 112 MJ, far out-weighing all the others.)

All the Energy

We now have a total of just under seventy megajoules of energy that must be delivered to the wheels during the journey, but the output of the engine will need to be rather greater than this. There are transmission losses, the result of friction in the chain of events between engine and wheels. Typically these might add 11 per cent, increasing the required energy to nearly 75 MJ. Then the engine must provide the energy needed for all the accessories: pumps, fan, lights, other electrical systems, etc. The power for all these has tended to increase as drivers have come to expect ever more sophisticated systems. We'll assume an average of 600 watts throughout the trip, giving a total of 6 MJ. (A car with power steering and brakes, electric windows, or worst of all, air conditioning, could require several times this.) We now have a grand total: 80.7 MJ of energy supplied by the engine during the journey, which is only 18.6 per cent of the 430 MJ provided by the petrol that it consumed. The internal combustion engine is a marvellously versatile, flexible, compact, and even cheap machine, but efficient it is not.

In the last chapter we looked at some of the reasons for this low efficiency. We also saw that the four-fifths of the energy 'lost' in the engine was dissipated as waste heat, carried away in the cooling system or the exhaust gases. The same fate of course awaits our 'useful' 81 MJ. Much of the kinetic energy lost as the car decelerates and the energy that might be gained in running down the hill will become heat in the brakes. Rolling friction means that the tyres become hot. Drag slightly warms the surrounding air. Friction generates heat in bearings and other moving parts. Electrical energy becomes heat in the wiring, fan motors, etc. And so on.

We have therefore answered the original question. The entire energy content of the petrol used for the Smiths' journey, enough to heat a house for a couple of days, has gone into warming the countryside.

More mpg?

Could we do any better? The answer is certainly yes. Over the years there have been considerable improvements in the miles-per-gallon or 'fuel economy'. (A strange name, considering the facts.) Table 6.1 shows the above data for the 200 km journey and the results of a few changes which are all within the realms of possibility. Indeed, 'concept cars' have been developed by various manufacturers who claim that they achieve the sort of fuel consumption shown in the table. It is a salutary thought that if all motor vehicles increased their fuel economy by 60 per cent or so like this, total world oil consumption would be reduced by about one-fifth and carbon dioxide emissions into the atmosphere by 3 billion tonnes a year.

Energy at Home

We obviously aren't doing very well when we travel, so how about staying at home? Table 6.2 shows the pattern of energy consumption in an average British household. It is of course most unlikely that any actual household uses exactly the average mix of

TABLE 6.1. *The car journey, and revised version*

The table shows the energy consumption for a journey of 200 km (125 miles) at an average speed of 20 metres a second (45 mph). Columns 2 and 3 refer to a present-day car and columns 4 and 5 to a possible improved version. (See the text for further details.)

Energy-using process	Details	Energy required (MJ)	Changes	Energy required (MJ)
Gaining kinetic energy	Accelerating (as described in the text) for 800 kg car	10.5	Mass reduced to 750 kg	9.8
Gaining gravitational energy	Climbing hills totalling 800 metres	6.4	Mass 750 kg	6.0
Rolling friction	Travelling 200 km, with C_R = 1.2%	19.2	Mass 750 kg, C_R reduced to 1.0%	15.0
Air drag	Travelling 200 km at 20 metres per second, with C_D = 30%	31.2	Improve vehicle shape to reduce C_D to 24%	25.0
Total energy delivered to wheels		*67.3*		*55.8*
Transmission losses	Add 11% to energy delivered	74.7	Reduce transmission loss to 9%	60.8
Accessories	600 W for 10000 seconds	6.0	Reduce by more efficient systems	5.0
Total energy output of the engine		*80.7*		*65.8*
Average engine efficiency		18.6%	Improved engine (see Chapter 5)	24%
Required energy input to the engine		*434 MJ*		*274*
Fuel requirement Fuel consumption	@ 160 MJ per gallon	2.7 gal 46 mpg		1.7 gal 73 mpg

TABLE 6.2. *Energy consumption in an average UK household, 1994*

Annual consumption		kWh	GJ	Cost[a]
Gas	17000 kWh	17000	61	£250
Electricity	5000 kWh	5000	18	£400
Solid fuel	$\frac{1}{3}$ tonne	2500	9	£20
Heating oil	160 litres	1500	$5\frac{1}{2}$	£20
Total		26000	$93\frac{1}{2}$	£590

[a] The cost data are estimates based on average 1994 prices paid by domestic consumers.

fuels. (Nor for that matter does any actual household include exactly two and two-thirds people.) As with many averages, this one hides very large variations—from single people to households of twenty, bed-sits to stately homes, and flats in South Coast apartment blocks to isolated cottages in the far North. But we'll use it as our example and try to see, as with the car journey above, how the average energy might be used.

Why does a house need energy? We can list four categories of use:

- essentially electrical: lighting and many appliances
- high temperature heat for cooking
- medium temperature heat for hot water
- lower temperature heat for space heating.

Notice that the order of these items is not arbitrary. It is easy to obtain from each type of energy any of those lower in the list. If you've got electricity, you can produce very hot water, and if you've got hot water you can easily produce warm water—by waiting if necessary. But producing hotter from colder is not so easy, and certainly doesn't happen spontaneously. (If you have read Chapter 5 this remark should ring bells: it is the Second Law in action again.) We'll return later to the significance of this for our uses of energy, in the home or elsewhere, but here we'll look at each of these uses in more detail, at the same time asking where there might be scope for improvement.

Lighting

The average household uses about 300 kWh a year for lighting; equivalent to running five 60-watt bulbs for three hours a day throughout the year. It seems unlikely that we'll use fewer lights in the future, or that we'll change to a different fuel. However, a very important point to notice is that less than a tenth of the 300 kWh actually produces useful light. All the rest immediately becomes heat, radiated and conducted away from the light bulb. It is not entirely lost, of course, as it helps to heat the house; but that is hardly the aim, and it's an expensive way to do it.

Why not convert all the energy into light, without the heat? The unfortunate fact is that this is impossible with an ordinary filament lamp (for reasons that we'll see in more detail in Chapter 11). Discharge tubes, however, are not subject to the same limit. Probably the most efficient easily available light source is the large sodium lamp used for street lighting. Using some 200 W of electrical power, this gives about five times the light output of two ordinary 100-watt bulbs. There are, however, a couple of problems. First, we don't want to live in a bright yellow glare, and secondly most of us don't need one lamp equivalent to ten 100-watt bulbs in the middle of the living room. We want nice, small, intimate lights.

The problem of colour has largely been solved in the fluorescent tubes, at the cost of some reduction in efficiency. Many 'low energy' bulbs of this type have come on the market in the past decade, but they have yet to become widely accepted, and do still have a few problems. One is the initial cost: ten times that of a conventional bulb. The energy saving will cover the difference in a couple of years with our 3-hour average daily use, and the fluorescent bulb should then continue to save money for at least another five years. Many people feel, however, that the 'light equivalents' claimed by the manufacturers are optimistic, and unlike conventional bulbs, these produce less light as they age. Other disadvantages are that the bulbs are bulky and unsuitable for use in many fittings; and must not be used with dimmer switches. Nevertheless, the design and light quality have both improved considerably in recent years, so we may yet see their more widespread use. After all, if every UK household cut its energy consumption for lighting by half, it would save about £20 a year—and reduce annual carbon dioxide emissions from power-stations by some 7 million tonnes.

Appliances

There are 8760 hours in a year, so to run something whose power rating is 100 W day and night, year round, uses 876 kWh of electrical energy, at a cost of about £70. Of course few appliances are used in this way. (A heated towel rail might be one possibility.) So, although the power rating of an appliance such as a refrigerator is relevant, we really need to know its average annual consumption in normal use. Table 6.3 gives such data for some household electrical appliances and equipment. How much electricity any particular household uses for such purposes will obviously depend on how many of these appliances they own and how they

TABLE 6.3. *Electricity consumption in UK households*

Appliances	Average annual consumption per appliance (kWh)	Household consumption (kWh/year)	
		light user	heavy user
Lighting	60	300	500
Vacuum cleaner, iron, toaster, kettle, radio, CD, tape deck, computer, etc.	<100	400	800
TV	1000	1000	1500
Fridge	180	180	180
Freezer	420	420	420
Washing machine	200	200	300[a]
Tumble drier	700		700
Dishwasher	600		600
Cooking	1000		1000
Total		2500	6000

[a] Includes electrical heating of water.

use them. So the third and fourth columns of the table show the consequences for two households.

The 'light user' of Table 6.3 is in fact close to the average householder. She doesn't use a dishwasher or electric tumble drier and heats and cooks with gas, but her use of lights, TV, and the customary kitchen appliances is about average. Her resulting electricity consumption for these purposes is about half the total shown in Table 6.2—leaving something for hot water and possibly space heating.

The 'heavy user' is different in several respects. This is an all-electric household, with electricity rather than gas for cooking and to heat the water for the washing machine. The dishwasher and electric tumble drier are used regularly, and lights and other small electrical equipment rather more than average. The household also has a larger TV—or watches it more. Or perhaps they use the remote control to 'switch off' rather than the power switch or wall socket; an expensive habit that could account for an extra few hundred kWh a year. The consequence of all this is an electricity consumption for appliances alone that is already in excess of the total for the average household.

Thermal Insulation

An important factor in determining the energy consumption of a refrigerator or freezer is how well it 'keeps the cold in'; or more accurately, how well it keeps the heat out. This question of thermal insulation is also important for the next three items in our energy consumption list, so we might look at it a little more carefully before proceeding.

Heat energy will flow through anything where the temperature on the two sides is different: the casing of a fridge or an oven, a hot-water tank, or the wall of a house. The rate of this energy flow depends on three things:

- the temperature difference between the two sides;
- the total area available for the flow;
- the thickness and insulating qualities of the material through which heat is flowing.

Most of these factors are fairly obvious. Of course you lose more heat through a large window than a small one, and on a cold day than a warm one. And of course a water tank consisting only of a thin layer of metal loses more heat than one with a thick insulating jacket. But how much more? There are various ways of specifying the quality of an insulator, but we'll concentrate on just one: the **U-value**. It is used mainly in the context of buildings: walls, roofs, windows, etc., and if you know the U-value, it is very easy to calculate the rate of heat flow:

heat flow through each square metre
= U-value × temperature difference.

Suppose we want to work out the heat loss through a window. If it is an old one, single-glazed, its U-value could be as high as 6, so on a day when the outdoor and indoor temperatures are 5°C and 20°C respectively, the heat loss rate through a large window, with an area of 2 square metres, will be

$$2 \times 6 \times 15 = 180\,W$$

which means that, if the temperatures remain the same throughout, the energy lost in 24 hours will be over 4 kWh! As we'll see when we come to space heating, reducing the U-value can halve this loss.*

The same idea can be applied to a hot-water tank. Suppose you keep your hot water at 65°C. The air around the tank is likely to be warm, say 25°C, so the temperature difference is 40°C. A reasonably well-insulated tank might be losing heat at a rate of 100 W under these conditions. But if you reduce the water temperature to 55°C, the difference becomes only 30°C and the loss rate falls to 75 W, a saving of more than 200 kWh over the course of a year.

The aim in a refrigerator or freezer is of course to keep the heat

---

* Readers who have studied some physics may wonder why the term 'thermal conductivity' has not appeared in this discussion. The answer is simple: the layers of air on the two sides of a window are as important for the heat flow as the conductivity of the glass itself, and U-values take this into account. The actual temperatures of the inside and outside of the pane are very different from the indoor and outdoor temperatures—as you can tell at once by putting your hand on the glass.

out, rather than in, but the reasoning is the same again. The lower temperature (the temperature inside) is likely to be fixed in this case, so it is the temperature outside that matters: the warmer the surroundings, the larger the temperature difference and the greater the heat flow into the interior. Making sure that the air around the refrigeration unit is as cool as possible brings a double benefit because, as we saw in Chapter 5, ('Refrigerators, etc.') the performance of the unit, the COP, is also better the smaller the temperature difference. So you have less heat to be pumped out and more efficient pumping as well. In the kitchen, with its refrigeration unit tucked cosily under a worktop in a pocket of warm air, your freezer could be costing you £20 or so a year more to run than if you put it in the garage or a garden shed. A clear-cut case, surely? Unfortunately not. Things are never that simple in the real world. Our reasoning has ignored the fact that the annual 400 kWh or so 'consumed' by the appliance turns into heat which could be helping to warm your house. So do you run the appliance less efficiently, paying more but gaining at least some benefit in heat, or reduce your electricity bill but lose the benefit?

Cooking

The average household uses about 1000 kWh a year for cooking with electricity, or about 1500 kWh for cooking with gas. This suggests that gas cookers are less efficient in their use of energy, which should not surprise us. As we've seen, there is almost always waste heat carried away by combustion products when a fuel is burned. (On the other hand, it could be that people who use gas cook 50 per cent more meals!) Cookers are on the whole a bright spot in the world of energy, having become much less wasteful in recent years. In principle, once an oven has reached the set temperature very little more heat input should be required—just enough to increase the temperature of the middle of the joint until it is done. In practice of course, even an empty oven will use gas or electricity while maintaining a steady temperature. The additional energy is needed to replace heat losses to the surroundings, and it is in this respect that ovens have improved—better insulation has considerably reduced these losses. Fans to improve heat distribution are now common, too—but they need motors, so they may be a doubtful advantage from the purely energy point of view. The trend to larger cookers also works against the improved performance, with a greater mass of material to be heated before you can cook your small pie.

Cooking—or rather re-heating—small pies brings us to the real energy-saver: the microwave oven. Consider the figures. Suppose you do want to heat up a pie. To bring a normal oven to the required temperature and maintain it for the necessary time will need gas or electricity at the 4 kW full supply rate for perhaps 15 minutes in all: a total of 1 kWh. The microwave, using 600 W, heats the pie in 10 minutes, for a total of one-tenth of a kWh. Of course, not all of us want to live on warmed-up pies; and it may also be relevant that you'll need to re-heat more than 2000 pies before the microwave oven pays for itself.

Hot Water

We like our hot water supply at between 55°C and 65°C, and we use between 50 and 80 litres of it a day per person. How much energy is used in producing this? We'll assume 65 litres, and that it enters the boiler or water heater at an average 12°C and is heated to 62°C. To heat one litre (kg) of water by 1°C takes 4200 joules. So one person's annual supply will need:

$$65 \times (62 - 12) \times 4200 \times 365 = 4.8 \text{ billion joules}$$

which is a little over 1300 kWh, giving an average annual household requirement of about 3500 kWh.

But we must remember the losses. If the household hot-water system includes any form of storage, an energy input is needed just to keep the water hot, because there will always be heat losses from the tank and pipes (see 'Thermal insulation', above). Incidentally, it follows that leaving the immersion heater on all night does waste energy. Keeping the water hot means continually replacing lost heat. With the heater off, the water cools, and as we've seen above, cooler water means a lower loss rate. So the total loss during the night—the energy that must be replaced—is less than if the water was kept hot all the time.

Insulating the tank and pipes makes an enormous difference to the energy loss. With very poor insulation, the losses from a full-sized hot-water tank can amount to 2000 kWh a year—and if the tank is in the roof, the house doesn't even benefit from the heat. Very good lagging can reduce this figure to perhaps 700 kWh, and the annual household requirement then becomes 4200 kWh. If the water is heated electrically this is all the energy needed, because an electric heater converts all its input energy into useful heat. (This figure is also about right for a system with direct electrical heating and no storage tank, as there will always be some slight losses.)

If the system uses a fossil-fuel boiler there will be further losses—up the flue or out of the sides. In the discussion in Chapter 4 ('Furnaces and Boilers') we saw that a well-run power-station boiler can convert over 90 per cent of the energy of its fuel into useful heat. This is unfortunately unlikely to be true of the average household central heating boiler. Unless the system is regularly tested and adjusted by a skilled engineer, its efficiency is unlikely to exceed 75 per cent, and there is reason to believe that many are very much worse.

Table 6.4 compares four households. The first has either direct electrical heating or a very well-insulated tank and pipes and an immersion heater. The second again has good thermal insulation, and uses an efficient gas boiler. (The figures would be not dissimilar for direct heating with an efficient gas heater.) The third is probably most representative of the UK average, a house with some tank insulation and a boiler of average efficiency. Then there is the last household, with no insulation, a boiler that hasn't been looked at for years, and a gas bill for hot water that is £100 a year more than it need be.

Hot Air

Finally, we like to keep warm. Again, the only reason for continuous heating is that the house is continuously losing heat, and there are two main ways in which this happens. The first is the one we've already seen: the inevitable flow of heat outwards through the windows, walls, roof, floor etc., as long as the interior

TABLE 6.4. *Producing hot water*

The figures show the input needed to produce 3500 kWh of useful heat—enough for hot water for an average household for one year. The four examples are (A1) a very well-lagged system, with immersion heater only, (A2) as A1 but with an efficient gas boiler, (B) an average UK system with gas boiler, and (C) a very poor system with little insulation and an inefficient boiler.

All energies are in kWh. Costs are based on 1995 UK domestic prices: 7.6 p/kWh for electricity and 1.6 p/kWh for gas.

	Energy to heat water	Tank and pipes			Energy input to tank	Boiler efficiency (%)	Total annual consumption	Cost £/yr
		Temperature (° C)	Insulation	Losses				
A1	3500	55	good	700	4200	N/A	4 200	340
A2	3500	55	good	700	4200	75	5 600[a]	90
B	3500	60	average	1400	4900	60	8 200[a]	130
C	3500	65	poor	2100	5600	45	12 400[a]	200

[a] The required quantities of fuels other than gas can be estimated by recalling that the energy content of a litre of oil is a little less than 10 kWh, of a tonne of coal a little less than 8000 kWh, and a tonne of wood about 4500 kWh.

is warmer than the outside air. As discussed in 'Thermal insulation' above, the U-value indicates how good—or rather how bad—each of these is as an insulator. We've seen that a single pane of glass can have a U-value as high as 6. With a modern window it might fall between 5 and 6, and double glazing can reduce it to about 3. Not surprisingly, it remains the case that, area for area, windows are the 'worst' (i.e. the best) transmitters of heat. The U-value of a single brick wall can be as high as 2 whilst the normal cavity wall value is about 1.5, which is reduced to less than 1 by filling the cavity with insulating foam.

The second cause of heat loss is the constant need to heat fresh air. Air may seem rather light stuff—airy, in fact—but nevertheless there is about a quarter of a tonne of it in the average small house. We need air changes for health and comfort, and each complete air change means heating this quarter-tonne of air. One complete change an hour is considered acceptable for an inhabited space (more if it is crowded). To heat one tonne of air by 1°C requires about a quarter of a kWh of energy, so if the outdoor and indoor temperatures are 10°C and 20°C respectively, each tonne will need 2.5 kWh. With one change an hour, the energy requirement for a day with these 24-hour average temperatures will therefore be

$$24 \times \frac{1}{4} \times 2.5 = 15\,\text{kWh}$$

To calculate the annual heating demand for the house, we need to put together all these data: the areas of windows, walls, roof, and floor and their U-values, the rate of air change—and the temperatures. The outdoor temperature is of course changing all the time, and published tables of 'degree days' for different locations are used in detailed calculations. We'll simplify things, however, by using average outdoor temperatures. We then need to decide

(*a*)　What temperature do we want indoors?

(*b*)　For how many hours a day is the house heated?

(*c*)　For how many months during the year?

(*d*)　What is the average outdoor temperature during those months?

We'll take two cases, as follows:

Case 1. (*a*) 20°C (*b*) 18 hours (*c*) 8 months (*d*) 7°C

This might be a typical well-heated British house—although it would look like hardship to many Americans.

Case 2. (*a*) 21°C (*b*) 24 hours (*c*) 12 months (*d*) 10°C

Some like it hot, and these people are obviously wary of British summers. Note, however, that the slightly higher average outdoor temperature during the heating period (the whole year here) does recognize that the summer months are warmer.

Possible data for three households are given in Table 6.5. The first two have the heating pattern of Case 1 above, with the difference that one house is very energy efficient and the other not. The third house is the same as the first, but with the Case 2 heating pattern. Comparing the final column with the figures in Tables 6.3 and 6.4 shows clearly that space heating is the dominant energy use for any of the households we've considered.

There are two further important factors to take into account in assessing the heating needs of a house. One is the 'free heat'. All the energy consumed by electrical appliances eventually turns

TABLE 6.5. *Heat losses from houses*

The figures are for three different semi-detached houses, each with 90 sq m (900 sq ft) of living area on two floors and a total external wall and roof area of about 140 sq m.

The house	Effective U-value of walls, roof, and windows (W/sq m/°C)	Heat loss rate per °C temperature difference		Annual heating hours	Average temperature during heating period			Total annual heat loss[a] (kWh)
		walls etc. + air change	total (W)		Indoor (a)	Outdoor (b)	(a) − (b)	
Energy-saving house Well-insulated walls and roof, double-glazed windows. Few draughts, so one air change an hour	1	140 + 80	220	4380[b]	20	7	13	12 500
The leaky house Normal cavity walls, some roof insulation, ordinary windows. Draughty, so two air changes an hour	2	280 + 160	440	4380[b]	20	7	13	25 000
The hot house Structure etc. as energy-saving house	1	140 + 80	220	8760[c]	21	10	11	21 000

[a] Loss rate per °C times temperature difference times hours.
[b] 18 hours a day for 8 months.
[c] 24 hours a day for 12 months.

into heat energy and helps to warm the house. The same is true of much of the heat from cooking and, if the house is sensibly designed, the 'losses' from hot water pipes, etc. Even an inefficient boiler contributes something, as not all its lost heat goes out of the flue. And finally, there are the inhabitants. People generate heat, at an average rate of about 75 watts per person, so they make an appreciable contribution. Table 6.6 shows some possible data, based on the 'light user' of Table 6.3 and intermediate cases from Tables 6.4 and 6.5. These lead to an annual total of nearly 8000 kWh, but this heat won't always come at times when the house needs it, so we assume that roughly half is useful.

The other factor is 'solar gain'. The sun shining on a wall or windows of a house warms it of course, and can provide an appreciable heat input—even in the British Isles in winter (see

TABLE 6.6. *'Free heat'*

Sources of heat	kWh
Appliances	2500
Cooker, $\frac{2}{3}$ of 1500 kWh	1000
Tank and pipe losses	1400
Boiler, $\frac{2}{3}$ of losses	2000
People, 12000 person-hours	900
Total heat generated	7800
Useful heat, about half of total	4000

TABLE 6.7. *How one household might use the energy*

Item	Consumption (kWh)	
	electricity	gas
Appliances (Table 6.3)	2500	
Cooker		1500
Hot water (Table 6.4)		
Gas boiler, $\frac{2}{3}$ of 8200 kWh		5500
Immersion heater, $\frac{1}{3}$ of 4900 kWh	1600	
Sub-totals excluding heating	4100	7000
National average annual household consumption		26000
Subtract sum of sub-totals		−11100
		14900
Add 'free heat' (Table 6.6)		4000
Energy available for space heating		18900

Chapter 11). For the present, however, we'll leave this contribution, returning to it below when we look at a really energy-efficient house.

Summing it up

We can now do a few sums to see how the figures for the different types of use might add up to give the 'average household' total. Table 6.7 shows the results. We assume the relatively modest 'light user' of appliances (Table 6.3) and add 1500 kWh for gas cooking.

For hot water, we take Case B of Table 6.4, but use the gas boiler during the winter eight months only, when the central heating is on. An immersion heater provides the summer third of the required 4900 kWh. These items bring the total to just over 11000 kWh, leaving about 15000 kWh of the average household consumption unused. To this we can add the 4000 kWh provided by the 'free heat', giving a total of 19000 kWh for space heating. Inspection of Table 6.5 shows that this would be sufficient for comfortable warmth in a house intermediate between our 'energy-saving' and 'leaky' cases.

We notice that the electricity consumption of our householder is rather less than the average, but there could be several reasons for this. First, she is the 'light user' of Table 6.3. Then we didn't include in this table the power needed to run the pumps of the gas central heating system (or a fan in a gas cooker). But we also know that some UK households, unlike this one, use electricity for their main heating and these probably use more than their 'share' of the total consumption. It is very important to remember that a national average is no more than one national total divided by another national total, and that it can hide very wide variations indeed.

The Low-Energy House

How many people in Britain—or other countries, for that matter—are aware that it is possible to have a comfortably warm house with no heating system at all? We are not talking about a house in the tropics, either, but places with average temperatures like those of the UK, or even lower. We've just seen that the average British semi-detached house might need a heat input of 20000 kWh a year just to stay reasonably warm. How could we manage with none at all? The answer, of course, is that we couldn't; but what we could do is to make maximum use of heat which is already available and make sure that heat losses are as low as possible. The result could be significant. About an eighth of Britain's total annual energy is used in warming houses, at a cost of some five billion pounds a year. Denmark, living largely on imported oil, decided in the

1970s that something needed to be done. Introducing building regulations that demanded much better insulation, and making maximum use of combined heat and power for district heating, they halved the energy needed to heat the average building within 15 years. Sweden, concentrating on improving existing houses, reduced their average heat requirement by more than a third during a similar period. How did they do it?

A good starting-point for the route to our low-energy house is Table 6.5, and we'll look at the items there to see where real savings can be made. We'll also add another source of 'free heat' to those in Table 6.6. Some of the improvements, as we'll see, are only practicable in new buildings, but others can be 'retro-fits' for existing houses.

Insulation

In contrast to the single-glazed window with its U-value of about 6, there are now 'super-insulating' windows with U-values as low as 0.7—nearly ten times better. How do they do this? The windows are triple-glazed so that the air layers between the glass act as good insulators. And they don't have metal frames! Their frames do however include 'heat barriers', insulating strips all round, within the frame, to reduce conduction through it. They also have weather-stripping (draught stripping) to prevent any air leakage.

With a window U-value of less than 1, something obviously needs to be done about the walls. Multi-layer walls, with a thick layer of insulation sandwiched between brick or other masonry, or wood, can bring the U-value down to 0.5 or less, with a similar value for the floor and even lower for a very well-insulated roof. With care, our low-energy house might achieve an overall U-value, for walls, floor, windows, and roof, of 0.5.

Fresh Air

Our super-efficient house will also be as airtight as possible. This is one of the most difficult things to achieve, requiring extremely careful attention to all joints between walls and floors, for instance, and to the roof structure. This is not intended to asphyxiate the inhabitants, but to give complete control of the air flow. So first you eliminate all accidental leaks and then you arrange to have ventilation when and where you want it. This also allows a heat exchanger to be incorporated, using the heat of the departing air and/or hot water to pre-warm the incoming air. Another advantage of a draught-free house (and windows that aren't cold on the inside) is that most people are then comfortable with a slightly lower air temperature, a further saving.

Solar Gain

It is fairly obvious that it is an advantage to have most windows on the south side of the house if possible—or at least not to have large north-facing ones. (Unfortunately not so obvious, it seems, to many builders of British houses over the past couple of centuries.) Even in Britain, the solar energy reaching each square metre of a south-facing window in the course of a year can be over 700 kWh. Supposing that your house has 8 square metres of south-facing window, that these transmit 70 per cent of the solar energy reaching them, and that one-third of this comes at times of the year when you need heat, the result is a useful gain of 1300 kWh a year.

Revising the Sums

The first two items above bring the annual heat loss for the house described in Table 6.5 down to perhaps 5000 kWh. In Table 6.6 we saw that even for a house with quite modest use of appliances, the useful 'free heat' from these, from cooking and the hot water system, and from the inhabitants could amount to 4000 kWh a year. Add the solar gain of 1300 kWh and we have eliminated the need for a heating system, with even a little to spare.

The main problem for our low-energy house is, of course, the cost. How much must we pay for all those super-insulating windows? Certainly several thousand pounds for the average British house. There is a well-known rule of thumb, that people will invest in energy-saving measures only if convinced that they will get their money back in two years. (This piece of folklore also appears in discussion of industrial and commercial energy saving.) It seems a rather short-sighted policy, but if true it means that there is little chance of more than a bit of loft insulation and newspaper stuffed in the worst of the gaps. Sweden achieved the 30 per cent reduction mentioned above by first training the craftsmen to do the work and then offering full government grants to pay for it. It is reported that after a few years people began to see the point, and the improvements continued even when the grants were reduced. But Sweden had a different starting-point. It is a salutary thought that the most recent building regulations designed to improve the energy efficiency of British houses just meet the specification that was the norm in Sweden 50 years ago. (Parts of the USA still have no insulation regulations at all.) And it is a bit discouraging to discover the date on an article published in Britain and containing most of the above ideas: 1978.

But perhaps this is unfair. True, the average British household uses about one-eighth more energy in the mid-1990s than twenty years ago, but we must remember that these twenty years have seen enormous growth in the number of useful but energy-consuming household appliances and a considerable change in the quality of space heating we expect. (It is also reported that we take more baths and showers!) There has been some government support for energy-saving measures too, in both Britain and the USA, although this has diminished in recent years. It will probably be some time before we see a majority of really low-energy houses anywhere, but perhaps we are gradually learning, and won't just sit and wait for the next energy crisis before taking a serious interest in reducing our fuel bills.

A Zero-Energy House?

We could of course go further, to the zero-energy or 'fully auton-omous' house. It is designed for minimum heat loss and maxi-mum solar gain, oriented to capture as much solar energy as possible, and with a long-term heat store to hold it: massive ma-sonry, or a large volume of water or rocks, well-insulated to retain the heat. Solar panels supply the household hot water. Electric power comes from photovoltaic cells or a wind generator, with rechargeable batteries for power when there is no input. Home-grown coppice, or biogas produced by anaerobic fermentation of wastes, provide fuels for cooking and additional heat.

A number of autonomous houses have been built—a very large number indeed, if we include those occupied by the billions of people who have no other option. Of those built from choice rather than necessity, most cheat, of course, by using the products of a modern industrial society (PV cells do grow on trees, but they are called leaves, and they don't make very good power supplies.) To be fair, most enthusiasts for this type of do-it-yourself housing experiment recognize that it will not appeal to everyone. Never-theless they make a point which should be attractive to just those supporters of modern technology who tend to reject their philos-ophy out of hand. Most of us living in the developed world are totally dependent for our way of life on technical devices and systems which we do not begin to understand. Centuries of scien-tific advance have led to a situation where the sequence of pro-cesses leading from the reservoir or coal-mine to the electric light is as much a mystery as thunderbolts from heaven were to our ancestors. Surely any serious technologist should welcome the idea of a world where people are not alienated from the mech-anical objects around them, where an elegant solution to a tech-nical problem might earn the same informed applause as a work of art or a display of sporting skill.

7

Electricity

―――

A New Force

Electrotechnology is a relative newcomer—compared with mining, say, or the working of metals, or paper-making. In 1831 Michael Faraday discovered the principle of virtually all our present-day generators: that a varying magnetic effect produces a voltage. The next fifty years saw one of the most remarkable periods ever of technological development. Within a decade came not only the electric motor but the first trials of electric trains and even an electric boat. Arc lamps followed, and rapid improvements to electrical machinery, and by the early 1880s the conditions existed for the first public electricity supplies. Generators were large enough and sufficiently reliable, transformers and insulated cables had been developed to distribute the power, and Edison's invention of the light bulb made electricity attractive to potential consumers. (Another essential for a public supply was also available: an early form of electricity meter.)

The initial growth of the generating industry, with output increasing at an amazing 30 per cent a year (Fig. 7.1), was probably faster than for any other new technology over a similar period. (Or has the personal computer already beaten this record?) The rate of increase then declined a little, but nevertheless maintained a remarkably steady $7\frac{1}{2}$ per cent a year for nearly 50 years, apparently ignoring wars, recessions, and energy crises. In recent decades demand has risen much less rapidly, but it is a salutary thought that we have used more electricity in the past 15 years than in the preceding 150.

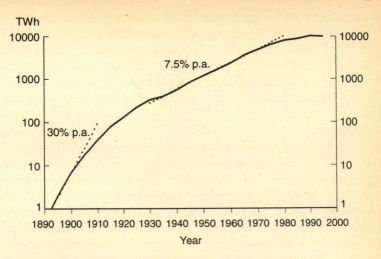

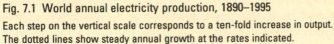

Fig. 7.1 World annual electricity production, 1890–1995

Each step on the vertical scale corresponds to a ten-fold increase in output.
The dotted lines show steady annual growth at the rates indicated.

The efficient production, distribution and use of electric power are accordingly important matters, and we shall look at some aspects of present methods in this chapter. With as wide and varied a field as electrical technology, we can of course only touch on a few topics, but there is one merit in this area of energy studies: the field may be wide but the central core of basic science is very compact. We shall need to extend the atomic picture of materials, and to introduce a few new laws dealing with the specifically electrical behaviour of things; but this will be enough to allow us to discuss in some detail several important technological matters.

Let us begin by returning to the atom, which we saw in Chapter 4 as the basic constituent of everything—solid, liquid, or gaseous. Closer investigation reveals that atoms themselves are composed of smaller entities. Almost all the mass of any atom is in its nucleus, a concentration of dense matter roughly at the centre. We shall say more about nuclei in Chapter 8, but here we are concerned with the outer part of the atom: a swarm of electrons, very light particles which contribute well under one thousandth of the total mass. One might visualize an atom as a miniature solar system; but when we try to explain how the fast-moving electrons are held in place, calculations show at once that gravity—the pull that holds the planets as they swing around the sun—is far too weak a force. If that were all, the electrons would fly off in all directions.

The force which holds an atom together and gives it its stability is the **electrical force** between the electrons and the nucleus, and this type of force differs in one extremely important respect from the force of gravity. Everything experiences the pull of gravity, not only towards the Earth but towards every other object to a greater or lesser degree. This is not the case for the electrical force, which affects different objects in different ways. Some are pulled towards each other, but others are pushed apart—and many are not affected at all. Imagine a strange substance which is pushed rather than pulled by gravity. A piece of it when released will shoot vertically upwards, and if you hold on to it, you will rise or fall depending on the relative strengths of the pull on you and the push on it. With a piece of suitable size, the two forces will just balance and you will float. There is of course no such 'negative-gravity' material, as far as we know, and the parallel with electrical forces is in any case not perfect, but it is the idea that is important: that we can have forces of repulsion as well as attraction and that these can cancel each other.

An atomic nucleus and an electron are electrical opposites. The nucleus is pulled one way by any outside electrical force and an electron the opposite way. The nucleus is said to have 'positive electric charge' and the electron 'negative electric charge', names which are of course quite arbitrary. (In Chapter 8 we meet particles called neutrons, which have no charge.) There is a strong electrical force of attraction between the nucleus and the electrons in an atom, and as long as the electrons stay near the nucleus—which they do with some tenacity—the atom as a whole is neither pushed nor pulled by outside electrical forces. It is electrically neutral because the positive charge of the nucleus is *exactly* counter-balanced by the negative charge of all the electrons. If we do manage to remove an electron from an atom, it can then move off under the influence of any outside force, leaving the atom (now properly called an **ion**) with a net positive electric charge.

All electrons are completely identical with each other—'as alike as the same pea in a pod'—and the number needed to make up the complete atom is the single most important characteristic of a substance. Atoms of the element copper, for instance, have 29 electrons (Table 7.1). They may lose one or two under some circumstances, but if the number in the complete, neutral atom is not 29, it is not copper but some other element. A carbon atom has six electrons, oxygen eight, and hydrogen only one. The whole of chemistry is a consequence of these electron numbers: they determine whether the element is a metal or a gas, what molecules the atoms will form with atoms of other elements, and—an important question, as we've seen in Chapter 4—how much energy is needed to take apart these molecules.

Amps

That some materials are much better conductors of electric currents than others is common experience. When a wire breaks, the current in the circuit stops because the air between the broken ends is a good insulator. The current in a household circuit flows in the copper wires and not out through the surrounding walls because copper is a much better conductor than the plastic insulation around the wire. When we ask why this is, we are really asking what it is that makes a metal metallic. The answer, in terms of the atomic picture, is that a metal has large numbers of free electrons. Every atom has released one or more of its electrons, and these move around freely within the metal at very high speeds. When we introduce an electric force along a wire, as we do in connecting a battery to, say, a torch bulb (Fig. 7.2), the whole assembly of free electrons is moved along by the force, and it is this drift of the cloud of electrons which constitutes the current. To allow a current to flow continuously there must obviously be a complete circuit: a loop. (Otherwise electrons would pile up at

TABLE 7.1. *The elements*

The upper left-hand figure is the number of electrons in the atom. The figure beneath the symbol represents the mass of the atom, and is further discussed in Chapter 8. One of the most interesting discoveries in chemistry is the repeating periodic pattern shown here, in which elements with similar chemical properties fall in the same vertical columns.

1H 1.008																	2He 4.003
3Li 6.939	4Be 9.012											5B 10.81	6C 12.01	7N 14.01	8O 15.999	9F 19.00	10Ne 20.18
11Na 22.99	12Mg 24.31											13Al 26.98	14Si 28.09	15P 30.97	16S 32.06	17Cl 35.45	18Ar 39.95
19K 39.102	20Ca 40.08	21Sc 44.96	22Ti 47.90	23V 50.94	24Cr 52.00	25Mn 54.94	26Fe 55.85	27Co 58.93	28Ni 58.71	29Cu 63.54	30Zn 65.37	31Ga 69.72	32Ge 72.59	33As 74.92	34Se 78.96	35Br 79.91	36Kr 83.80
37Rb 85.47	38Sr 87.62	39Y 88.91	40Zr 91.22	41Nb 92.91	42Mo 95.94	43Tc (97)	44Ru 101.1	45Rh 102.91	46Pd 106.4	47Ag 107.87	48Cd 112.4	49In 114.8	50Sn 118.7	51Sb 121.8	52Te 127.6	53I 126.9	54Xe 131.3
55Cs 132.91	56Ba 137.34	57–71 (see below)	72Hf 178.5	73Ta 180.95	74W 183.85	75Re 186.2	76Os 190.2	77Ir 192.2	78Pt 195.1	79Au 196.97	80Hg 200.6	81Tl 204.4	82Pb 207.2	83Bi 209.0	84Po (209)	85At (210)	86Rn (222)
87Fr (223)	88Ra (226)	89–103 (see below)															

Lanthanides														
57La 138.9	58Ce 140.1	59Pr 140.9	60Nd 144.2	61Pm (145)	62Sm 150.4	63Eu 152.0	64Gd 157.3	65Tb 158.9	66Dy 162.5	67Ho 164.9	68Er 167.3	69Tm 168.9	70Yb 173.0	71Lu 175.0

Actinides														
89Ac	90Th	91Pa	92U	93Np	94Pu	95Am	96Cm	97Bk	98Cf	99Es	100Fm	101Md	102No	103Lr

	Element	Atomic number		Element	Atomic number		Element	Atomic number		Element	Atomic number
Ac	actinium	89	Er	erbium	68	Hg	mercury	80	Sm	samarium	62
Al	aluminium	13	Eu	europium	63	Mo	molybdenum	42	Sc	scandium	21
Am	americium	95	Fm	fermium	100	Nd	neodymium	60	Se	selenium	34
Sb	antimony	51	F	fluorine	9	Ne	neon	10	Si	silicon	14
Ar	argon	18	Fr	francium	87	Np	neptunium	93	Ag	silver	47
As	arsenic	33	Gd	gadolinium	64	Ni	nickel	28	Na	sodium	11
At	astatine	85	Ga	gallium	31	Nb	niobium	41	Sr	strontium	38
Ba	barium	56	Ge	germanium	32	N	nitrogen	7	S	sulphur	16
Bk	berkelium	97	Au	gold	79	No	nobelium	102	Ta	tantalum	73
Be	beryllium	4	Hf	hafnium	72	Os	osmium	76	Tc	technetium	43
Bi	bismuth	83	He	helium	2	O	oxygen	8	Te	tellurium	52
B	boron	5	Ho	holmium	67	Pd	palladium	46	Tb	terbium	65
Br	bromine	35	H	hydrogen	1	P	phosphorus	15	Tl	thallium	81
Cd	cadmium	48	In	indium	49	Pt	platinum	78	Th	thorium	90
Cs	caesium	55	I	iodine	53	Pu	plutonium	94	Tm	thulium	69
Ca	calcium	20	Ir	iridium	77	Po	polonium	84	Sn	tin	50
Cf	californium	98	Fe	iron	26	K	potassium	19	Ti	titanium	22
C	carbon	6	Kr	krypton	36	Pr	praseodymium	59	W	tungsten	74
Ce	cerium	58	La	lanthanum	57	Pm	promethium	61	U	uranium	92
Cl	chlorine	17	Lr	lawrencium	103	Pa	protoactinium	91	V	vanadium	23
Cr	chromium	24	Pb	lead	82	Ra	radium	88	Xe	xenon	54
Co	cobalt	27	Li	lithium	3	Rn	radon	86	Yb	ytterbium	70
Cu	copper	29	Lu	lutetium	71	Re	rhenium	75	Y	yttrium	39
Cm	curium	96	Mg	magnesium	12	Rh	rhodium	45	Zn	zinc	30
Dy	dysprosium	66	Mn	manganese	25	Rb	rubidium	37	Zr	zirconium	40
Es	einsteinium	99	Md	medelevium	101	Ru	ruthenium	44			

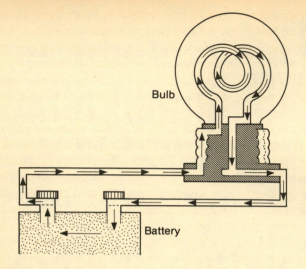

Fig. 7.2 An electrical circuit

some point, producing a massive electric charge there, and stopping the flow.) The same current must thus be flowing at every point along the wire, and also through the supply. If the bulb filament is broken, no current flows at all, because none can pass across the gap. Air, like other insulators, does not normally have many free electrons and therefore will not carry much current. (Of course, if something happens which breaks up the atoms, producing free electrons, then a current can flow: we've all seen sparks, and streaks of lightning.)

We'll return to the supply, the cause of the current, shortly; but for the moment let us look at an important effect of the current. As the cloud of high-speed electrons drifts down the wire, they collide continually with the ions of the metal, and these collisions have two consequences. First, they tend to slow down the electrons. In other words, they provide **resistance** to the current flow; and secondly, they increase the motion of the ions, the vibrations which, as we saw in Chapter 4, are related to the temperature. They heat the metal.

The amount of current that is flowing in a wire obviously depends on how many moving electrons there are and how fast they are moving. We could measure electric currents as we measure traffic flow: the number passing per second. However, this would not be very convenient, owing to the very small amount of electric charge carried by each electron, so we use a more practical unit: the ampere, usually abbreviated to **amp**. (One ampere corresponds to about 6 million, million, million electrons passing per second.) Apart from the supply, two main things determine the current flow. It depends on the particular metal, not only because different metals have different numbers of free electrons, but because the electrons in different metals flow at different rates, for the same supply conditions. There are good and bad conductors, even among metals, and a copper wire will carry about six times as many amps as an identical iron wire with the same supply: the resistance of the iron wire is six times that of the copper. Then of course the area available for the current flow matters, so that if we compare two otherwise identical wires, one with twice the area for the electrons to flow through, the latter will carry twice as much current, all other things being equal—a very important point, as we'll see, for the transmission of electric power.

Volts

Basically it is an electric force which causes a current to flow, and what a battery or the generator in a power-station does is to provide this force. A useful way of visualizing the process is through an often-used analogy: the flow of water along a pipe. Water flows along a pipe because there is a pressure difference between the ends. How this is produced—by a reservoir or by a pump—doesn't matter. In either case, the larger the pressure difference the greater the flow rate. The analogous 'pressure difference' between the two ends of a wire carrying a current is the voltage difference. (It is customary to drop 'difference' and speak of the 'voltage across' a wire, or any component in a circuit, the word 'across' meaning in this case 'between one end and the other'.) It is the voltage maintained across the wire which causes the current to flow, and the greater the voltage, the greater the current. Notice that this voltage is needed even to keep the electron cloud moving along at constant speed—just like the water in the pipe. This is because the electrons continually give up energy to the ions of the metal; and the supply is therefore doing two things. It acts as a 'pump', bringing electrons 'up' from the low voltage end of the wire so that they can flow back in at the high voltage end; and as it does this, it is continually replacing the energy lost in collisions: the energy which is heating the metal. *A voltage supply is an energy supply*.

Voltages are of course measured in volts. For ordinary metals, we find in practice that the current is proportional to the voltage: doubling the voltage causes the current to double, and so on. If the voltage measured in volts is divided by the current in amps, the figure obtained is the resistance (measured in ohms) of the wire. With a little rearrangement, this statement can be written as

$$voltage = current \times resistance$$

or more briefly, if less elegantly,

$$volts \ equal \ amps \ times \ ohms.$$

Watts

Power is the rate at which energy is converted from one form to another (joules per second, calories per day, or barrels of oil equivalent per year). To see what this is for our simple electrical circuit consisting of a supply and a wire, we follow a sample electron around the loop. It is given energy as it is 'lifted up' by the supply, and this energy is then dissipated as heat during the journey along the wire. So energy is converted from the electrical energy of the supply into thermal energy of the metal at a rate which must depend on the energy gained by each electron and the number of electrons flowing per second. In other words, the power is proportional to the voltage and to the current.

To make life simple, the unit we call one volt has been chosen so that the power in watts (joules per second) is just equal to the voltage in volts times the current in amps. Another simple rule:

watts equal volts times amps.

A slight complication in practice is that the normal mains supply does not provide a steady voltage, like a battery, but an alternating voltage which changes direction every hundredth of a second (in Europe, or every hundred-and-twentieth in the USA); so the picture must be of an electron flow which switches to and fro at this rate. However, if we use suitable average values for the varying voltage and current, the two rules (above and in the previous section) still apply, at least where heating effects are involved. These averages are what we mean when we talk about the 230 volt a.c. mains, or 13-A wiring—wiring which can safely carry a current of 13 amps without becoming too hot.

Transmission and Distribution

The cost, in both energy and money, of transporting any energy from the place where we find it to the place where we want it is an important factor in decisions about the systems we use. There are energy costs in carrying coal or oil and in pumping liquids and gases along pipes, but here we are concerned with the costs of transmitting electric power. These can be very high: in financial terms, up to half the cost we pay as consumers, and in energy terms a waste of from 10 per cent to as much as 40 per cent of the generated power. Moreover, there can be few people who think that a series of large metal structures supporting a network of cables actually improves the landscape. To see why (or perhaps whether) these are really necessary, we need only carry out a simple calculation based on the results of the past three sections.

Suppose that electric power is to be supplied to a village fifty kilometres from the power-station, and that the peak requirement is just one megawatt. The total current flowing, into all the houses in the village, must then be about 4000 amps (Table 7.2); and this current must also flow along the connecting lines from the power-station, generating heat as it does so. We decide that we do not want to lose more than one-tenth of the power in heating the

TABLE 7.2. *More power to the people*

The aim	To deliver power to a village without losing too much of it as heat in the transmission cables
The data	The power needed by the village is 1 MW, the normal supply voltage is 240 V and the village is 50 km from the power-station
The specific requirement	The energy wasted as heat in the cables should not exceed one-tenth of that supplied to the village, i.e. 100 000 W
Step 1	Find the current that must flow to the village to supply 1 MW at 240 V

$$\text{watts} = \text{volts} \times \text{amps}$$
$$1\,000\,000 = 240 \times \text{amps}$$

The required current is therefore about 4200 A

Step 2	Find the voltage drop along the cables, if 100 000 W of heat is developed when a current of 4200 A flows

$$\text{watts} = \text{volts} \times \text{amps}$$
$$100\,000 = \text{volts} \times 4200$$

The voltage drop along the cables must not therefore exceed 24 V

Step 3	Find the maximum permitted cable resistance, for a voltage of 24 V with a current of 4200 A

$$\text{volts} = \text{amps} \times \text{ohms}$$
$$240 = 4200 \times \text{ohms}$$

The resistance of the total 100 km of cable must not therefore exceed about six-thousandths of an ohm

Step 4	Using known data for different sizes of copper wire, estimate the required diameter

wire diameter (mm)	resistance of 100 km of wire (thousandths of an ohm)
20	5500
50	880
100	220
200	55
500	9
600	6
1000	2

countryside, so the total voltage drop along the 100 kilometres of cable must not exceed 24 V. This means in turn that the entire resistance of the cables must be less than about six thousandths of an ohm. We have a table showing the ohms per 100 kilometres for different thicknesses of copper wire—about the best conductor there is. Inspection shows that we need cables about 600 mm, or two feet, in diameter!

This is evidently not feasible; yet we know that electric power is transmitted, and over longer distances and at higher rates than in the example. How is it done? To see the answer we work backwards. We need thinner cable, and thinner cable means greater resistance. So the only way to keep the heating effect low is to reduce the current in the cables. How can one megawatt be delivered with less than 4200 amps? By having a higher supply voltage. If this were 100 times greater—24 kV instead of 240 V—then the current, for the same power, need only be 42 A, which could be carried without much loss in quite a modest cable. The answer, then, is to use much higher voltages; but this solution brings with it two immediate problems. Both are related to the fact that the greater the voltage the better the insulation needed to prevent currents flowing where they should not. In the first place, a household supply at 24 kV would be very unsafe—or, at the least, would require impossibly massive insulation. So the 24-kV transmission voltage must be reduced to an acceptable 240 V, and this requires transformers, which of course cost money and which themselves lead to some additional energy dissipation.

The second problem comes from the fact that high voltages mean high pylons. The 240-V supply to a house can use cables slung on wooden poles or buried in a simple conduit, but transmission at tens or even hundreds of kilovolts requires a very different order of insulation. (For long distances, 400 kV is quite widely used, and 800-kV lines are being introduced.) As in so many cases, we have again a 'trade-off' situation. We, the consumers, want ever more electric power, and we'd like it as cheaply as possible. It is probably the case that generating costs show economies of scale, at least up to power-station outputs of several hundred megawatts: enough for a population of a few hundred thousand people. If we then add that power sharing makes it desirable to inter-connect these large units, we begin to see the need to transmit many megawatts over many hundreds of miles. Burying high voltage cables is more expensive than carrying them on pylons overhead; but no one likes the visual pollution of the latter method.

There doesn't seem to be any simple 'technical fix' to get us out of this difficulty. Better and cheaper methods of insulating underground cables are being developed all the time, but slowly. Superconducting cables (for some, the answer to all problems) do not seem likely to be with us for a while yet. Superconductivity, the disappearance of all resistance and with it all heating effect, sounds like the perfect solution, but unfortunately the superconducting metals turn out to be rather expensive alloys, often difficult to handle, and needing to be kept at temperatures well below freezing in order to remain superconducting. The cost of manufacturing and maintaining such a system makes this, for the present, a rather expensive way of economizing, and we seem to be left with the usual three-way balancing problem, weighing against each other cost, energy efficiency, and the environment.

Generators

The generation of electric power plays such an important role in our use of energy, and as we've now seen many times, is responsible for so much waste heat and so many environmentally undesirable products, that an understanding of how a power-station works is almost essential for any serious discussion of ways in which we might improve the management of our energy world. The present-day power-station is the subject, therefore, of the rest of this chapter. First we need to look at the essential component: the generator. Then we can bring this together with information from earlier chapters in order to analyse the inputs and outputs of energy and materials in a large modern power-station.

The input to almost all present generators is mechanical power. There are other possibilities: a battery uses chemical energy and a photocell uses light, but these contribute only tiny fractions of the

world total power. In all other cases, from a 10-kW diesel generator to a 1000-MW nuclear power-station, some mechanical force
causes a machine to rotate and thus generates a voltage. The
mechanical force itself can be produced by almost anything (even
a person cranking a handle), but by far the most common means is
a turbine driven by hot steam. (A lesser, but appreciable contribution comes from hydroelectric plants, where water provides the
driving force. These are discussed in Chapter 9.)

The principle of the generator is very simple, and like many
simple principles it took a genius to discover it. In 1831 Michael
Faraday found the link which is the basis of almost the whole of
electro-technology:

- a voltage is generated wherever there is a changing magnetic
  effect.

Magnetic effects have of course been known for centuries. The
compass needle, a small magnet aligning itself with the magnetic
field produced by the Earth, was probably known to the Chinese
3000 years ago, and was certainly used by European navigators
in the Middle Ages; and the Romans already knew that a piece
of iron brought near a magnet becomes 'magnetic' itself. The
understanding that the two separate fields, electric and magnetic,
were very closely related came, however, only in the nineteenth
century, culminating in a series of great discoveries which have
led not only to the electrical industry as we know it, but to tele-
vision and the transistor radio and other delights of modern
civilization.

A voltage is produced if the magnetic field through a loop of
wire changes. *Change* is of the essence, because only as long as
there is change is the voltage maintained; and the faster the change
the greater the voltage. This is why continuous motion is required.
A generator must therefore have three essential features: a *coil*, a
magnet, and a method of *moving* the one with respect to the other.
Fig. 7.3 shows a very simple possibility. If we were to connect a
light bulb to the two leads A and B and rotate the coil, a current
would flow in the filament of the bulb, just as if a battery were
connected. (This particular generator would produce an alternat-

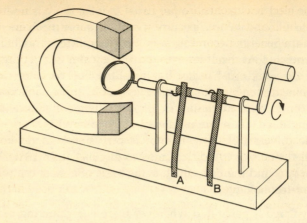

Fig. 7.3 A very simple generator

As the coil of wire is rotated, the changing magnetic effect produces a voltage. Two springy metal strips rubbing against metal bands connected to the ends of the wire provide a continuous path for the current.

ing current, changing direction every time the coil flipped over in the magnetic field.) The construction is on a rather grander scale, but the principle is the same, for a power-station generator. The main differences apart from size are that the latter has a fairly complex system of coils wound on an iron core to give the greatest magnetic effect, and the magnet itself is an electromagnet: a separate set of coils also wound on a suitable shape made of iron or a magnetic alloy. This again increases the magnetic field, and also gives better control.

For an energy analysis of the generator we must start with the mechanical input power. In our hand-cranked example, this is the energy used per second in pushing the handle round and round. The output power is of course the voltage across the lamp multiplied by the current flowing in it, and the difference between input and output must be the losses due to friction and to the heating effect of the current in the generator wires. (In a large generator there are further losses as energy is dissipated in all the iron, both in magnetizing and demagnetizing it continuously and because some electric currents are produced in it.) If there is no load—no light bulb and hence no current and no output power—then all the input energy becomes losses, a very inefficient way of running a generator. At the other extreme, if the losses are very small, we can see what must happen as the light bulb is connected. The voltage produced in the coil depends on how fast it is rotated (one reason why speed control is very important in power-stations). Suppose we crank the handle at absolutely constant speed. With no load, very little force is needed, but as soon as someone connects the bulb, we find that it is necessary to push harder to keep the crank turning. We must change our rate of energy input to match the new rate of energy output—the power used in the lamp. The argument is precisely the same on the large scale. If the TV programme ends and 100000 people plug in their electric kettles, the power-station must find a great deal of additional push— and find it fast, or there will be complaints about the 'drop in supply'.

Running under optimum conditions, large modern generators are extremely efficient energy-conversion machines, with losses that can be as little as 1 per cent of the input power. Unfortunately their efficiency falls off when they are required to run at much less than their rated output, a problem for the power-station engineers who have to deal with the widely varying demands we place on the supply system in the course of a day or a year.

A 660-MW Power-Station

In the decades following World War II the size of the average power-station rose steeply almost everywhere. In the immediate post-war years, 'small' plants, generating perhaps 5 MW—enough at the time for a town of about 20000 people—were common throughout Europe. Within little more than twenty years, the typical output was a hundred times this; large coal-fired plants located near their sources of fuel distributed power to a million people over distances of hundreds of miles. With a few exceptions, the growth of individual generating units then levelled off, with outputs of 500–700 MW regarded as optimum. Where the available fuel supply, distribution system, and demand make a larger installation the preferred option, it has become more usual to have several turbo-generators in this range, rather than one very large set. We therefore take as our example a 600-MW system; coal-fired because world-wide this is still our main source of power and also because it presents some of the problems in their most acute form.

The two diagrams in Fig. 7.4 show the flows of materials and energy. There will be some variations depending on the nature of the coal, and of course differences if other fuels (oil gas, MSW, nuclear) are used, but in general the figures are representative of any plant of this size. A glance at Fig. 7.4(*b*) shows that the energy input is 5600 GJ an hour. Remembering that one watt is one joule per second, we see that this is about 1.6 GW, or 1600 MW. The useful electrical output is 600 MW, so the overall efficiency of the plant is about 38 per cent, and energy is being 'lost' at a total rate of about 1000 MW. To see where it all goes, we'll follow each stage from fuel input to electrical output.

The Boiler

About 1500 tonnes an hour of water pass through the boiler, to be converted to superheated steam at about 550°C and a pressure of nearly two hundred atmospheres. The energy for this comes from the combustion of a little over two hundred tonnes of coal, requiring over three thousand tonnes an hour of air. This is equivalent to using all the air in an average house every second, and the pumps to draw it in consume about 5 MW of electrical power. In Chapter 4 we saw the inventory of hot gases and particulates leaving the boiler, and these carry away about a tenth of the original energy.

The Turbine

After further small heat losses en route, the 1500 tonnes of steam an hour reaching the turbine carry a little under five thousand gigajoules of energy. The turbine might achieve 45 per cent efficiency under optimum conditions (Chapter 5), giving an hourly

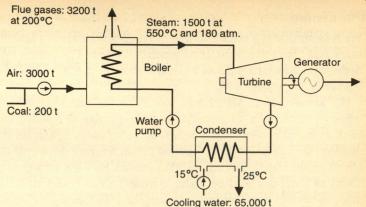

(a) Flows of materials (tonnes per hour)

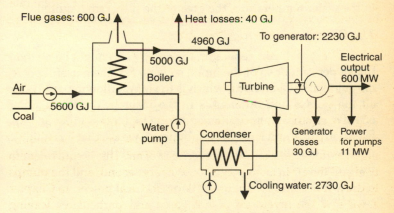

(b) Flows of energy (gigajoules per hour and megawatts*)

* 1 MW = 3.6 GJ per hour

Fig. 7.4 A 600-MW coal-fired power-station

output of 2230 GJ of useful energy. The remaining energy becomes 'waste heat' that must be removed in order to condense the steam leaving the turbine. As we saw in Chapter 5, failure to do this would reduce the conversion efficiency of the turbine.

The Condenser

We'll assume that a constant flow of cooling water is available to carry away the waste heat. How much is needed? The answer will depend on how far we allow its temperature to rise, as the following reasoning shows.

We know that 4.2 MJ of heat will raise the temperature of a tonne of water by 1°C. Suppose we allow a rise of ten degrees. Each tonne of cooling water will then carry away 42 MJ. As the diagram shows, heat is to be removed at an hourly rate of 2730 GJ, which can be translated into 760 MJ a second. So we need a flow of about 18 tonnes of cooling water a second. (You could visualize this as a six-foot depth of water flowing in a six-foot wide channel at a speed of about ten miles an hour.) Assuming that the water must be pumped up ten metres or so, at least 2 MW of pumping power will be needed. Obviously, the smaller the permissible rise in the water temperature, the greater the flow rate required.

The Generator

With a very well-run generator, the energy loss might be no more than a per cent or so of the input, so we'll assume a useful power output of 2200 GJ an hour, which is 611 MW. Allowing 11 MW for all the pumps and other uses in the plant leaves the required 600 MW electrical output. Remembering that transformer and distribution losses still have to be subtracted, we see that it is unlikely that even one-third of the original energy of the coal reaches the final consumer.

Conclusions

The conclusions of this little study are all there in the figures. Two-thirds of the energy laboriously extracted by the miners is thrown away in slightly warm water or a plume of hot air. In Chapter 5 we looked at some options for dealing with the waste heat; but this is by no means the only problem. There are the undesirable material products too, as we've seen in Chapter 4. Changing to a different fossil fuel might help a little, but would by no means eliminate the problem. The suggestion that we might dramatically reduce our electricity consumption is unlikely to be very popular. So are there other options? There certainly are, and we'll be investigating them in the rest of this part of the book; but as we'll see, they too have their difficulties. Unfortunately, whilst we all seem to want more and more of our energy in this particular form, Nature and the engineering professions have yet to provide us with a clean, cheap, and plentiful source for it.

8

Nuclear Power

Introduction

In the mid-1990s the world has nearly 450 nuclear power-stations in thirty different countries. They represent about a sixth of the world's total generating capacity and produce a little over a ninth of the total annual output of electricity. Four countries obtain more than half their power from this source: Lithuania with a little under 90 per cent, France with nearly 80 per cent, and Belgium and the Slovak Republic both with more than 50 per cent.

The first self-sustaining controlled operation of a nuclear reactor was achieved in December 1942 at the University of Chicago, and in 1956 the first power-station linked into a national grid system started operating at Calder Hall, in Cumbria on the north-west coast of England. (The site subsequently became Windscale, and later again Sellafield.) The rate of growth, for a technology whose scientific basis was discovered only sixty years ago, has indeed been rapid; but events within and outside the nuclear industry have put constraints on development during the 1980s and early 1990s. We'll look at some of these factors later, but here we are concerned with the science and technology.

To understand how a nuclear reactor works and why it produces energy, we must penetrate more deeply into the atom and ask about the structure of the nucleus itself. This will be the first task, and the rest is then a progression: from the nucleus to the fission process, then to the reactor using this process and ultimately to specific types of reactor. Safety must feature in any account of nuclear power, and a section on radioactivity establishes a background for the later discussion of its effects in Chapter 13. We finish this chapter with a brief look at the 'other' nuclear power process: fusion.

Nuclear power, rather like education, or modern architecture, is a subject on which almost everybody has opinions, with the experts just as polarized in their views as the laymen. To discuss the subject at all is to invite a hail of response from the committed on both sides, and to embark on our usual journey from basic ideas to current technology in just a few short pages must be rash indeed. The missiles are surely waiting: 'over-simplification', 'omission', 'bias'. Each will no doubt find a target; but perhaps a minimum measure of the objectivity of this account will be the extent to which it attracts equal fire from the cannons to the left and to the right.

Nuclei

At some time during the fifty years since the first nuclear reactor, two words at the very centre of the energy vocabulary seem to have extended their meaning. The terms 'fuel' and 'burning' have come to include materials and processes very different from the hydrocarbons and chemical reactions discussed in Chapter 4. The 'fuel' in a nuclear reactor is quite unlike any fossil or biomass fuel, and its 'burning' doesn't involve a reaction with oxygen, or indeed any chemical process in the usual sense. When a uranium nucleus splits into fragments the change is much more profound than a mere rearrangement of atoms within molecules. It is a realization of the dream of the alchemists down the ages: the transmutation of one chemical element into another. An element is characterized by the number of electrons making up a complete, electrically neutral atom (see Table 7.1 in the previous chapter), and this number is determined by the need to balance the positive electric charge of the nucleus. So if the nuclear charge is altered, a different number of electrons is needed and you have a different atom, a different chemical element.

Let's now look at the nucleus of any atom. It has a positive electric charge equal to some exact multiple of the charge of an electron, and it accounts for most of the mass of the atom. Consider the implications of the first of these remarks. A child whose building-blocks are two-inch cubes will build towers whose heights are multiples of two inches. Similar reasoning suggests that perhaps all nuclei have the same basic 'building-block', an entity with just that basic electric charge. A nice tidy idea, but unfortunately it falls down the moment we look at the masses. Table 8.1 shows a few examples. The atomic number is the number of basic charge units—the building-blocks proposed above. The masses are shown in **unified mass units** to bring out their relationships more clearly than if we used kilograms, and the table reveals three important features:

- There are nuclei with the same number of charge units but quite different masses: a particular element can have several **isotopes**.
- Unlike the charges, the masses are not exact multiples of the smallest.
- They are however nearly exact multiples; the nearest whole numbers are the **mass numbers** shown in the table.

The first of these observations immediately disposes of the idea of a single building-block; but if we ignore for the moment the slight discrepancy in the multiples, the third suggests an alternative. It is that there are two building blocks, with the same mass but one having electric charge and the other not. This is indeed our present view; we call the particle with electric charge a **proton** and the neutral one a **neutron**, or refer to them collectively as **nucleons**. So the atomic number of each nucleus in Table 8.1 is the number of protons and the mass number is the number of nucleons. The nucleus of the uranium isotope U-235, for instance, has 92 protons and 143 neutrons, whilst U-238 has three more neutrons.

A look at the world around us reveals that most atomic nuclei are extremely stable objects. We just don't see elements changing into other elements. Oxygen remains oxygen, gold stays as gold, lead as lead. Iron Age tools may rust, but this is a chemical reaction, a rearrangement of the outer electrons of iron and oxygen

Table 8.1. *Nuclear masses*

Masses are in 'unified mass units'. $1\,u = 1.66043 \times 10^{-27}\,kg$.[a]
The masses of a single proton and a single neutron are
respectively $1.0073\,u$ and $1.0086\,u$. For the elements up to
bismuth, the masses of only the most common isotopes are
shown.

Element	Atomic number	Mass of nucleus	Mass number
hydrogen	1	1.007	1
		2.014	2
helium	2	4.002	4
carbon	6	12	12
		13	13
iron	26	55.92	56
copper	29	62.91	63
		64.91	65
krypton	36	83.89	84
		85.89	86
strontium	38	85.89	86
		87.89	88
iodine	53	126.87	127
barium	56	137.87	138
gold	79	196.92	197
lead	82	207.93	208
bismuth	83	208.93	209
thorium	90	234.04	234
uranium	92	232.99	233
		234.99	235
		238.00	238
plutonium	94	239.00	239

[a] The original idea behind the unified mass unit was that it would
be the mass of the smallest known nucleus, so that all the others
could be given as numbers of these, just like the charges. However,
for practical reasons it was found better to base it on one type of
carbon nucleus rather than hydrogen, so $1\,u$ is exactly one twelfth of
the mass of a carbon-12 nucleus.

atoms to link them together. The iron nuclei are the same ones that
existed thousands of years ago.

There is however evidence of unstable nuclei. There is radioactivity, the process in which a high-speed particle spontaneously

shoots out of a nucleus. Closer investigation shows that all the heavier nuclei are radioactive, the heaviest truly stable one being bismuth-209, with 83 protons and 126 neutrons. If this is so, how is it that we can go mining for uranium? The answer is that uranium decays only very slowly. Starting with a piece of U-238 today, you would need to wait 4500 million years before half the nuclei had emitted particles and changed into thorium. For U-235 the time is shorter—only 700 million years—which is why there is less of it today. These facts explain why uranium is at the centre of our interest. On the one hand it exists, at least a few million available tonnes of it. Unlike other radioactive elements, it hasn't yet decayed away. On the other hand it is certainly unstable, and the emission of high-speed particles means that energy is released when it disintegrates.

Fission

Natural radioactivity is important because it shows that nuclei can be unstable and can release large amounts of energy, but it is **fission** which offers the prospect of a continuous supply of power. Fission is the splitting of a nucleus into two roughly equal parts. It does occur spontaneously, like radioactivity, but the very important point is that *we can also make it happen*. To see how, we note two facts:

• Fission can be induced by a neutron.
• Fission produces surplus neutrons.

Together, these suggest the possibility of a **chain reaction** (Fig. 8.1). Neutrons from a first fission induce further fissions, and the neutrons from these induce even more, and so on. If each fission event releases energy, we have a process which will generate ever more power until the supply of suitable nuclei runs out.

Of course there are questions. Will the chain reaction actually happen in practice? If it does, how much energy is produced? Then—the crucial question—can we control the process? Once the multiplication has started, can we govern the rate? After all, we control combustion by limiting the supply of fuel and oxygen, but

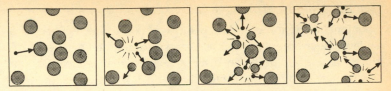

→ Neutron
● Fissile nucleus
● Product nucleus

Fig. 8.1 A chain reaction

a nuclear chain reaction doesn't need a supply of anything as long as there are suitable nuclei still present. How can we ever switch it off?

Nuclear processes can be represented by equations rather like those used for chemical reactions. We can write the equation for the fission of the nucleus U-235 in the form

$$^{235}_{92}U + {}^{1}_{0}n \rightarrow X + Y + \text{energy} + \text{neutrons}.$$

Notice that, at least on the left-hand side, we keep track of the mass numbers and atomic numbers by superscripts and sub-scripts. The right-hand side as it stands, however, is a bit vague and imprecise. The trouble is that 'fission of U-235' is not a single well-defined reaction at all, but a process leading to a range of possible results. In order to understand enough about these to follow the events in a nuclear reactor, let us take each item of the above equation in turn.

The Uranium

The isotope U-235 is the only naturally-occurring fissile material, 'fissile' meaning that the nucleus can be induced to split by an encounter with a not particularly energetic neutron. About 0.7 per cent of natural uranium is U-235, roughly one atom in 140. If a reactor needs more concentrated fuel than this, the uranium must be 'enriched' to increase the U-235 content.

Two other fissile nuclei are known, plutonium-239 ($^{239}_{94}Pu$) and uranium-233; but these do not occur naturally and must be 'bred', a process we'll return to later.

The Initiating Neutron

Spontaneous fission does occur but is a rare event, whereas if a suitable neutron encounters a U-235 nucleus the chances of induced fission are high. To discuss exactly what is meant by an 'encounter' or by a 'high' chance would take us into rather too much detail, but the word 'suitable' must certainly not pass without comment. A fact which is crucial in the design of reactors is that a slowly moving neutron is at least 100 times more likely to induce fission than a fast one.

What do 'slow' and 'fast' mean? A better term than slow is 'thermal', in the sense in which we discussed thermal energies in earlier chapters. A thermal neutron is simply one which has bounced around in some material until it has the same average energy as the surrounding atoms or molecules. If the temperature inside a reactor is a few hundred degrees, the average speed of a thermal neutron will be a few kilometres a second. In contrast, the neutrons produced in fission move 10000 times faster, with 100 million times the kinetic energy of a thermal neutron. To be as effective as possible they must be slowed down, and we return to this shortly.

The Fission Products

X and Y in our equation (sometimes called the fish 'n chips!) are new nuclei resulting from the splitting of U-235. There are usually two of these and they account for all the protons and most of the neutrons of the original nucleus. On the small scale of the nucleus, fission is a violent process and we cannot predict its outcome in detail, so X and Y must stand for a variety of possible new nuclei. We can however make a few remarks about the average result from many fission events.

X and Y tend to be unequal, one with an atomic number in the high thirties and one in the low fifties, with the mass split in a ratio of about 95:140. (A glance at Table 7.1 will show why we find the gases krypton, iodine, and xenon and the solids strontium, caesium, and barium in the inventory of reactor products.) It would be surprising if the initial explosive fission led to fragments with just the right proton-neutron combinations for stable nuclei, and indeed it doesn't; so the products are almost always radio-active, emitting particles and changing through a series of forms until they reach a stable state.

Energy and Mass

Energy is released, appearing in the first place mainly as kinetic energy of the fission products and the excess neutrons. In terms of the large-scale world, the energy released in a fission event is extremely small: about one-thirtieth of a billionth of a joule; but a few comparisons might show why words like 'enormous' tend to creep in. The fission of one nucleus releases about 20 million times as much energy as the combustion of one natural gas molecule. Complete fission of a pound of pure U-235 would release the energy equivalent of about 1500 tonnes of coal. A 600-MW power-station could run for a year on the U-235 in 100 tonnes of natural uranium. The energy equivalent of a ten-gallon tank of petrol is a tiny sphere of U-235 about one millimetre across.

What is the source of all this energy? One explanation is much like the answer to the similar question about the energy released in combustion. Energy would be needed completely to take apart a nucleus into its constituent nucleons; and conversely the same energy, the **binding energy**, would be released if the nucleus were to be assembled from its constituents. It follows that if the binding energy of the original uranium nucleus is smaller than the combined binding energies of the product nuclei, there will be energy to spare when fission occurs. (The actual process does not of course involve complete dissociation and reassembly; it is only the net difference that matters.)

So what is the source of the energy? The idea of binding energy is useful, but it doesn't really explain anything. (Rather as though we ask why things fall to the ground and are told, 'It's because the ground is lower down.') We know that the origin of the energy released in a chemical process lies in the electrical forces holding molecules together: chemical energy is electrical energy. Electrical forces play a role in the nucleus too, but they certainly don't hold it together. Observing that particles with the same type of electric charge repel each other, we can calculate that there is a great deal of electrical energy waiting to be released if the 92 protons of a uranium nucleus were allowed to spring apart. Opposing this tendency, providing as it were the elastic band which holds the spring compressed, is the **nuclear force** of attraction between nucleons. This is a third force, different from the other fundamental forces of gravity and electricity, and it is this which makes a stable nucleus possible. When a thermal neutron interacts with a U-235 nucleus, a delicate balance is tipped, the nucleus splits and the fragments fly apart, with kinetic energy which comes largely from the stored electrical energy of the original nucleus.

How we measure the binding energies of nuclei is in itself an interesting piece of physics. Because fission is not a single process, detailed energy changes cannot be measured directly. They can however be calculated. Einstein provided the method when—over thirty years before the discovery of fission—he developed the Special Theory of Relativity, an essential consequence of which is that *mass and energy are equivalent quantities*. The mass of a system is not a fixed, unchanging quantity, but depends on its total energy. The measured mass of the U-235 nucleus is nearly 1 per cent less than the total mass of 92 protons and 143 neutrons, and this difference is the mass equivalent of the binding energy.

The conversion factor relating mass and energy appears in the well-known equation

$$E = mc^2$$

in which the quantity 'c' is the speed of light in empty space, a universal constant which plays an important role in the theory. Its value is about 300 million metres a second, so the conversion is

energy in joules = $9 \times 10^{16} \times$ mass in kilograms.

Looking again at Table 8.1, we can predict that if a U-235 nucleus splits into two roughly equal parts, together with a few spare neutrons, the total mass will decrease by about one-fifth of a unified mass unit. It is the conversion of this into energy units which gives the thirtieth of a billionth of a joule mentioned above.

(We should note that there is nothing special here about nuclear reactions. Mass changes will accompany any reactions which produce or absorb energy, but for chemical processes they will be extremely small: combustion of one tonne of coal, for instance, leads to a mass decrease of less than half a milligramme. Not easy to detect.)

The Product Neutrons

There is a simple reason why extra neutrons are released in fission: the ratio of neutrons to protons is greater for the heavy nuclei than for the stable light ones. In practice, as we've seen, the product nuclei are not stable; they are radioactive precisely because they start life with too many neutrons. Nevertheless, there are usually about two free neutrons released in each fission event.

These survive as free particles for a ten-thousandth of a second or less, during which time one of them on average must initiate a further fission if a constant rate of energy production is to be maintained. This is however only one of many possible fates awaiting a free neutron. It could for instance escape altogether, and be lost in the surrounding material. It could, as we'll see, interact with the 'wrong' isotope, U-238, or with other nuclei present in the fuel. It could even interact with U-235 without inducing fission. All these processes compete for the available neutrons.

One way of increasing the chances of fission is to slow down the neutrons, and this is the method adopted in most present reactors—the so-called 'thermal reactors'. If this is not done, the reactor must be designed to maintain a constant fission rate using the less efficient high energy or **fast** neutrons direct from the fission process. It is then called a **fast reactor**. Whatever the design details, it is evident that control of the output of a reactor can be achieved if a way is found of controlling the numbers of free neutrons and hence the rate at which fission occurs and energy is produced. When the desired condition is reached, with exactly one neutron from each fission event inducing a new fission, the reactor is said to be 'critical'.

A Significant Side-Effect

Absorption of a neutron by U-238, dismissed above as a loss process, is in fact the start of the extremely important series of events shown in Table 8.2. We see that the resulting U-239 is radioactive, emitting an electron (negligible mass but one unit of negative charge) and turning into neptunium-239, which is similarly radioactive and turns into plutonium-239. The significance of this is that *Pu-239 is fissile*. The interaction of the neutron with non-fissile U-238 has bred a new fissile nucleus. It has increased the fuel content of the reactor. A thermal neutron can now induce fission of the Pu-239, releasing about the same energy as in a U-235 fission.

Materials like U-238, whose interaction with neutrons leads to new fissile nuclei, are called **fertile**, and the second important instance is thorium-232, which breeds fissile U-233. Present commercial reactors all use uranium fuel, however, and consequently breed plutonium. The term 'breeder reactor' is reserved for systems which actually produce more fissile material than they consume, and this is not the case for current thermal reactors. Let us take a simplified example to see how the figures work out.

We'll follow the fate of 1000 uranium nuclei in a reactor during the period of one year between insertion of a fresh fuel element and removal of the spent fuel. Table 8.3 shows the figures. With enriched fuel, about 32 of the original nuclei are U-235 and the rest U-238. At the end of the year, analysis of the spent fuel reveals about nine remaining U-235 nuclei in our sample, and six Pu-239 nuclei. Table 8.3 also incorporates a further piece of information: that for every ten neutrons absorbed by U-235, about six are absorbed by U-238 to breed plutonium. With these numbers, we see that nearly one-third of the total fission events are not U-235 at all

TABLE 8.2. *The breeding process*

U-238 captures a neutron and becomes U-239	$^{238}_{92}U + ^{1}_{0}n \rightarrow ^{239}_{92}U$
U-239 emits an electron and becomes Np-239	$^{239}_{92}U \rightarrow ^{239}_{93}Np + ^{0}_{-1}e$
Np-239 emits an electron and becomes Pu-239	$^{239}_{93}Np \rightarrow ^{239}_{94}Pu + ^{0}_{-1}e$

TABLE 8.3. *Uranium and plutonium in a thermal reactor*

Data: Fresh fuel contains 3.2 per cent U-235 and no plutonium.
Spent fuel contains 0.9 per cent U-235 and 0.6 per cent Pu-239.
80 per cent of interactions between neutrons and U-235 nuclei lead to fission.
For every 10 neutrons absorbed by U-235, 6 are absorbed by U-238 to produce Pu-239.

Analysis of a fuel sample containing initially 1000 uranium atoms		Fission events
U-235 nuclei		
At the start: 3.2 per cent of 1000	32	
At the finish: 0.9 per cent of 1000	9	
Consumed	23	
Of which 80 per cent undergo fission		18
Pu-239 nuclei		
At the start	0	
Bred from U-238: $^6/_{10}$ of 23	14	
At the finish: 0.6 per cent of 1000	6	
Consumed in fission events		8
Total number of fission events		26

but Pu-239—a third of the energy comes from the plutonium process.

The significance of this little analysis lies not in the precise figures, which will vary from reactor to reactor and which are in any case over-simplified, but in three specific implications. There is the fact that any uranium reactor is a plutonium producer, and if our figures are at all typical, the total fissile content of the spent fuel can be as much as twice that of natural uranium. This is the argument for reprocessing spent fuel in order to make better use of resources. An alternative is to design reactors to produce *and consume* as much plutonium as possible, avoiding the need for reprocessing.

Finally, we have the true breeder reactor, designed to convert so much U-238 into plutonium that it is a net producer of fissile material, which can then be extracted for use in other reactors. In principle this would increase the fuel potential of uranium more than a hundred-fold, from 0.7 per cent to nearly 100 per cent (see Breeders, p. 195).

Radioactivity and Radioactive Substances

Nearly all the special problems of the nuclear industry can be traced to a single, essential feature of fission reactors. This unique characteristic, not found in any other power system, is the unavoidable presence of intense radioactivity. Radioactivity brings complex new problems for engineers, adds considerably to costs, and is at the centre of public concern about reactor safety and waste disposal. Questions of industrial safety and the disposal of dangerous wastes are not unique to the nuclear industry of course; they are equally important in coal-mining or the production of toxic chemicals. A significant difference, however, is that mines or chemical plants are not designed for the production of thousands of megawatts of power. If there is a justification for what the nuclear industry sees as the disproportionate attention paid to its slightest mishap, it must surely lie in this conjunction of very large power potential and the presence of an invisibly lethal material for which there is no neutralizer or antidote.

It is by no means easy to assess the potential hazards of nuclear reactors or the effectiveness of measures to make them safe. We'll start optimistically with a series of questions we'd like to answer:

- What is radioactivity?
- What causes it?
- Why are radioactive substances produced in reactors?
- What is produced, how much and what happens to it?
- What are the relevant effects of radioactivity?
- How much produces what sort of effect?
- How can radioactivity or its effects be prevented?
- What are the safety measures in present systems?
- Have they been successful?
- Will they be successful in the future?
- How about new systems?

Some of the answers are straightforward enough and we'll deal with them at once. Others involving matters of detail about reactor design and safety systems are treated briefly here and taken up again in other sections of this chapter. Biological effects are discussed later in Chapter 13, together with other environmental issues, and as we'll see, controversy over the facts then begins to emerge. Finally, there are really difficult questions to do with prediction and the assessment of risk, and we shall try to analyse some of the many conflicting answers to these later too.

Radioactivity

We've already seen that this is a natural phenomenon; that certain nuclei emit particles and turn into different nuclei. Let us start with the particles. The heaviest object emitted is a complete helium nucleus, known as an alpha (α) particle. As one might expect, alpha decay is particularly common in the heavier nuclei and an example we've already met is U-238 which decays to produce thorium:

$$\ce{^{238}_{92}U} \xrightarrow[4.5 \times 10^9 \text{ yr}]{} \ce{^{234}_{90}Th} + \ce{^{4}_{2}He}.$$

The time shown under the arrow is called the **half-life** and is the time needed for half the U-238 in any sample to decay. It is a very important quantity and from it we can deduce a number of other facts about the radio-isotope concerned, as we'll see shortly.

Not all radioactive nuclei emit alpha particles. Some produce beta (β) particles, and these are a little surprising because they are simply electrons. A negative particle coming from a positive nucleus? It may seem odd but it's not impossible provided that the positive charge increases by one unit to conserve the overall net charge. The electron carries away very little mass so the mass number is unchanged, and effectively we have the conversion of one neutron into one proton. Two beta emitters of some importance are strontium-90 and tritium:

$$\ce{^{90}_{38}Sr} \xrightarrow[28 \text{ yr}]{} \ce{^{90}_{39}Y} + \ce{^{0}_{-1}e}$$

$$\ce{^{3}_{1}H} \xrightarrow[12 \text{ yr}]{} \ce{^{3}_{2}He} + \ce{^{0}_{-1}e}.$$

The short half-lives explain why these isotopes are rare in nature. They are artificial radioisotopes produced in reactors.

The third radioactive emission is the only one which really is radiation in the usual sense. The gamma (γ) rays are electromagnetic waves, like radio waves, or light or X-rays. The special feature of gamma rays (and X-rays too) is that they have extremely short wavelengths and oscillate very fast, and this gives them their penetrating power. In emitting gamma radiation a nucleus of course gives up energy, but there is no change in the numbers of nucleons; it is a sort of settling-down process which often follows alpha or beta decay.

Other types of radioactivity are known but these three are the most common and—together with neutrons—are the main 'radiations' which give rise to concern about nuclear reactors.

An Effect Without a Cause

The basic rule of radioactive decay is that the number of nuclei that will emit a particle in the next second, hour, year, or century is simply proportional to the number present when you start counting. If half the nuclei decay in the first eight days then half the remainder will decay in the next eight days, half the new remainder in the next eight, and so on. Let's take U-238 as an example—though the reasoning is equally good for any half-life, whether it is as long as the age of the universe or as short as a millionth of a second. Table 8.4 shows the method, and the result for U-238 with its very long half-life is that only an extremely tiny fraction of the nuclei in any sample will decay in the next second. But the number of nuclei present is likely to be very large: even 1 gram of U-238—a tiny sphere about 5 millimetres across—has many many millions. So the resulting **activity** in this case is about 12 500 particles per second. This is a very weak source, because U-238 has a very long half-life. A gram of spent fuel direct from a reactor can produce several million, million particles a second.

We can use the U-238 example again to bring out a crucial characteristic of radioactivity. Suppose we take a tiny fragment of uranium containing 'only' 1000 million atoms, and watch it for

TABLE 8.4. *Radioactive decay rate and half-life*

The basic rule. The number of nuclei which decay in any one year is always a certain fraction of those present at the start of that year.

The number remaining at the end of the first year is *one minus one Nth* of the original number:

$$\left(1-\frac{1}{N}\right) \times \text{original}$$

At the end of the second year it is one minus one Nth of the '*one year*' number:

$$\left(1-\frac{1}{N}\right) \times \left(1-\frac{1}{N}\right) \times \text{original}$$

and after a third year

$$\left(1-\frac{1}{N}\right) \times \left(1-\frac{1}{N}\right) \times \left(1-\frac{1}{N}\right) \text{times,}$$

or more concisely

$$\left(1-\frac{1}{N}\right)^{3} \times \text{original}$$

The number continues to fall in this way, until after 4500 million years there remain

$$\left(1-\frac{1}{N}\right)^{4.5\times10^{9}} \text{ of the original number.}$$

However, if 4.5×10^{9} years is the half-life (for U-238), then the number remaining must be just one half of the original number:

$$\left(1-\frac{1}{N}\right)^{4.5\times10^{9}} = \frac{1}{2}.$$

We want to know what N must be, for this to be true. What fraction must decay each year if one half remains after 4500 million years?

Provided the fraction one Nth is very small there is a simple rule for calculating N. It is

$$N = 1.44 \text{ times the half-life.}$$

For U-238, N is thus about 6500 million: one nucleus in 6500 million decays in a year, or five per million, million, million in each second. Now 1 gram of U-238 contains about 2500 million, million, million atoms, so the rate of decay will be about 12500 per second, and this is therefore the number of alpha particles emitted per second.

6000 years. We can confidently predict that about 1000 nuclei will decay in this time, but what we cannot predict at all is which nuclei. Right up to the moment it happens there is absolutely no way to tell that a nucleus is about to decay. And this is not just a matter of poor technology. It's not even that the physicists haven't found how the hidden clock ticks. On the contrary, they firmly believe that there is no hidden clock. Unlike any other process we've studied, radioactive decay is *an effect without a cause*, and the practical implication is that we ourselves can neither cause nor prevent the decay of a particular nucleus. We could of course smash it with a sufficiently fast sub-nuclear projectile, but this is not a practical way of dealing with large quantities of material. Otherwise, once we've produced radioactive material there's no way to stop the radioactivity. We can only wait for enough half-lives for it to die out naturally.

Reactor Products

As the fuel in a reactor burns, the inventory of radioactive nuclei which builds up has three main constituents:

- Unstable fission products, mainly beta- or gamma-active and contributing over three-quarters of the activity of the spent fuel. Their half-lives are mostly rather short: hours, days, or a few years.

- Heavy isotopes resulting from non-fission interactions. Known as actinides, these are mainly alpha- and gamma-emitters with half-lives from decades to thousands of centuries, and account for about one-quarter of the activity.

- Isotopes produced, mainly by neutron bombardment, in the fuel cladding, structures, etc. They vary widely, and contribute a few per cent of the total radioactivity.

An important distinction is that, if all goes well, the first two of these should remain inside the enclosed fuel elements whereas the third obviously does not. In discussing safety and the 'escape of radiation' we should be clear whether we mean the escape of the substances themselves or the penetration of containers by emissions from enclosed substances. For the latter the penetrating powers are obviously important, and these are very roughly as follows:

- Gamma rays and neutrons are the most penetrating, needing thick concrete or specially selected absorbing materials to stop them.
- Beta particles are stopped by, say, a thick metal sheet.
- Alpha particles are stopped by almost anything: a sheet of tissue-paper, or about an inch of air. Virtually the only way they can cause harm is if the source is either eaten or inhaled.

This last point brings out a major practical problem: that some reactor products are gases, and gases—unlike solids—will not just stay where you put them.

Containment

It is evident that if radioactive substances are potentially harmful the total containment system of a reactor must ensure that during normal operation the fuel cladding remains intact and the core is adequately shielded, and that in the event of an accident no radioactive substance—gas, liquid, or solid—can escape into the surroundings. Containment of spent fuel is equally important during removal, transport, reprocessing, and ultimate storage, until enough half-lives have passed for the danger to become negligible.

Reactors

The first problem for the designer of any nuclear reactor is to get the neutrons right. The composition of the fuel and the choice of other materials, the sizes and shapes of the component parts of the reactor, the methods used to extract heat energy, are all governed by the need to ensure that precisely one neutron from each fission event induces another fission. Too few neutrons and you don't have a power plant; too many and you have a catastrophe.

Now reducing the number of neutrons is relatively straightforward. Certain materials are good neutron absorbers and will very effectively cut down the neutron flux when introduced into the reactor core. So control is a negative process: the reactor is designed to produce too many neutrons and the excess is absorbed. A common control system is a set of rods, any of which can be inserted or withdrawn as necessary.

Producing an excess of neutrons in the first place is a matter of putting in enough U-235 at sufficiently high concentration to allow for all losses and still have more than one spare neutron per fission. There is thus an inter-relationship between the composition and form of the fuel elements, the type of material used to thermalize the neutrons (the moderator) and the nature of the coolant which flows through the core and carries away the heat. Table 8.5 lists the main reactors currently in use for power generation, all but one of them thermal reactors. Their main differences come from the choice of moderator and coolant, a choice which is crucial in determining the entire structure of the reactor.

Moderators and Coolants

The ideal moderator should reduce neutron energies as efficiently as possible. That is, quickly and with the minimum neutron loss. At first glance, hydrogen should be best because it has the lightest atoms, which means that a neutron gives up its energy in the fewest collisions. (A fast-moving billiard ball gives up most of its energy when it collides almost head-on with a much slower or stationary one. A fast-moving billiard ball colliding with a twenty-

TABLE 8.5. *Types of reactor*

Reactor	Fuel	Moderator	Coolant
PWR	enriched uranium	light water	light water
BWR	enriched uranium	light water	light water/steam
CANDU	natural uranium	heavy water	heavy water
MAGNOX	natural uranium	graphite	carbon dioxide
AGR	enriched uranium	graphite	carbon dioxide
VVER	enriched uranium	light water	light water
RBMK	slightly enriched uranium	graphite	light water/steam
LMFBR	highly enriched uranium	none	liquid sodium

pound cannon ball bounces off with very little energy loss.) Ordinary water contains plenty of hydrogen, is cheap, and has the further advantage that it can also act as coolant. Unfortunately however, it is a rather heavy absorber of neutrons. They combine with the hydrogen nuclei (protons) to form deuterons, nuclei of the hydrogen isotope deuterium. (Only in the case of hydrogen are the isotopes given names of their own. They are deuterium, written as either $_1^2D$ or $_1^2H$, and tritium, $_1^3H$.) The absorption of neutrons by water is so great that natural uranium is too dilute to sustain a chain reaction. So all reactors using ordinary water (light-water reactors or LWRs) must be fuelled with enriched uranium.

Deuterium itself is an excellent moderator. The neutrons need more collisions than with hydrogen but they will travel literally for miles in heavy water (D_2O) with very little loss. In consequence heavy-water reactors (HWRs) can use natural uranium. But the 500 tonnes of heavy water needed as moderator and coolant in a large reactor must be obtained by separating out the small fraction of deuterium in natural hydrogen (about one atom in 7000); a factor to be balanced against the saving on uranium enrichment.

The third common moderator is the one used in the first reactor ever: carbon in the form of graphite blocks. Although the atoms are relatively heavy, the neutron loss is only a quarter of that in light water. Graphite cannot of course circulate, so something else must act as coolant. In most British reactors this is carbon dioxide gas. The first generation (called the Magnox reactors, from the alloy with which their uranium metal fuel was clad) could use natural uranium, but the later Advanced Gas-Cooled Reactor (AGR) needed slightly enriched fuel.

The LMFBR, being a fast reactor, has no moderator. It is sufficiently different from all the others that we shall discuss it separately.

Structures

Certain basic requirements determine the general form of all the reactors discussed here. The fuel must be distributed at the right density, in good contact with the coolant, and surrounded by the moderator. Given the high level of radioactivity once the reactor has been running, replacement of spent fuel must be handled from outside. Hence the common use of tubes or 'pins' assembled into bundles, with the fuel (normally now uranium oxide, which can withstand higher temperatures than uranium metal) in the form of slugs or pellets inside a metal cladding (Fig. 8.2).

Coolant must stream freely past the hot fuel, at the highest possible temperature and pressure for maximum efficiency. This has a major effect on the design, because the material of any pipes for it to flow through will absorb neutrons, so only those reactors with very low neutron loss in the moderator and coolant can afford the additional absorption by individual pressure tubes. In many light-water reactors and the AGR the whole core is therefore submerged in the flowing coolant in a single large pressure vessel.

Materials as well as people can be harmed by exposure to intense irradiation. This must be taken into account in the choice of reactor components, and the growth of the nuclear industry has led to many developments in materials science. The need for remote handling of all monitoring and control, inspection, and maintenance has required new specialized instrumentation techniques. Consider for a moment the interior of a reactor core. The coolant mustn't occupy too much space, so it must flow fast in

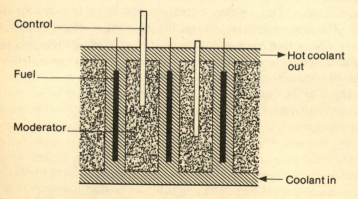

Fig. 8.2 Essential features of a thermal reactor core

order to carry away the heat. We thus have a very hot fluid streaming at high speed and high pressure through narrow gaps and channels past long thin fuel rods. It is not surprising that materials and measuring instruments, even when they survive the combined effects of temperature and pressure, chemical attack, and bombardment by sub-nuclear particles, have sometimes shaken themselves to pieces. But the designer must ensure that fuel rods do not distort, that control rods can move freely without jamming, and that nothing is ever allowed to impede the flow of coolant.

Safety

The first essential is a way to stop the chain reaction—in a hurry if necessary. This shouldn't be difficult, because almost anything inserted near the fuel will absorb enough neutrons. One 'fail-safe' method has the control rods suspended so that they can if necessary fall in, without the need for any drive. We must remember, however, that the inside is at high pressure, so anything inserted from outside will meet resistance. It is fairly common these days to have a back-up system which can inject a neutron absorber into circulating coolant.

Any major loss of coolant can have particularly serious consequences in a nuclear reactor. In a coal-fired plant the mass of hot coal could be rather an embarrassment, but stopping the input of fuel or air can at least prevent the generation of more heat. Not so in a nuclear reactor. Even after the chain reaction has stopped, the generation of heat continues. It comes from the energy released in the radioactive decay of all the fission products, and immediately after shut-down can be almost one-tenth of the full normal output. Fortunately the half-lives of many of the products are very short, and within an hour the rate of heat production should have fallen to 1 per cent or less of full power. Nevertheless, the heat produced during this time is enough to melt the core and perhaps the floor of the reactor building as well: the scenario for the China Syndrome—the fictional idea that the contents might set off for the diametrically opposite point on the globe. The likelihood or otherwise of a core melt-down, and the measures adopted to prevent one, must be a central issue when we ask about the safety of different reactor designs.

The fear that the fuel of a thermal reactor will somehow turn into an 'atomic bomb' is probably not well-founded. Any explosion—nuclear or chemical—is the result of a runaway energy-producing chain reaction, multiplying so fast that the energy doesn't have time to escape by the normal 'peaceful' means, as heat and light. Instead, the energy density rises until the bonds holding the material together are broken and it blows apart. In the words of the unfortunate spokesperson after one accident in the USA, it is indeed an 'energetic disassembly'—but we'll call it an explosion. A nuclear explosion therefore requires a rapid multiplication of neutrons, and for this to occur there must be a high density of fissile nuclei in a large enough lump to make the neutron loss out of the surface negligible. About 10 kg of pure U-235 will do it, or about 5 kg of Pu-239. If the fissile material is diluted in any way the mass needed becomes greater, and if there are fewer than about 1 in 10 fissile nuclei it can't happen at all. So the only way for a thermal reactor to become a nuclear bomb would be for a large number of the U-235 or Pu-239 nuclei distributed throughout 100 tonnes of core to bring themselves miraculously to one place. At Chernobyl in 1986, where the bottom of the reactor vessel was blown downwards and the molten fuel flowed out, scientists were concerned for some time that a self-sustaining chain reaction might re-start, but eventually found that the fissile material had been diluted by a simultaneous flow of large quantities of the sand forming part of the screening around the core: an interesting but somewhat unplanned 'safety system'.

This reasoning does not of course exclude an 'ordinary' explosion resulting from the generation of too much heat. The 1979 accident at the Three Mile Island plant in the USA resulted in a chemical explosion—the 'energetic disassembly' mentioned above—but the containment held. The explosions at Chernobyl were even more straightforward: the effect of uncontrolled heating, building up steam pressure until the structure blew apart. (See 'Risk' in Chapter 13 for further discussion of these events.)

Efficiency

A feature common to all present nuclear power-stations is that they use the conventional method for producing electric power: steam turbines driving generators. The coolant carries away the energy as heat which produces hot steam. Steam temperatures and pressures in nuclear plants have always lagged behind those of fossil fuel systems, partly because of the more severe conditions which materials must withstand. Consequently, thermal efficiencies are lower (34 per cent turbine efficiency is considered good) and the waste heat output is greater. Heat losses should be least if the coolant itself becomes the steam, and this is the method adopted in boiling water reactors (BWRs). The others all use two circuits, with the primary coolant giving up energy in a heat exchanger (steam generator) to a secondary flow of water.

The concept of 'overall efficiency' is not a very clear one for a nuclear plant. What do you take as starting-point? What is counted as energy input? At the mines (Fig. 8.3), natural uranium is extracted—or to be precise, an ore of natural uranium. This is treated to give an oxide (U_3O_8) known as yellowcake, which is in turn processed before use as fuel, even in a reactor using natural uranium. Increasing the proportion of U-235, if necessary, is an expensive process consuming a twentieth or more of the power

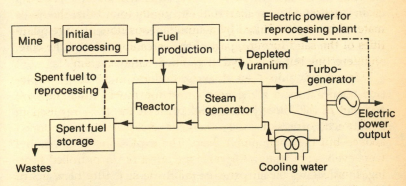

Fig. 8.3 Uranium fuel processes

output of the plant. The useful life of a fuel element ceases when the build-up of neutron-absorbing fission products starts to limit the chain reaction, so the spent fuel may have a fissile content equal to half that of a fresh element. On the other side of the account-book, as we've seen, some Pu-239 which wasn't even there to start with will have contributed to the output.

Types of Thermal Reactor

We've seen how reactors work and to some extent why they are as they are. It remains to look at some actual structures. Of the many reactor types developed in the past fifty years, just a few now dominate the world market. The American-designed light-water reactors (PWR and BWR) account for about three-quarters of the total, and the Canadian CANDU design has been adopted in a few countries. The Advanced Gas-Cooled Reactor was adopted for Britain's nuclear power programme in the mid-1960s, as successor to the original Magnox type. Seven twin-reactor (2×660MW) AGR power-stations joined the eleven Magnox plants in the following couple of decades, but by the time the seventh was completed, the decision had been made to change to PWRs for future plants. The first of these, Sizewell B, was commissioned in 1995. The ex-USSR has an equally long period of development of different systems, resulting in two main types. One, the VVER, is a form of pressurized-water reactor but with significant differences from the American PWR, having for instance several separate coolant circuits rather than a single pressure vessel. The other Russian type, the RBMK, is a 'mixed' reactor, with water coolant but graphite moderator. (The Chernobyl reactors are of this latter type.) Space doesn't allow detailed accounts of all these different systems, so we'll briefly discuss just three examples, emphasizing the main differences between them.

PWR

Figure 8.4 shows the structure of the core of a PWR. It consists of little more than the fuel elements, perhaps 50 000 long thin metal tubes containing the 100 tonnes or so of fuel. Assembled into

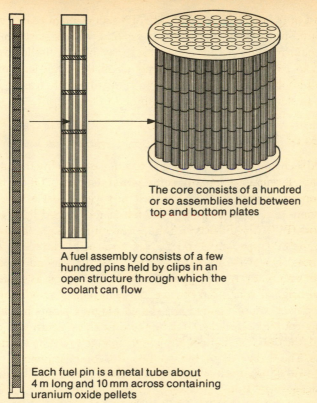

The core consists of a hundred
or so assemblies held between
top and bottom plates

A fuel assembly consists of a few
hundred pins held by clips in an
open structure through which the
coolant can flow

Each fuel pin is a metal tube about
4 m long and 10 mm across containing
uranium oxide pellets

Fig. 8.4 Fuel arrangement in a pressurized-water reactor

bundles, these are held in place by top and bottom plates, and the
whole is submerged in water in a pressure vessel some forty feet
high with walls eight inches thick (Fig. 8.5). The water, acting as
both moderator and coolant, circulates through the pressure vessel and through steam generators near it. High pressure (over 100
atmospheres) prevents the water from boiling even at its maximum temperature of over 300° C. Maintaining this pressure is very
important, as the cooling requires water—not steam, which
would carry away much less heat. The danger of a massive loss of
coolant is taken very seriously, because if one of the large pipes

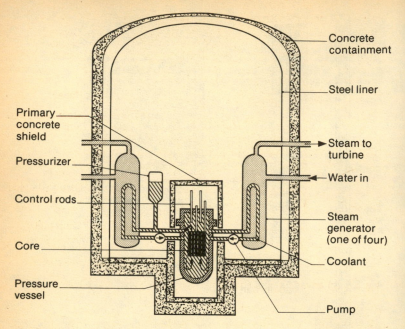

Fig. 8.5 A pressurized-water reactor

were to fracture, the water would flash to steam and be lost in seconds.

A point in favour of the PWR is that any loss of coolant is also loss of moderator, so the chain reaction should in any case stop. Nevertheless, a fast and effective emergency cooling system is needed, and the American PWRs have several, including large tanks holding water under pressure, which can be released instantly into the core, and various pumped systems.

AGR

With its solid moderator, the AGR is of course structurally completely different from the PWR. Instead of the open lattice of thin tubes, the core, about thirty feet across, is made of solid graphite, pierced by several hundred vertical channels into which the fuel clusters slide (Fig. 8.6). There are 2000 or so of these clusters, short

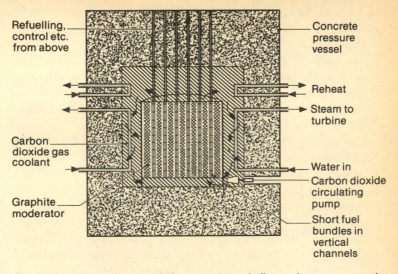

Refuelling, control etc. from above

Concrete pressure vessel

Reheat

Steam to turbine

Carbon dioxide gas coolant

Water in

Carbon dioxide circulating pump

Graphite moderator

Short fuel bundles in vertical channels

Fig. 8.6 An advanced gas-cooled reactor: core, boiler, and pressure vessel

and chunky, not long as in the PWR. The carbon dioxide gas coolant is pumped through the core at a pressure of about forty atmospheres. Gas temperatures as high as 600°C were planned, but there have been difficulties in achieving these.

The pressure vessel is a massive reinforced concrete structure, a system which is claimed by advocates of the AGR to be less likely to suffer catastrophic failure than the steel vessel of the PWR. Other claimed safety advantages are the fact that the coolant is already a gas and the ability of the heavy graphite core to absorb heat if the cooling did fail. On the other hand, the planned on-line refuelling (without needing to close down the system), which should give the AGR an advantage over the PWR, has not proved very successful in practice.

CANDU

Twenty or so CANDU (Canadian Deuterium Uranium) reactors with heavy water as coolant and moderator provide power for Canada's nuclear power-stations, and this is also the only system to have made any dent in the domination of the international market by LWRs.

The CANDU uses to advantage the low neutron absorption in heavy water. It has separate circuits for moderator and coolant (Fig. 8.7). The short fuel bundles lie in hundreds of horizontal channels and the coolant flows past them inside double-walled tubes. The moderator is thus kept cool enough that it need not be under pressure to avoid boiling. Refuelling is on-line.

The whole network of fuel channels and horizontal and vertical control rods is in a horizontal steel cylinder called the 'calandria', which for a 600-MW reactor is about 8 metres in each dimension. Surrounding the reactor is a concrete radiation shield and the entire system is inside a containment building some 70 metres high.

The use of many small pressure tubes makes sudden total loss of coolant unlikely (though a fracture could still lead to local over-

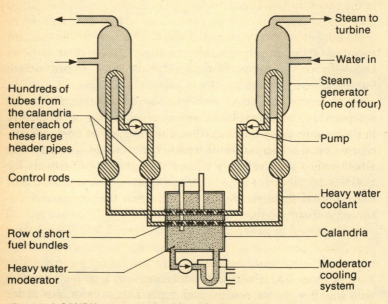

Fig. 8.7 A CANDU reactor: calandria and steam generators

heating), and as in the AGR, the mass of moderator should hold the temperature even if the coolant pumps failed. The disadvantage that loss of coolant is not loss of moderator is recognized by a dual SCRAM system, with control rods to drop in and provision for injecting a neutron absorber.

With a coolant temperature only a little above 300°C the CANDU has poor thermal efficiency, but its efficient use of uranium compensates for this. Overall it is capable of producing about a quarter more power per tonne than the LWRs. The CANDUs have also proved the most reliable nuclear reactors on the whole, their 'availability factors' of 80 per cent or so indicating that they are seldom out of service for unplanned reasons.

Breeders

Breeder reactors are not new. The first ever 'nuclear' generation of electric power used heat from an experimental breeder in the USA in the 1950s. Britain had a small demonstration fast reactor (DFR) and then a larger prototype fast reactor (PFR) at Dounreay in Scotland, but both are now closed and to be decommissioned, and there are no plans at present for another. Other countries with breeder programmes include Japan, India, and France, where Superphénix, the world's largest breeder, was restarted in 1994 after a four-year closure. The fuel-saving attraction of these reactors was a main reason for early interest in their development, but for many years they have been the subject of fierce debate, centred on the two issues of whether they were necessary and whether they were safe. We'll leave the question of necessity for the later discussion of future energy supplies, but a few details of the essential features are needed in order to understand the concerns about safety.

We have seen how a breeder works in principle ('A Significant Side-Effect', above), and it is obvious that for the breeding reaction to proceed, each fission must result in more 'useful' neutrons than the single one required to keep the fission going. Fast neutrons give slightly greater neutron yield per fission, and also better conversion of U-238 than thermal neutrons, so the breeder is a **fast**

reactor. However, as we've seen, fast neutrons are much less efficient in inducing fission, so the fuel must be considerably more highly enriched than in a thermal reactor: mixed oxides of uranium and plutonium have been used with up to 20 per cent fissile nuclei. The more concentrated fuel means greater heat production per cubic metre, but the coolant must neither slow down nor absorb the neutrons. Sodium is used, a metal which is liquid at the high temperature in the reactor.

Figure 8.8 shows in outline one form of Liquid Metal Fast Breeder Reactor (LMFBR). The core sits in a 'pool' of liquid sodium, with the heat carried away by a flow of the same liquid metal in an intermediate circuit. Sodium is chemically extremely active, igniting on contact with air and reacting violently with water, so it is

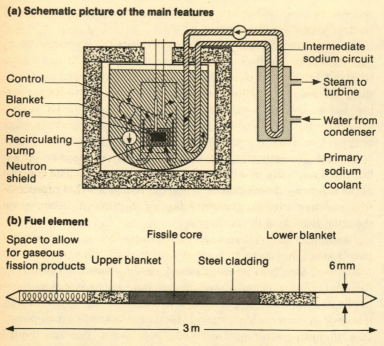

(a) Schematic picture of the main features

Control
Blanket
Core
Recirculating pump
Neutron shield

Intermediate sodium circuit
Steam to turbine
Water from condenser
Primary sodium coolant

(b) Fuel element

Space to allow for gaseous fission products
Upper blanket
Fissile core
Steel cladding
Lower blanket
6 mm

3 m

Fig. 8.8 An LMFBR

essential that both sodium flows are very securely contained. The central part of the system consists essentially of the core where fission is maintained and the surrounding blanket of U-238 where breeding occurs.

The main concerns about a breeder programme centre on its fuel, for three reasons:

- the concentration of fissile material,
- the necessity for reprocessing,
- the central role of plutonium.

The concentrated fuel raises the question whether a runaway nuclear reaction could occur. A fully efficient 'atomic bomb' isn't possible, and even a 'nuclear fizzle' would require a number of improbable conditions simultaneously. Nevertheless, there is some disagreement about probabilities, and the unlikelihood does seem to be of a different order than the virtual impossibility of a nuclear explosion in a thermal reactor.

Similarly with reprocessing. The USA does not reprocess spent fuel from civil reactors. Britain has reprocessed from early days (the original Magnox design was influenced by the need for plutonium for military purposes). The new Thermal Oxide Reprocessing Plant (THORP), and France's new plant at the La Hague facility both started work in 1994, and offer a reprocessing service to other countries, extracting uranium and plutonium from their spent fuel. The important point, however, is that this is an option but not a necessity in a thermal reactor programme. The concern about extensive development of breeder reactors is that reprocessing, and in particular the extraction of plutonium, becomes an essential feature of the fuel cycle.

To see why this causes concern we must look at the nature of plutonium. One central fact is that with enough of it a bomb can be made. Not, it should be emphasized, easily. Plutonium is a nasty material, very poisonous, and in any but skilled hands is more likely to lead to an unpleasant death than to unlimited power. (Indeed, its extreme toxicity and the consequent blackmail power of a threat to distribute it is another reason for concern.) Bombs can of course also be made from fissile U-235, but the very important difference is that in natural uranium or spent fuel from any type of reactor the U-235 is mixed with a large amount of non-fissile U-238, and separating two isotopes like this requires complex and costly plant. Fissile Pu-239 does have 'diluting' isotopes (also produced in reactors) and true 'weapons grade' material should have less than 7 per cent Pu-240; but the plutonium from breeders containing 80–90 per cent Pu-239 can still be used in a weapon, if a rather unreliable one. There can be little doubt that the safest policy would be to design thermal reactors to burn as much plutonium as possible and then to leave the residue in the highly radioactive spent fuel.

Unfortunately it appears that we may be too late, and that in the mid-1990s the world is already seeing the beginnings of a 'black economy' in plutonium. Weapons, of any type, are not the subject of this book, but it is relevant to mention that between 50 and 100 tonnes of weapons grade plutonium are becoming 'available' following the decommissioning of nuclear weapons by Russia and the USA. Several groups of concerned scientists have tried to reach agreement on a method for making this safe. It could be used as a fuel in reactors, which would reduce the quantity and also 'poison' any remainder with radioactive fission products. However, not all ordinary thermal reactors are suitable, and those that are could consume plutonium only very slowly. The Superphénix breeder could in principle convert a couple of tonnes a year, but is not considered sufficiently reliable. Other options include mixing the plutonium with other wastes and burying it. Unfortunately there remains no agreed method, and at the time of writing it looks increasingly as though neither side really wants to dispose of it irreversibly. (To put the quantity in context, about 5 kg of weapons grade plutonium are required for a bomb, and the total quantity of plutonium in existence is thought to be over 1000 tonnes—a million kilograms.)

Footnote on Fusion

Fusion is the coming together of two lighter nuclei to form one heavier one. As it is the reverse of fission we might expect it to consume rather than produce energy, and this would indeed be so if we tried to persuade strontium and xenon to fuse into uranium. However, if we start with two very light nuclei we find completely the opposite. The fusion of two deuterons, producing He-3 and a neutron, releases energy. The masses tell us so. Table 8.6 shows the figures, and reveals why billions of dollars, roubles, etc. have been spent on fusion research. Fusion, it seems, offers 'clean' energy from a fuel so plentiful that it will last for millions of years. No mining, no radioactive fission products, no reprocessing, no plutonium. Only one problem. We don't know how to do it. Not even in

---

TABLE 8.6. *Energy from fusion*

Fusion reactions

Fusion of two deuterium nuclei leads to hydrogen and tritium nuclei:

$$_1^2H + _1^2H \rightarrow _1^1H + _1^3H$$

Fusion of another deuteron with the triton produces a helium nucleus and a neutron:

$$_1^2H + _1^3H \rightarrow _2^4He + n$$

The neutron is unstable and decays, with a half-life of 16 minutes, into a proton, an electron, and a neutrino

$$n \rightarrow _1^1H + e + \nu$$

The net effect is that three nuclei of deuterium have become two of hydrogen and one of helium.

Particle masses (u)		*Energy*
proton	1.0073	The total nuclear mass has decreased by 0.0247 u, about one 240th of the total mass of the original three deuterons.
neutron	1.0086	
deuteron	2.0136	
triton	3.0155	This 'lost mass' is the energy produced ($E = mc^2$), some 360 million megajoules per kilogram of deuterium consumed.
helium-4	4.0015	
		360 million megajoules will run a 600-MW power-station (30 per cent efficiency) for roughly two days.

Sources of deuterium

Water is H_2O. As an oxygen atom is 16 times as heavy as a hydrogen atom, there are 2 kg of hydrogen in 18 kg of water.

1 in 7000 hydrogen atoms is deuterium, so there is 1 kg of deuterium in 63 000 kg (about 60 tonnes) of ordinary water.

A 600-MW power-station therefore needs a net fuel input of 30 tonnes of ordinary water a day!

---

the laboratory. The only fusion power we have achieved so far in any quantity is the hydrogen bomb.

It is easy to see in a general way why there is a difficulty. Two nuclei can only fuse if they come close enough together for the strong nuclear force of attraction to take over. Until this happy state is reached the repulsive electrical force dominates, pushing ever harder the closer they approach. Only if they can be given enough initial energy to overcome this enormous electrical barrier can they reach the promised land flowing with fusion energy.

We'll finish, then, with a very brief glance at one of several attacks on the problem. (The reaction being sought is not exactly the one shown in the table, but the idea is the same.) The thermo-nuclear method aims to give particles high energies by using the fact that hotter means faster. A temperature of some millions of degrees is needed, and a major technical problem is how to contain the mass of 'hot' particles. If they touch anything they will share their energy and cool down. One answer is a 'non-material' container, and a great deal of work has gone into the magnetic bottle, which holds the particles by surrounding them not with atoms at all but with a strong magnetic field. Designing this is difficult enough, but it is only the first step. There is the question of how to get the fuel in and the energy out. And how about side effects? Is it really going to be clean? Tritium is radioactive, and pollution of water by this hydrogen isotope is not an appealing prospect.

Optimists believe (as they have done for many years) that we shall see controlled fusion within the next few decades, but no one expects fusion power-stations until well into the twenty-first century, and there are so many unknowns that it is quite impossible to incorporate this potential source realistically into present plans. A number of recent studies, while feeling that research should continue, have questioned the current scale of investment. Should we really try to fuse all our eggs in this one basket, which may prove either dirty or bottomless?

9

Energy from Water

Introduction

In Chapter 4 we encountered one renewable energy source, in the form of the world's biomass. Now we move on to others: moving water, flowing air, and the origin of almost all our energy, the sun. The present chapter is called simply 'Energy from Water', but as we'll see, this title covers some very different systems—different in their basic principles as well as their present states of development.

The natural flow of water in rivers has been used for thousands of years to drive machinery. It was the energy source for some of the world's first power-stations a hundred years ago, and hydro-electricity now contributes about a fifth of all the world's electric power. So this is a very well-developed technology. The other natural flow, the tides, also has a long history, with tide-mills used to grind corn for centuries. In this case, however, recent development has been much more limited, which at first sight seems odd because tidal power uses much the same technology as conventional hydro-power. We'll need to look a little more closely into the reasons for this difference. Then there are the waves. They certainly carry energy, but as we'll see, they don't involve much actual flow of water at all. So harnessing wave power involves rather different techniques, and these are still very much under development. Finally, we'll come to a system that is totally different from all the others: a mid-ocean thermal power-station. We start, however, with an issue of some importance for national power systems in general and for the integration of renewables in particular: how to store surplus energy for later use.

Storing Energy

We do tend to take for granted the flexibility of our energy supplies. In the early hours of the morning, demand is low. Then the central heating switches on, we all get up, take showers, put on the kettle, make the toast—a sudden demand for gas and electricity that could amount to several kilowatts per household, thousands of megawatts for a large city. Half an hour later, we have abandoned all this power and are demanding equally large amounts in an entirely different form—to travel to work, school, the shops, etc. Then in the evening, we all sit down to watch the TV, and that really tests the system. Not the sitting down, but the getting up at the end of the programme: millions of us if it's a popular one, and we all go and switch on the kettle, increasing demand by tens of millions of kilowatts. This is so predictable that the engineers controlling the electricity grid also sit watching particularly popular programmes in order to anticipate the surge in demand. Some of the largest have followed major sporting events. As the 1990 World Cup match between England and Germany came to its dramatic end, the engineers watching the penalty shoot-out were ready—but the surge didn't come. Then it did, a couple of minutes late. Perhaps thirty million people were sitting stunned? That match, with a rise in demand of 2800 MW, still holds the record. The almost identical events in the 1996 European Cup produced 'only' 1600 MW. Explanations include the suggestions that after-match drinks were rather stronger than tea or that people just retired to bed in despair.

How do our present systems meet these fluctuating demands for different sorts of energy with the reliability we have come to expect? The answer is of course to have enough power-stations, gas supplies, and petrol pumps; but behind all these is the requirement for sufficient storage. If a power station or petrol pump is to provide output on demand it must be able to draw immediately on a store of fuel. As we have seen in Chapter 4, our present fuels, whatever their other disadvantages, are excellent energy stores. So a problem arises when we consider replacing them with renewable sources. The sun, the tides, the winds, and the waves are extremely large stores of energy, so that's not the problem. The difficulty is that they, not we, determine how much power we can draw at any time. To take an obvious example, it's no use expecting a solar plant to deliver the power needed to cook breakfast at 7 am in mid-winter in Britain. The tides pose similar problems, whilst the wind and waves, being unpredictable, are even more of a difficulty.

With the exceptions of direct solar heating and some uses of biofuels, most of the renewables are seen as potential sources of electric power. So a solution to the problem of irregular supplies would be to generate as much power as possible when the energy is available and then keep it until it is needed. And that raises the real problem: we don't have any means of storing large amounts of electrical energy. It is important to note that it is not only with the renewables that this problem arises. Nuclear power-stations in particular cannot conveniently vary their output to follow the short-term demand variations described above, and power-stations of any kind are most efficient when run at full output, so in order to make best use of our existing generating systems we need a means to store surplus output for later use.

Suppose we consider a large modern plant, generating 600 MW. How can we store a few hours of output overnight in order to meet the peak demand next day? Rechargeable batteries are at present our most common way of storing electrical energy, but as Table 9.1 shows, they are hardly practicable for large-scale use. Considerable research effort has been devoted to improved batteries in recent years, but even optimists don't expect changes of the order needed here. (See also Chapter 15, 'The all-electric economy'.) Table 9.1 lists some other possibilities, with the storage capacities of existing fuels for comparison, and we'll look briefly at each of the options in turn.

The first item is steam under the conditions used in a normal fossil-fuel power-station. It would be possible in principle to produce the steam, using concentrated solar radiation for instance, to

TABLE 9.1. *Some possible energy stores*

The second column gives the stored energy in kilowatt-hours and the third column the length of time for which each store could provide 600 MW of electric power, at present efficiencies.

Storage medium	kWh stored	Time
100 tonnes of steam at 540° C and a pressure of 180 atmospheres	100 000	$3\frac{1}{2}$ minutes
100-tonne flywheel	30 000	3 minutes
100 tonnes of car batteries	20 000	2 minutes
100 tonnes of concrete heated to 100° C	5 000	2 seconds
100 tonnes of water at a head of 100 m	30	$\frac{1}{5}$ second
100 tonnes of natural gas	1 500 000	1 hour
100 tonnes of natural uranium	15 000 000 000	1 year

store it, and then to release it to drive a turbine when the power is needed. The figures show that the quantity required to store the overnight output of a large plant would already make this option impracticable, but a more serious factor is that the resulting electrical output would be well under half the original input, because a steam turbine is subject to the Second Law limit (Chapter 5). This applies to any system that stores energy in the form of heat, and as the example of hot concrete shows, heat storage at relatively low temperatures is quite useless if the aim is to produce electric power.

The second idea in Table 9.1 has been seriously studied. The flywheel is brought up to high speed using an electric motor—converting electrical energy into kinetic energy. It continues to spin with little loss of energy, and power is provided when required by coupling it to the generator. Flywheels have the major advantage over heat storage systems that the efficiency of conversion from kinetic energy to electrical energy is limited only by frictional and electrical losses, which can be made quite small. (Conversion from heat energy is not involved, so there is no Second Law limit.) The total energy that can be stored by a particular flywheel depends on its rate of rotation and the amount and distribution of its mass, and there is a maximum for the simple reason that if the wheel spins too fast it flies to pieces. As the table shows, flywheel storage of the surplus from a large power-station is unlikely to be practicable, if only because it would require large numbers of large wheels, with constant switching between them. The method has however been used in other contexts, and its supporters claim that new 'strong' materials could allow greater maximum speeds and therefore more stored energy. Energies per tonne of material which are several hundred times greater than the figure in Table 9.1 have been mentioned, and if these could be achieved reliably and cost-effectively, flywheels might become serious contenders, at least for medium-sized power plants.

Pumped Storage

So, finally, to water. The stored energy shown in the table is the energy needed to raise the 100 tonnes of water through 100 metres height difference. We can treat this as stored energy because if we allow the water to flow down again, it can be used to drive a water turbine or other machinery. The water in the high reservoir is therefore said to have **potential energy**. In Chapter 6 ('A Short Drive in the Country') we saw that the energy in joules needed to raise anything through one metre vertically is equal to its weight; and that the weight of anything is equal to about ten times its mass in kilograms.*

We now have a result that is very important for this method of storage:

- stored energy in joules = 10 × mass in kg × height difference in metres

When we think of water in a reservoir, the stored volume is easier to visualize than the mass, so we'll reformulate the equation using

---

* Technically, the weight of an object is the force pulling it towards the Earth. Forces are measured in units called newtons, and 'about 10' represents the force pulling on 1 kilogram of mass. The actual figure depends on where you are on the surface of the Earth. At sea-level in London, for instance, the force on each kilogram is 9.8118 newtons (approximately!). We shall continue to use 10, however, as the 2% error is not significant for most of our purposes.

the fact that one cubic metre of water has a mass of 1000 kg. We'll also change the terminology slightly, calling the height difference the head of water. So we have

- stored energy in joules = 10 000 × volume in cubic metres × head in metres

or converting to megajoules,

- stored energy in MJ = ($\frac{1}{100}$) × volume in cubic metres × head in metres

As 1 kWh is 3.6 MJ, we could use an even more useful version:

- stored energy in kWh = ($\frac{1}{360}$) × volume in cubic metres × head in metres

But why the interest, when the amount of energy shown in Table 9.1 is so small? The answer is simple: 100 tonnes, which is 100 cubic metres, is a 'small' quantity in terms of reservoirs. Consider the following. A lake 400 metres in diameter and 20 metres deep holds about $2\frac{1}{2}$ million cubic metres of water. At a height of 500 metres this would store about $3\frac{1}{2}$ million kWh of energy, nearly six hours' output of the 600 MW power-station. With the high conversion efficiency which is possible for hydro-plant, it could release this again on demand with relatively little loss.

Figure 9.1 shows the scheme. Surplus electric power is used to pump the water up to the reservoir, where it is held until demand rises. It is then released and runs back down, generating power. There are two nice technological advantages in this system. The first is that a suitably designed electric generator will also serve as an electric motor: instead of mechanical input and electrical output, you have the reverse, electrical input producing mechanical output. Even better, the other part of the system is also reversible, because a suitable water turbine can be run 'backwards' as a water pump. So we have the system shown in the drawing: turbo-generator becomes electrically driven pump, and it is not necessary to invest in two sets of machines. There is another advantage, too. Unlike a thermal power-station, a hydro-plant doesn't need to 'raise steam' before it can generate power, so it can respond extremely quickly to changes in demand.

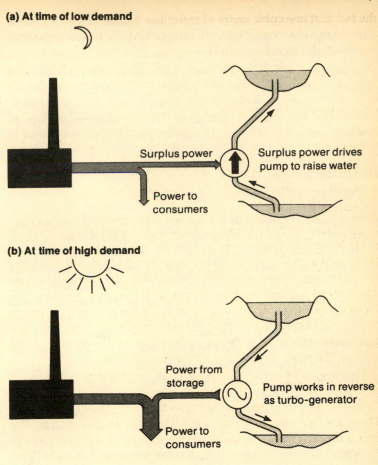

(a) At time of low demand

Surplus power

Surplus power drives pump to raise water

Power to consumers

(b) At time of high demand

Power from storage

Pump works in reverse as turbo-generator

Power to consumers

Fig. 9.1 Pumped storage

With the growing importance of electricity supplies, increasing numbers of pumped storage systems are appearing in many countries. Switzerland, with 8000 MW of capacity, even offers a service to neighbouring countries needing temporary storage for their surplus output. The UK has one of the world's largest pumped storage plants, the Dinorwig power-station in Wales. Its upper reservoir, 500 metres above the outflow, stores nearly 7 million cubic metres of water and its six 280 MW generators produce nearly three times the output of our example above. The overall pumping-to-generating efficiency is about 80 per cent (minus a few per cent more to run the plant). With the turbine already spinning in air, the system can go from zero to full output in 10 seconds—about the time it takes to fill one of those millions of kettles.

Hydroelectricity

The Resource

Conventional hydroelectricity doesn't, of course, depend on electric motors to pump the water uphill. The sun does it for us. Solar radiation provides the energy to evaporate water from oceans or lakes and drives the convection currents and winds that deliver the water vapour over land masses. Some of it then condenses and falls as rain or snow on hills and mountains, resulting in streams which feed rivers, and occasionally, natural storage in lakes or glaciers. We've seen how to calculate the total energy stored in a high lake, but now we need to know how much power can be delivered by a particular flow of water. The answer is easy to find, because the power is the rate at which the water delivers energy (1 watt = 1 joule per second). As we've seen, the energy depends on the volume of water and the head, so the power depends on the volume flowing and the head:

- power in watts = 10 000 × flow in cubic metres per second × head in metres

or, changing to kilowatts:

- power in kW = 10 × flow in m^3/s × head in metres

A nice simple relationship, which can be used to find whether it is worth building a small hydro-plant on a local river, or to assess the total world potential for hydroelectric power.

At present, as we've seen, hydro provides about a fifth of the world's electricity, but estimates suggest that the potential is there to produce five times the total output of all present power-stations. Such 'total resource' figures must be treated with care, however. Much of this running water is in very inaccessible places, often far from any possible consumers. And then there is the issue, already arising in the more developed countries, of whether we want to imprison all our streams and rivers behind walls and in pipes. Or, in the developing world, the even more difficult question whether some people should be driven from their homes in order to improve life for other people. 'Not in my backyard' takes on an entirely new interpretation when you are about to lose not only your backyard but your house, family land, and entire way of life.

Turbines

Cold water is very different from hot steam, and not surprisingly, water turbines are different from steam turbines. They are also different from each other, because the sites for hydro-plants can offer very different conditions (Fig. 9.2). Water from the high mountain reservoir or lake, falling through as much as 1000

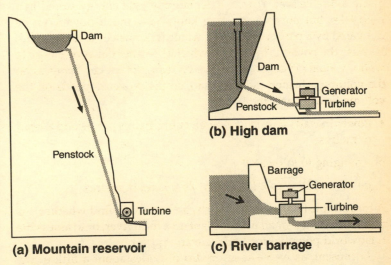

(a) Mountain reservoir

(b) High dam

(c) River barrage

Fig. 9.2 Hydroelectricity sites

metres, could arrive at the turbine as a narrow high-speed jet delivering perhaps 5 cubic metres a second. In contrast, the flow from the reservoir behind a dam might be many times this, but might still deliver the same 50 MW of power because the head is lower. Very different situations which call for very different turbines.

Figure 9.3 shows the rotating part—the **runner**—of a few types of water turbine. The Pelton wheel, used when the head is very high, spins as the high-speed jet hits each of its double 'cups' in turn. The energy input to the turbine and the generator it drives is the *kinetic energy* of the fast-moving water. The other types work in

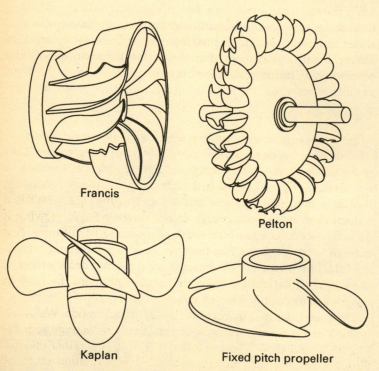

Francis

Pelton

Kaplan

Fixed pitch propeller

Fig. 9.3 Turbine runners

a very different way. Their runners operate totally submerged, with the water swirling over them, and it is mainly the pressure of water that pushes the turbine round. In a Francis turbine with a head of, say, 200 metres, the pressure where the water enters the turbine would be near to 20 atmospheres, and with normal atmospheric pressure on the other side, at the outflow, this pressure difference provides the driving force. Most of the world's large hydroelectric plants use Francis turbines, including the largest of them all, the huge Itaipu plant on the Parana River between Brazil and Paraguay. Each of its 18 Francis turbines has an output of 700 MW: a total capacity of 12 GW, ten times that of a large coal-fired or nuclear plant. At the other extreme are little mini-hydro plants generating less than a thousandth of this power, but still using the same turbine design. The 'propeller', the third main type of turbine, operates on a similar principle but the structure is rather different, being adapted for use with large volumes of slowly flowing water—on big rivers, for instance, or in tidal plants; which brings us to the next topic.

Tidal Power

Although we take very little power from the world's tides at present, they are nevertheless constantly dissipating energy. Like many dissipation processes this one involves friction: the drag of the tidal flow over the sea-bed and along coastlines generating heat at a total rate of a few million megawatts. The result is a reduction in the kinetic energy of the rotating Earth, slowing it down by about one six-hundredth of a second per century. Not enough to worry about. Nor need we be concerned about extracting tidal energy for our own use, as we'd need to draw a third of the world's total annual energy consumption from the tides in order even to double this tiny effect.

There are tides mainly because the Earth has a moon. We usually think of the moon as going round the Earth, but a more accurate picture would show a sort of folk dance with two rather unequal partners circling each other, completing one rotation every 28 days. The force that holds them in position is of course gravity: the pull of the Earth on the moon and the equal and opposite pull of the moon on the Earth. But not all parts of the Earth are at the same distance from the moon. The parts on the far side are both further away and circling faster, with the result that they have a tendency to fly away. The reverse is true for the parts facing the moon: its pull is greater and they are also moving more slowly, so they tend to fall towards it. These differences are far too small to pull the Earth apart, but they have a noticeable effect on the water on its surface. Water on the far side from the moon bulges outwards slightly and water facing the moon bulges towards it—which is again 'outwards' as viewed on the Earth. Where there is water there are always these two bulges, locked on to the moon's position. The Earth, however, rotates on its own axis once every 24 hours, taking its oceans with it, of course. So the high and low tides that we see are the changes in level of our local piece of water as it is pulled out into a bulge and then released. The time between high tides is not exactly 12 hours but about 25 minutes longer, because the moon has moved on a bit each time we come round. The sun is another complicating factor. Although it is 30 million times more massive than the moon, its effect is much less because the difference in distance to the near and far sides of the Earth is so much smaller than the distance from the sun. It does have some effect, however, giving us the fortnightly spring tides at new moon and full moon—when the sun and moon are along the same line—and the smaller neaps in between.

Unfortunately, or perhaps fortunately for tidal power, the tides we actually have are also affected by many other factors. The shapes of coastlines, the effects of inlets and islands, their directions and dimensions, are crucial in determining tidal patterns and therefore the energy we might extract. Full, detailed flow calculations are beyond even the largest computer, but a simple picture, drawing on everyday experience, allows us to see why some features might lead to particularly large tidal ranges. Consider the waves you can set up in a bath or bowl by moving your hand to and fro at one end. If you get the timing just right you can build up a big displacement, with the water swinging from one end to the other. The right timing depends on the size of the container, and it is this type of 'resonance' effect that builds up large tides. If the size of an inlet, bay, estuary, or other partially enclosed stretch of water is right for the 12½-hour swing of the tides, a large movement will be maintained. Other factors, such as drag by coastline or sea-bed can affect the result, but if the picture is even approximately correct, it carries a warning: we must be careful that the barrages and breakwaters of the power installation don't change the shape and destroy the very effect we are relying on.

Once the body of water is chosen, it is possible to make a rough calculation of its energy potential. We'll use as our example the only existing tidal power-station of any size. It is based on a barrage across the estuary of the river Rance in Brittany and has been operating since 1966. The tidal range is about 10 metres and the barrage encloses an area of some 20 square kilometres (20 million square metres). This means that when the basin is full it holds about 200 million cubic metres of water at an average height of 5 metres above low water level. Using the equation earlier in this chapter, we find that this represents a little under 3 million kWh of stored energy. The next question is how best to extract it.

The machinery is not the issue; with this low head there is no doubt that propeller turbines (Fig. 9.3 above) are the most suitable, and these are used at La Rance. The question is how to run them. It might seem that the best method would be to capture the water at high tide, hold it until the next low tide, and let it run out through the turbines as fast as possible while the head is still high (Fig. 9.4(a)–(c)). This would certainly extract the most energy, but at a cost, as Fig. 9.4(d) shows. A 'spike' of very high power every 12½ hours is not the most useful input for a national power system, and the turbines to handle this power are going to be expensive machines that then sit idle for much of the time. Is it possible to improve on this?

It is, but at the cost of reduced total output. The pattern originally adopted at La Rance, generating on both ebb and flood tides, running the turbines at less than the maximum head, and incorporating an element of pumped storage, certainly produces a more uniform supply (Fig. 9.4(e)). The rather complex pattern of use of the turbines did, however, give some trouble, and it has been

(a) Water flows into the basin through open sluices as the tide rises

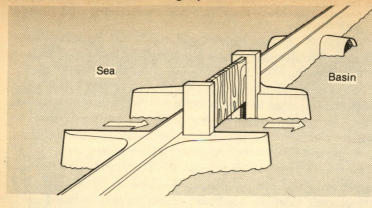

(b) The sluices are closed at high tide, so the basin level stays high as the sea falls

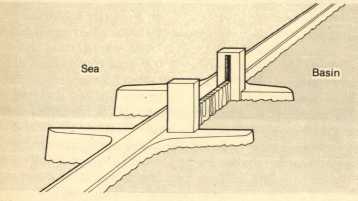

(c) At low water when the head is greatest, the turbines are opened and the water rushes out, generating power at a high rate

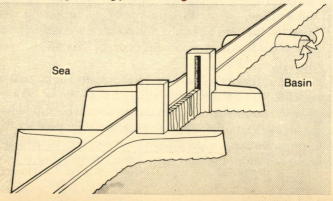

Fig. 9.4 A simple tidal power system

(d) This shows the changing level in the basin, and the power output, over a period of about twenty hours. (The times corresponding to (a), (b) and (c) are indicated)

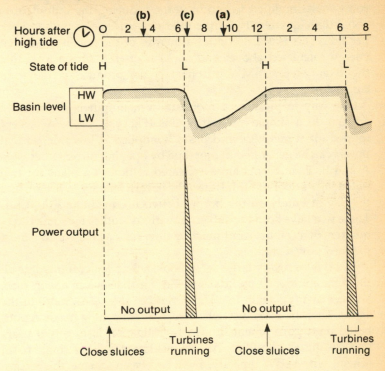

(e) A more uniform output is obtained by generating during the rise and fall of the tide

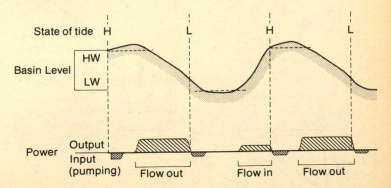

Fig. 9.4 *Continued*

somewhat simplified in recent years, reducing the output from about three-quarters to a little over two-thirds of a million kWh per tide. This is a little under a quarter of the maximum stored energy calculated above, and about a quarter of the total that the twenty-four 10 MW turbines could produce if they ran constantly.

One way to produce a more uniform output is a two-basin scheme. In a simple version of this (Fig. 9.5), Basin A is kept topped up at high tide and Basin B emptied at low tide, so that power can be generated at any time by opening turbines between A and B. Twin basins have appeared at times on plans for two potentially important tidal sites: the Severn Estuary in Britain and the Bay of Fundy on the border between Canada and the USA. These two have been the subject of various studies for some three-quarters of a century, and must by now rank as the world's most planned power-stations.

You'd need a very large set of bookshelves to accommodate all the different reports on tidal schemes for the Severn: one in 1920, another in 1933, again in 1944, several in the 1960s, more in the 1970s. Then in 1981, just what we needed: a new major report, based on a government-funded investigation lasting two years and costing £2.3 million. After considering a large single-basin scheme with 12 GW capacity, and a two-basin scheme, this recommended a smaller, one-basin plan (Fig. 9.6). The installed capacity

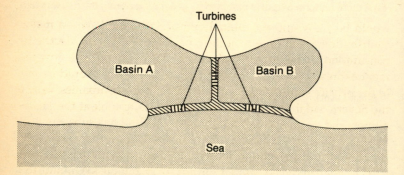

Fig. 9.5 A two-basin system

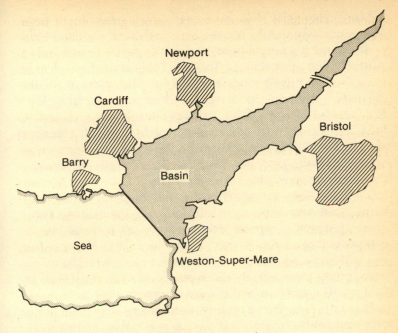

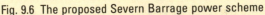

Fig. 9.6 The proposed Severn Barrage power scheme

A single barrage from Lavernock Point to Brean Down.
Installed capacity: 7.2 GW from 160 turbines.
Estimated annual output: 13 000 million kWh.
Estimated cost (1981): £5600 million.

would be 7 GW and the annual output 13 billion kWh—a major
contribution amounting to some 6 per cent of total UK electricity
consumption. The capital cost would be £5.6 billion. The government expressed interest, but felt that development should be left
to the private sector. A consortium of six major companies, called
the Severn Tidal Power Group, was formed to look at the possibilities, and some £15 million of public funding has subsequently
been invested in studies of environmental and other issues. At
the time of writing, the proposed installed capacity has risen to
8.6 GW, the predicted annual output to 17 billion kWh, and the
estimated cost to over £10 billion.

Many other tidal sites have been investigated. In England, Morecambe Bay and the Mersey have both been studied. World-wide, interest has ranged from Alaska to Cape Horn and Siberia to Australia; but other than La Rance, all this effort has led to no more than a relatively modest 18 MW Canadian plant on the Bay of Fundy and a couple in Russia and China each generating just a few hundred *kilo*watts. Why is this potentially large resource so little developed? Environmentalists might hope that concern about the wildlife of tidal estuaries is the reason, but such 'green' arguments haven't stopped the development of conventional hydroelectric power-stations in many parts of the world. It seems much more likely that sheer cost is the inhibiting factor. Tidal barrages are very expensive, and designing the plant so that it doesn't just produce a pulse of output every $12\frac{1}{2}$ hours adds to the cost per unit of output, as we've seen. The 'fuel' is of course free, and with some refurbishment, the system could well last for 100 years, producing extremely cheap power once the initial costs are paid off. The problem is that most investors want their money back in rather less than a century. Calculations show that, for the proposed Severn scheme, just paying reasonable interest on the money would cost 5p per unit of electricity produced—nearly twice the total price that other power-stations receive for their output. It may be that tidal power, like other renewables, will find its place if we become really worried about the effects of burning fossil fuels; but until then it seems that it will have to wait for a benefactor with £10 billion to spare.

Wave Power

So much for the tides. How about the waves? It is not difficult to see that they are a potential source of energy. Just stand on the shore and look at the sea; or listen to the continuous roar of the surf, day and night, year in, year out, on an exposed beach. The power of the sea, built up by winds over thousands of miles of open ocean, is obvious. Obvious, but how much? What is the power of the sea? How many kilowatts?

Let's start with a simple calculation that uses little more than the evidence of our eyes. Two features of a wave are clear from even a casual glance: the water moves incessantly and is lifted up intermittently. Kinetic energy and potential energy are both involved. We'll make an estimate of the gravitational potential energy first. Consider a long slice of water one metre wide running out across the waves. In Fig. 9.7(*a*) the wave height is 2 metres and the distance between peaks, the wavelength, is 160 metres. The water lifted up is the shaded area—it would of course just fill the corresponding trough if there were no wave. For the simplified squared-off wave in (*b*) it is easy to see that the raised volume is 80 cubic metres, and as this is raised through 1 metre, the energy stored is 0.8 MJ. It will, of course, be less for the curved wave, and more detailed calculation shows that it is in fact just half as much: 0.4 MJ, or 400 000 joules.

A further calculation—rather too complex to include here—shows that the kinetic energy of all the moving water in the same strip of wave is exactly the same as the stored gravitational energy. It also shows that on average just half the total energy flows past during a complete wave cycle, which brings the figure back to 400 000 joules. Suppose now that the time for this to happen is 10 seconds for our 160 metre wave. 400 000 joules in 10 seconds means 40 000 joules per second, which is 40 kW. We still need to ask how much of this could be collected, but if the figure is even

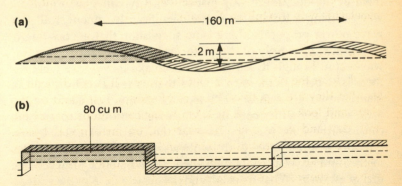

(a)

← 160 m →

2 m

(b)

80 cu m

Fig. 9.7 Gravitational energy of a wave

approximately correct, the power is enough to be interesting. A 1-MW plant would need to capture the energy from a width of at least 250 metres across the waves, so it's not exactly a compact source; but it could mean a fuel-free power supply, and one, moreover, that would normally be greatest at just the times of year when demand in cooler countries reaches its peak. The estimated wave-power potential around the coasts of Britain is some 60–80 billion kWh a year, enough to meet a quarter of the nation's demand for electricity. So it does seem worth looking at.

Many have indeed looked (and hundreds have filed patents) but very few devices have moved off the drawing board or out of the test tank and into the sea. In the 1960s the Japanese developed a bobbing buoy in which oscillating water compresses air to drive a small turbo-generator whose 100-W output gives enough power for a navigation light. Several hundred of these are in use, but they remain the only wave-power devices to be produced in any quantity. Everything else has been virtually 'one-off'—and an extraordinary assembly they are: bobbing and nodding, bending and wagging, tanks with a sort of cat-flap, even great squashy sacks full of air. Moreover, it seems that every few years there is a new collection of these oddities (in itself a suggestion that all might not be well with wave-power technology).

Why is this? After all, in our studies of water power so far, whether the source was a fast-running stream or the slow movement of the tide, there was just one energy conversion system: water forcing a turbine to rotate. Significantly, amongst all the wave-power proposals, there is no suggestion that energy might be collected by simply putting a turbine in the sea and letting the waves run through it. All this should make us wonder whether there isn't perhaps more to a wave than is revealed by a casual glance from the beach, so we'll look a little more closely.

Breakers are rather complicated, so we'll move out to sea and consider the long rolling waves of the deep ocean. These are typically a few metres high, with wavelengths of 100 or more metres, and travel at 10–15 metres per second (about 30 mph). The first question is, 'What travels?' and the answer is, 'Not the water.' There is definitely not a 30 mph flow of water, which is why the turbine in the sea would be no good. What does travel is the wave—the shape, the pattern of peaks and troughs. And most important of all, energy travels. A moving wave delivers energy from one place to another.

If it doesn't travel with the wave, then, what does the water do? The answer is that it goes round and round in circles. That it goes up and down is obvious; but if you ask yourself where the water comes from to make a peak, or goes to out of a trough, it becomes equally obvious that there must be a to-and-fro movement, along the direction in which the wave travels, as well. This motion of the water becomes less and less as you go deeper, falling to half the surface movement in little more than a tenth of the wavelength (16 metres for our 160-metre wave). Figure 9.8 shows how the circular motion of an individual particle near the surface fits into the

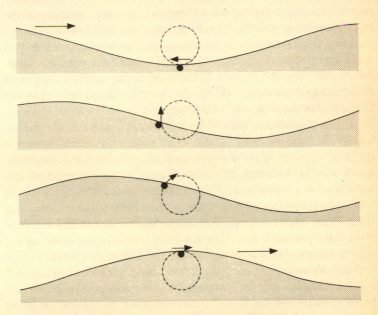

Fig. 9.8 Circular motion of a water particle as a wave passes

The wave height and therefore the circular motion is much exaggerated compared with the length of the wave.

pattern of the travelling wave, and we see that the water on the crest is moving forwards, in the trough backwards and on the front slope vertically upwards—facts well known to swimmers, surfers, and sailors of small boats in large seas.

The above facts are also important for the designers of wave-power devices, so we'll now look at some of their ideas. It might be useful to start with a couple of general principles:

- If energy is to be extracted at all, there must be relative movement: not only something that is moved by the waves but something else that isn't, or is moved less, or moved differently.
- Somewhere in the system there must be a 'one-way' component: something to ensure that, as the water moves up and down or round and round, the energy doesn't go in and out but in and in. (This component is often called the 'rectifier'.)

Almost anything that satisfies these two requirements could extract some energy from the waves, but if the plant is to be worth building the amount must be reasonable. Size is one critical factor, not merely because the bigger the collector the greater the output, but in the way the system is matched to the waves. Anything designed to oscillate should ideally have a natural time of swing that matches the time interval between successive waves, and long devices or structures should be suitably matched to the wavelength. Then there is the question whether the system needs to respond equally well to waves from all directions. But perhaps the most important feature for success is reliability—or perhaps 'survivability' is a better term. We are talking about structures which will spend their lives facing some of the world's nastier seas; and the maintenance engineer, far from being on the premises, might not be able to reach the plant at all for weeks on end during the winter storms. We'll look at a couple of plants that already exist and just a few of the many others that have yet to be built, and it is interesting to consider whether some designs have reached their present stage not because they are elegant or extract the most energy but because they stand a chance of surviving the 'fifty-year wave'.

The TAPCHAN

The Norwegian plant called the TAPCHAN (Fig. 9.9) satisfies the first of the above two requirements in a simple way: it is on the land and doesn't move at all, so there is just the movement of the water relative to the fixed structure. The 'rectifier' is provided by the walls, as water is carried in over them and can't escape out again. The clever part, which gives the system its name, is the tapered channel. Waves arriving at its wide mouth are forced onwards into the ever-narrowing space, with the consequence that the water level rises until it is high enough to spill over the wall. (In places with rocky coasts penetrated by underground channels, such as some of the Hawaiian islands, this same effect occurs naturally and can lead to spectacular water spouts through holes in the channel roofs.)

The final part of the TAPCHAN system uses normal hydro-technology, with the water flowing back to the sea through a propeller-type turbine which drives a generator. The maximum

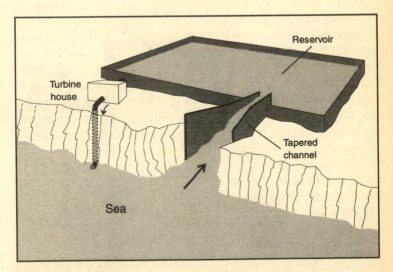

Fig. 9.9 The TAPCHAN

output of 350 kW seems rather modest for such a big structure, and this type of installation has the disadvantage that it obviously can't be used in places where there is a large tidal range. However, it does have two advantages. First, it works—and has done so for ten years—and secondly, the use of a reservoir means that it incorporates its own storage element to smooth out at least the short-term variations in wave power. At the time of writing, the Norwegians are about to start building a 1-MW TAPCHAN in Java.

Oscillating Water Columns

Another type of plant currently favoured is the shore-based oscillating water column (OWC) with an air-driven Wells turbine (Fig. 9.10). Here again the structure is fixed while the water moves, but the method of extracting the energy is rather different. The changing water-level constantly pushes and then sucks back the air

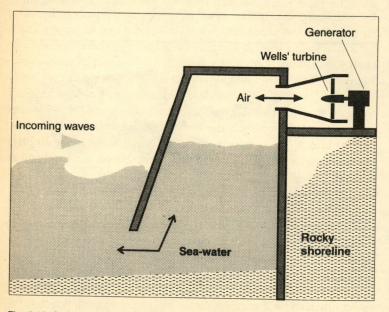

Fig. 9.10 A shore-based oscillating water column

above it, producing an alternating air flow through the turbine, and it is the turbine which is the ingenious part here. A Wells turbine is rather like the sort of propeller used in wind turbines (see Chapter 10), but its blades have no twist and are not tilted. They look the same from both sides, with the important consequence that they continue to rotate in the same direction regardless of the direction of the air flow. So for this system the Wells turbine is the rectifier.

A number of small plants operating on this principle and generating 100 kW or so have been in use for a few years: Japan has several; a 150-kW plant on the island of Islay in Scotland has been operating since 1985; India has one plant and plans a 15-unit, 1.6-MW system; Portugal is building one. (Another was built in Norway in 1985, near the TAPCHAN, but at the end of 1988 it was ripped away from the cliff and destroyed by severe storms.)

Clams and Ducks

It is surely significant that, apart from the small Japanese 'bobbing buoys', the most successful wave power devices so far are land-based. Nevertheless, it remains the fact that there is far more energy in the waves out at sea, so we'll finish this brief survey with a look at a couple of systems whose designers hope to capture it. The Clam, shown in Fig. 9.11(*a*) is successor to a whole series of 'squashy bag' devices. The full-scale structure would be 60 metres or so across, perhaps half the length of a typical deep-sea wave, and the idea is that as the waves pass across it, some of the air bags are being squashed at any moment, while others are expanding. Air is therefore pushed to and fro through the large tubes connecting the bags, and in these tubes are Wells turbines with their generators. Only experimental models have been tested so far, but it is claimed that under the right wave conditions, a full-size Clam could capture as much as 90 per cent of the power of the waves.

Our next example is the Duck (Fig. 9.11(*b*)). This device, first proposed some twenty years ago, is a much more 'engineered' system than those described above. The outer section, which is the moving part, is carefully designed to extract the maximum energy

(a) The Clam

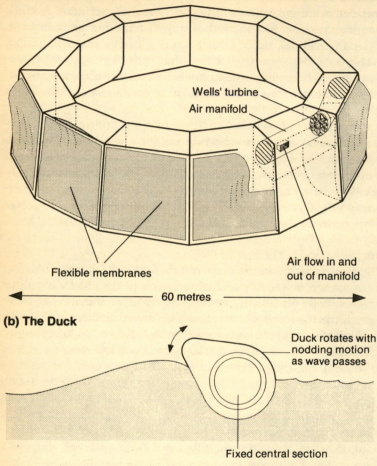

Wells' turbine

Air manifold

Flexible membranes

Air flow in and
out of manifold

← 60 metres →

(b) The Duck

Duck rotates with
nodding motion
as wave passes

Fixed central section

Fig. 9.11 Floating wave-power devices

from the waves. Some method is obviously needed to keep the
fixed part from turning with it, so that power can be extracted
from the relative motion. An early idea was to have a string of
ducks on one spine, longer than the width of the average wave

crest so that it would stay put as the ducks in different positions nodded at different times. Other schemes have included mounting a gyroscope in the fixed part, and attaching an arm to it which would be held in place by mooring lines anchored in the sea-bed.

Unhappily, neither of the above two sea creatures at present seems destined for a prosperous future. In the decade following the energy crisis of the early 1970s, wave power was a favoured renewable resource in the UK. Then the energy crisis passed, and a government review in 1982 concluded that wave-power systems were not likely to be viable in the near future, so support was withdrawn. There is, however, some present interest within the European Union, and things certainly look brighter for at least one sea-bird: the OSPREY. The Ocean Swell Powered Renewable Energy device, with a planned output of 2 MW, is an OWC/Wells air turbine system designed to stand on the sea floor in some 15 metres of water. The first OSPREY, funded in part by the EU, was 'launched' on the north coast of Scotland in 1995. Disaster followed when, before its steel ballast tanks could be filled with sand, five-metre waves which shouldn't have been there at all in August struck the 100-foot-high structure and the whole thing collapsed. Fortunately it was insured against 'peril of the sea', and at the time of writing there are hopes that a new one will rise from the ruins of the old. (A watery Phoenix perhaps?)

OTEC

Ocean Thermal Energy Conversion: a thermal power-station in mid-ocean? It sounds an odd idea, but is based on simple observation. In the tropics, ocean surface water can be quite warm, perhaps 25°C (80°F), but at depths of several hundred metres, the temperature may be no more than 5°C. A steady, almost unchanging temperature difference. Just what is needed for a thermal power-station. Of course, you can't produce high-pressure steam at 25°C, but there are liquids that 'boil' at lower temperatures: ammonia, for instance, or the heat transfer fluid used in ordinary refrigerators. Figure 9.12 shows the idea. The fluid, boiled by a

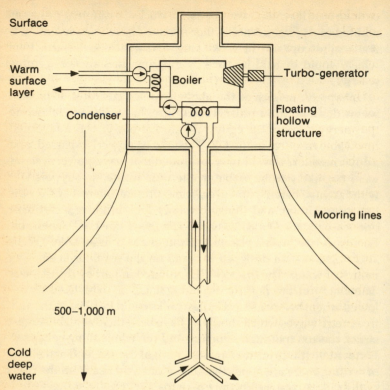

Fig. 9.12 An OTEC power-station

constant flow of warm surface water, would run a turbine, just as in a steam plant, with a constant flow of cold water pumped up from the depths to provide the necessary cooling.

The energy conversion efficiency would not be very high. Suppose the fluid was warmed to 20°C and cooled to 8°C. The heat engine rule (Chapter 5) tells us the maximum possible efficiency:

$$\text{eff}_{\text{max}} = 1 - (273 + 8)/(273 + 20) = 1 - 281/293 = 0.04$$

This is 4 per cent, which means that at most one twenty-fifth of the input energy becomes useful output. A 1-MW plant, for instance, would need to extract heat energy from the warm water at a rate of at least 25 MW. The flow of cold water would then have to be sufficient to carry away 96 per cent of this without itself warming up by more than a degree or so. Knowing that about 4 MJ of energy added or removed will change the temperature of a tonne of water by one degree, we can see that we are talking about flows of several tonnes of water a second, even for this rather modest power-station. A really large plant, generating a few hundred megawatts, would need water flows comparable to those of some of the world's largest hydro-plants.

There is, of course, plenty of water in the oceans, so in itself this need not be a problem. But very large volumes mean very large structures, and even with an inexhaustible supply of free energy, there is a limit to the capital cost if the system is to be economically viable. A few mini-OTEC plants were tried experimentally in the 1970s, but as with wave power, there are many technical problems still to be solved—not least the question of getting the power ashore. So OTEC is certainly not going to provide a short-term solution to the need to replace fossil fuels.

Nevertheless it remains an attractive idea. Unlike almost any other known system, its input is absolutely guaranteed. It doesn't depend on short-term variations in solar energy because the top hundred metres or so of water act as a massive heat store. There will be seasonal variations, but in suitable locations these can be small, so the OTEC plant can run day and night, year in, year out, following demand fluctuations if necessary, as long as the ocean exists and there is a sun in the sky.

10

Wind Power

The Winds that Blow

The energy of the winds is stored solar energy. A few per cent of the sun's radiation reaching the Earth is absorbed in the atmosphere, and the resulting uneven heating of the air leads to large-scale circulation patterns. During most of the year the tropics receive appreciably more energy per square metre than the polar regions, so the redistribution of this over the Earth's surface before it is radiated back into space means a massive energy flow, carried partly by the great ocean currents but mainly as the kinetic energy of moving air: the winds. This energy is gradually dissipated by friction with the ground, but in low latitudes the total annual flow is a few hundred thousand exajoules a year, several hundred times the present world total energy consumption.

Not all this energy is available, of course. For a start, we aren't (yet?) building mile-high windmills, so we can count as useful only the fraction of a per cent within a few hundred feet of the ground. If we further discount the flows in the world's more inaccessible regions, we reach a figure which is perhaps twice the present world total electricity consumption. More significantly, recent studies have concluded that it would be possible to replace about 10 per cent of the world's generating capacity by wind plants within 30 years. If true, this would probably make wind power the winner in any race to reduce carbon dioxide emissions in a hurry.

Wind and water, together with humans and animals, were the

major sources of power for the whole of recorded history until a couple of hundred years ago. In the eighteenth century, Britain alone is thought to have had some 10000 windmills (and 20000 water-mills). Wind machines didn't disappear with the Industrial Revolution, either. The multi-bladed wind pumps used for raising water, a familiar feature in Western movies, have by no means vanished today, even in the USA, and world-wide there are thought to be millions of them. Nor is the use of wind machines for power generation a new idea, but their output has increased enormously since about 1980. Not the output of individual machines, which hasn't changed much in recent years, but a hundred-fold increase in the number of them, in little over a decade. There do exist large machines with outputs above 1 MW, and there is also a specialized market for 'micro' battery-charging systems generating 100 W or less; but on the whole the wind power industry has settled for 100–500 kW as the preferred size. Wind-farms consisting of dozens or even hundreds of machines in this range have become a frequent sight in many countries and there are estimated to be over 20000 machines operating world-wide. Their total contribution is still only a few thousandths of the world's electrical output, but it certainly looks set to grow. So once again we need to ask how, when, and where this energy is available, how it can be extracted, and what it will cost in financial and environmental terms.

Delivering the Power

Calculating the power of the wind is not difficult. It carries kinetic energy, and we know how to find this for any specified mass and speed (Chapter 6, 'A Short Drive in the Country'). Table 10.1 shows that the energy carried by each cubic metre of air in a 20 mph wind (technically a 'fresh breeze') is little over 50 joules. We can then find the rate at which this energy is delivered to a wind machine. For simplicity, we consider one whose blades have an area of just 1 square metre, as in Fig. 10.1. (It would have a diameter of a little over 1 metre—about 4 ft.) The volume of air reaching this in one second is the volume in a cylinder 9 metres

TABLE 10.1. *Power from a fresh breeze*

Data	Wind speed = 20 mph = 9 metres per second Mass of 1 cubic metre of air = 1.3 kg Area of wind machine = 1 square metre
Calculations	Kinetic energy of 1 cubic metre of air = $\frac{1}{2} \times 1.3 \times 9 \times 9$ = 53 joules Volume of air reaching the machine in 1 second = 9×1 = 9 cubic metres Energy reaching the machine in 1 second = 9×53 = 474 joules 474 joules per second is 474 watts of input power.

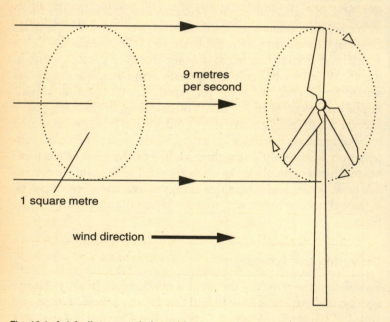

Fig. 10.1 A 4-ft-diameter wind machine

long, i.e. 9 cubic metres, so we reach the final result that the delivered power is somewhat under 500 W. Notice that if you double the diameter, the area—and therefore the power—becomes 4 times greater; in other words, the power is proportional to the square of the diameter of the machine. Even more important:

doubling the speed increases the power by a factor of 8, because the kinetic energy per cubic metre depends on the square of the speed and the number of cubic metres again depends on the speed; so the 9 m/s enters the calculations three times. Putting all these factors together, we can write a formula for the approximate power in kilowatts delivered by the wind:

• Power (kW) = $(^1/_{2000})$ × (diameter)^2 × (wind speed)^3

The next question is how much of the power can be extracted. It obviously can't be the lot, because if you remove all the kinetic energy you stop the wind altogether; and where does the air go then? There is in fact a theoretical maximum, the largest fraction of the delivered energy that any machine open to the winds can extract. It is equal to $^{16}/_{27}$ths, or just under 60 per cent, and is known as the 'Betz limit' after its discoverer. Figure 10.2 shows the power delivered per square metre and the maximum that could be extracted, for different wind speeds. So much for the theory. Now we need to ask what can be achieved in practice.

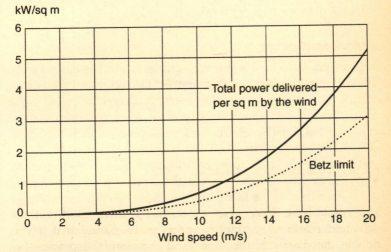

Fig. 10.2 Wind speed and wind power

The Betz limit is the maximum power that could be extracted by an ideal wind machine.

Wind Turbines

Windmills have always come in many shapes and sizes. Figure 10.3 doesn't include the most picturesque historic ones, but the four it shows demonstrate the variety of styles that are still in use in different parts of the world. Notice the contrasts: two rather 'solid' and two much slimmer; two on horizontal axes and two on vertical ones. The general principle of operation is of course the same for all four. Forces produced by moving air cause the machine to rotate, transmitting the power to a millstone, drive-belt, water-pump or—in the majority of the modern machines—an electric generator. So the question becomes, how do these forces work?

We try the simplest approach first. Air has mass, so the wind hitting a blade is just as though people stood throwing stones at it. Naturally it is pushed away. Unfortunately it is very difficult to explain on this theory why flimsy structures like (b) and (d) in Fig. 10.3 extract more power than (a) and (c). Surely most of the air must miss those thin airfoils? The stone-throwing theory of wind machines is clearly not going to explain everything. Nevertheless we'll try it, to see how far it takes us.

The Savonius Rotor

The Savonius machine is not very efficient, and has tended to be used in simple do-it-yourself systems. (One version is based on an oil-drum sawn in half down the centre.) But a careful look at it will reveal a few points which are important when we come to more sophisticated devices. Figure 10.4 shows the rotor in a 20-mph wind. The wind pushing on the concave side of vane A will certainly push it backwards, but this isn't the complete picture. Vane B is moving into the wind, so there will be an opposing push on it. Then there is the fact that if the outer tip of A is moving at, say, 15 mph, the wind speed it sees, the **relative speed**, is only 5 mph. Meanwhile someone sitting on the corresponding tip of B is moving into a 35-mph head wind. If the machine is to produce useful power at all, the drag force of the 5-mph wind past A must

Horizontal axis machines

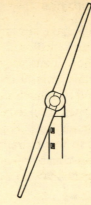

(a) Multi-bladed wind pump

(b) Two-bladed airfoil

Vertical axis machines

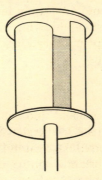

(c) Savonius rotor

(d) Darrieus 'egg beater'

Fig. 10.3 Four types of wind turbine

be greater than the drag force of the 35-mph wind on B. That's why curved vanes are essential in this machine.

Drag force is a topic we have already discussed in the entirely different context of a moving vehicle (Chapter 4, 'A Short Drive in

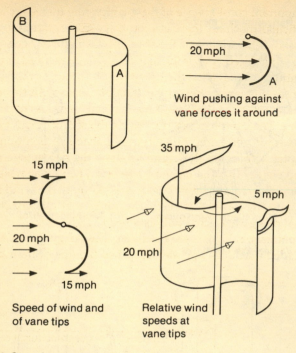

Wind pushing against
vane forces it around

15 mph

20 mph

15 mph

Speed of wind and
of vane tips

35 mph

5 mph

20 mph

Relative wind
speeds at
vane tips

Fig. 10.4 Savonius rotor

the Country'). There we saw that the energy used during the journey in overcoming drag on the car increased in proportion to the square of the speed of the vehicle relative to the air. This is equally true of the energy extracted by a vane being moved by the drag force of its relative wind. A coefficient of drag (C_D) can be defined for the vane just as for a car: the higher the C_D, the greater the drag force. If the Savonius rotor is to work, the C_D for the side pushed by the wind must be much greater than for the other side, to compensate for the fact that the relative wind speed is less. In the example shown in Fig. 10.4, the squares of the two relative speeds are in the ratio 49:1, so the C_D for the wind-catching side of a vane would need to be about fifty times the C_D for the other side, if the motion is to continue.

An important consequence of these competing forces is that, for any particular machine, there is a 'best' speed of rotation for each wind speed. What matters is the speed of the blade (v_B) compared with the wind speed (v_W). If the blade speed is measured at its tip, the quantity v_B/v_W is called the **tip-speed** ratio, and a graph showing how the efficiency of energy extraction varies with this quantity is characteristic of the type of machine, more or less regardless of the size. The curves in Fig. 10.5 show the characteristics of the Savonius rotor and some other types of machine mentioned in this chapter. (Note that these graphs show the percentage of the delivered energy that the machine extracts. The rate at which the energy is delivered, the input power, will rise with the wind speed according to the formula in the earlier section of this chapter, so the actual energy extracted will also rise.)

The contrasts in Fig. 10.5 are striking. The heavy Savonius and multi-bladed machines operate best when the tips of their blades

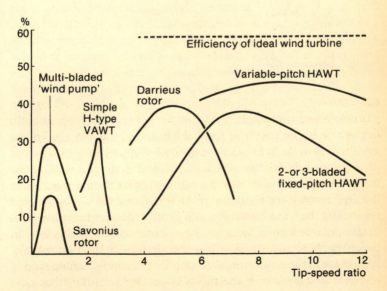

Fig. 10.5 Rotor efficiencies of some wind turbines

move at about the speed of the wind, but others have tip speeds up to ten times the speed of the wind that drives them. These are the airfoils, which we'll look at now.

Airfoils

Wind machines like (b) or (d) in Fig. 10.3, now normally called **wind turbines**, are quite clearly not much like a rotating oil-drum, and the first step in understanding how they work is to realize that they are in fact flying machines. Those thin blades are shaped like the wings—or perhaps the propellers—of aircraft, and for very similar reasons. So we'll start by looking at the effect of a flow of air past such an airfoil shape, and then see how the ideas can be applied to a wind machine.

The important thing we learn from diagram (a) in Fig. 10.6 is that the air above the airfoil moves faster than the air below it. The crowding-up of the streamlines tells us this. (Think of water flowing in a narrowing pipe.) And the important consequence of this speed difference is that the air pressure is less above the airfoil than below. A lower pressure above than below means a net upward force, which is of course what keeps an aircraft airborne. The airfoil of a wind turbine need not of course be horizontal; in some types it will be vertical and in others its position will constantly change as the machine rotates, but this force at right angles to the relative wind (Fig. 10.6(b)) is still generally referred to as the **lift**.

Along the direction of the relative wind there will be, as with any moving object, a drag force as well, and a major aim in the design of airfoils is to make the ratio of lift to drag as high as possible, so that the overall force is almost in the direction of the lift. We've already seen how drag increases with wind speed, and the lift increases in a similar way. So it makes sense to talk of a **lift coefficient**, and the lift–drag ratio is then the ratio of these two coefficients. This ratio, which can be as high as 100:1, depends on the shape of the airfoil and also on the angle of attack (Fig. 10.6(c)). As we'll see shortly, the angle of attack of a turbine blade depends on how fast it is moving, and this is important, because if the angle becomes too large there is an abrupt loss of lift. A wind turbine, like an aircraft, can stall.

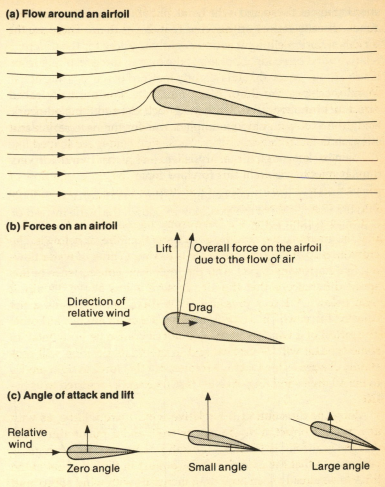

(a) Flow around an airfoil

(b) Forces on an airfoil

Lift

Overall force on the airfoil
due to the flow of air

Direction of
relative wind

Drag

(c) Angle of attack and lift

Relative
wind

Zero angle

Small angle

Large angle

Fig. 10.6 Airfoils
The lengths of the arrows show the strengths of the forces.

Horizontal-Axis Wind Turbines

Now we need to see how the lift makes the blades go round. We'll take as our example a three-bladed horizontal-axis wind turbine (HAWT). Let us suppose that it is facing straight into the wind and rotating at high speed. If the blade speed is several times the wind speed, the relative wind will be as shown in Fig. 10.7, coming almost directly at the leading edge. Now let us re-draw Fig. 10.6(*b*) for this situation, tilting it round slightly to allow for the different relative wind direction. Looking at the overall force resulting from lift and drag, we see that it is slightly forward of the axis line of the turbine. Despite the drag, it is pulling the blade round in the direction of motion. (It is also trying hard to bend the blade back along the axis, with obvious implications for the necessary blade strength.)

Going back through this analysis we can see that two conditions must be met to maintain this forward force:

- The lift–drag ratio must be high, or the overall force will point to the wrong side of the axis, slowing down the blade instead of pulling it round.
- To keep the angle of attack small so that the blade doesn't

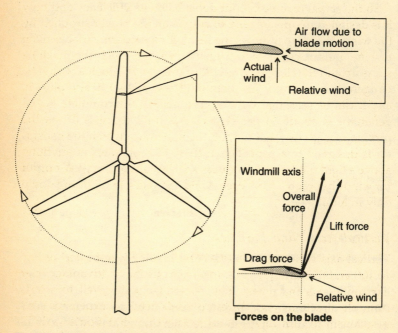

Forces on the blade

Fig. 10.7 Action of a horizontal-axis wind turbine

stall, the blade speed needs to be large compared to the wind speed.

For any airfoil shape there is a 'best' angle of attack which gives the greatest lift-to-drag ratio. The extraction of energy from the wind will be most efficient at the ratio of blade speed to wind speed which produces this angle, and this is of course reflected in the curves we have seen in Fig. 10.5. For a simple straight airfoil, there isn't just one angle of attack, however. The speed at which the blade cuts the air will increase as you move out along its length, so the angle of attack will decrease. Introducing a twist in the blade can compensate for this—making the turbine more like a propeller than a set of wings. Another option which allows a constant rate of rotation over a range of wind speeds is to turn the complete blades, and the effect of this 'variable pitch' in smoothing the efficiency curve can again be seen in Fig. 10.5.

So the actual turbine output depends on its efficiency and how it is designed to operate, and of course on the power supplied by the wind. Figure 10.8 shows the result for a modern variable-pitch turbine, indicating the cut-in wind speed at which the machine starts up and the close-down wind speed above which it would be dangerous to operate. The Betz limit (see above) is also shown, and it can be seen that the output power of the complete turbo-generator is about 80 per cent of this until it levels off as the turbine reaches its rated output, the maximum which the generator is designed to accept. This turbine thus operates in anything above a light breeze and produces a fairly constant 225-kW output for winds between a fresh breeze and a strong gale, shutting down only in a full gale.

Vertical-Axis Wind Turbines

Vertical-axis wind turbines (VAWTs) like the 'egg-beater' of Fig. 10.3(d) and the turbine in Fig. 10.9 have one major advantage over horizontal-axis machines: they respond equally well to winds from all directions and therefore don't need an expensive yaw mechanism to turn them round to face the wind. Some VAWTs also take advantage of the fact that the generator can be placed at

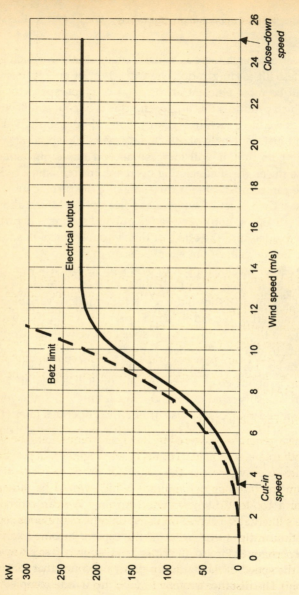

Fig. 10.8 Power and wind speed for a wind turbine

Normal operation in a light wind

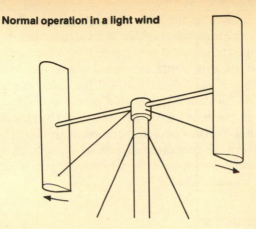

Fig. 10.9 A vertical-axis wind turbine

ground level and driven by a shaft straight down from the turbine above. As Fig. 10.5 shows, they operate at rather lower blade speeds than the HAWTs for a given wind speed, but the principle is the same, with the narrow blades pulled round by lift forces. Whilst some elegant designs have been developed, and a few hundred VAWTs are in use world-wide, at present their manufacturing cost makes them uncompetitive with the two- or three-bladed HAWTs.

Running the Generator

Running a generator powered by a wind turbine should be simple: they both rotate, so you just connect them together. In practice it is not quite so easy, because the generator needs to rotate at up to 1000 rpm (revolutions per minute), which would be rather startling for a 100-foot diameter wind turbine. We can estimate the turbine's likely rate of rotation using data from previous sections. The optimum tip–speed ratio for the type of turbine likely to be used is perhaps 8 (Fig. 10.5). With a wind speed of, say, 9 m/s, this makes the speed of the blade tip 72 m/s. (Notice that this is over 160 mph!) The distance travelled by the tip in one complete revolution is roughly three times the diameter: about 90 metres for a

30-metre turbine. So the time taken per revolution is about 1.3 seconds, which means just under 50 revolutions per minute. Gearing is going to be required to increase this to the 1000 rpm or so of the generator. Gears would be needed in any case, as the speed of the turbine will vary slightly whilst the speed of the generator must remain constant if it is to feed power to the grid. This complex linkage, combined with the fact that the turbine must turn to face the wind, explains why the simplest method is to house all the machinery in a self-contained nacelle, which can turn on the top of the supporting tower, and then bring the power down to the ground in an electric cable.

Wind Distributions

We now need to consider how much energy a wind generator will actually produce in the course of a year. It is not good enough just to estimate the average wind speed, look up the output on a graph such as Fig. 10.8 and multiply by the hours in a year. The wind never blows at a steady speed for 24 hours a day throughout the year; it is always variable, and as the graph shows, the power depends very critically on the speed. Assessing the pattern of winds at a prospective site is therefore very important. Is there a windy season, and if so, when? Does a regular afternoon wind blow from the sea? Are the strongest winds the 'wild North-Easters', or is there useful energy in balmy southern breezes too? How fierce are the strongest gusts? For how many hours is it too calm even to start up a wind machine? What we need is a wind distribution graph (Fig. 10.10). This divides up the wind speeds into bands: less than 1 m/s, 1 to 2 m/s, 2 to 3, etc. It then shows the number of hours when the wind speed lies in each band, in an average year. This information is becoming available for an increasing number of sites, but it takes time to accumulate, and wind power developers sometimes have to make informed 'guesstimates' based on sample readings and data from similar sites.

Suppose we have the wind information and propose to build a turbine with the characteristics shown in Fig. 10.8 at a site with the

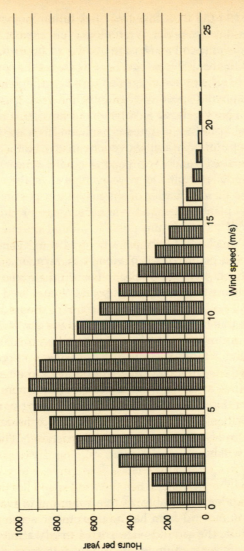

Fig. 10.10 Wind speed distribution

The bars show the number of hours in a year when the wind speed lies in each band. The average speed at this site is 7 m/s.

pattern in Fig. 10.10. Predicting the total annual output in kilowatt-hours is now possible. We multiply the power at the speed in the middle of each band by the number of hours for that band and add all the results together. For this case, the answer is about 680 000 kWh. (The recipe suggested above, multiplying the output at the mean wind speed by the hours in a year, gives less than 500 000 kWh.) Now if the 225-kW generator ran constantly for a full year, it would produce just under 2 million kWh, so we see that the actual output is only a little over one-third of this. This is a 'good' figure, because we chose a good site, with a mean wind speed of 7 m/s, about 16 mph. On more average sites, the output might be no more than a quarter of the maximum possible. An average fossil-fuel plant, if demand is sufficient, can produce up to three-quarters of its maximum possible annual output—two or three times as much electricity per kW or MW of generating capacity as the wind plant. This is obviously an economic factor to set against the fact that the 'fuel' for the wind turbine costs nothing. It also means that to replace a 500-MW coal-fired plant you need to install not 500 MW but over 1000 MW of wind farm capacity. Not that this necessarily puts wind power out of court.

The best wind farms are already competitive with coal-fired power-stations, and although electricity from the average UK site still costs nearly twice as much as from a gas turbine plant, costs should continue to fall as wind turbines become more standardized and therefore cheaper. Before contemplating a wind-dominated electricity system, however, we need to consider two further important questions: the environmental effects and the variability of the winds.

Environmental Effects

Wind shares with other renewable sources a number of environmental advantages. A wind-farm has no unpleasant waste products, does not pollute the ground-water, or adversely affect plant life. Sheep may safely graze under its turbines. It produces no carbon dioxide, and its only atmospheric effect is to reduce the strength of the wind.

Why then are there active opponents of wind power? There

seem to be two main causes of concern: noise and visual intrusion. Both are particularly important because the best wind sites are likely to be in rural areas. Few people want their peace and quiet disturbed by a steady *grr-swishsh* at half-second intervals—or a whole orchestra of such sounds. Noise reduction is therefore a problem which has concerned the turbine manufacturers, who obviously want to sell their products. Two or three 50-foot blades cutting through the air at 100 mph are probably never going to be silent, and in many older turbines, the noise from the rotating machinery inside the nacelle has been as much a problem as air-generated sound from the blades. Denmark, with a far greater density of wind machines than any other country, has a regulation that the noise level at the house nearest to any turbine must be less than 45 dB(A)—about the level of a conversation. For a turbine of the most common type, this is equivalent to placing it no closer than about 150 metres from the building; and then not everyone wants even a quiet conversation constantly outside their windows. On the other side of the argument, surveys of people living near wind-farms built recently in Britain show that fewer than one in twenty are unhappy with them.

The main cause of unhappiness, and of objections to proposed wind-farms, is frequently not noise at all, but the visual effect on the landscape. A wind-farm producing only one-hundredth of the output of a large modern coal-fired or nuclear power-station might consist of some fifty turbines, standing 200 ft high from base to blade tip and occupying a total area of two or three square miles. Unfortunately, there is little point in tucking them away in the bottoms of valleys or behind screens of large trees. They are by their nature going to be in prominent positions, and when these positions are in areas of unspoilt natural beauty, we should not be surprised that there are objections. The situation is perhaps a little less clear when the proposed site is on agricultural land, and some supporters of wind-farms have been moved to point out that the turbines can be considerably more attractive than many modern farm buildings—or the pylons of present electricity distribution systems.

One suggested solution to both the above problems is the development of off-shore wind-farms. There are many coastal sites throughout Europe with average wind speeds as high as 8 m/s. Denmark, very much in the lead in wind energy in general, already has one off-shore array, with the towers standing in relatively shallow water. The scope for development around the British Isles is considerable, with Scotland and the west of Ireland offering some of the best sites in Europe. The potential annual output for the UK alone has been estimated to be greater than its present total electricity consumption. Which brings us to a final problem.

Prospects

A hundred or so 1000-MW clusters of wind turbines, sited in shallow waters or on flat coastal land, might be the most environmentally acceptable way of satisfying Britain's demand for electric power into the next century. But would it? It certainly couldn't do so alone because of the variability of the winds. So if acceptability depends on cost, and the total cost depends on the amount of variation the rest of the system must allow for, the fluctuations in wind strength are going to be very important. It isn't surprising, then, that some effort has been devoted to studies of these variations and their effects on the scale of individual turbines, wind-farm arrays, or whole generating systems.

The results are not unexpected, but the detail is none the less important. The first observation is that wind speeds vary in a number of different ways. On a very short time-scale there are gusts, sudden changes within seconds or minutes. Then there are lulls and freshenings over a period of an hour or a few hours; the sort we experience as successive rain storms pass on a blustery day. Next are the very important daily changes such as the drop in wind strength at sunset. There is the weather, windy or calm over periods of days or even weeks; and finally we have the overall annual variation with the seasons. Looked at with a wind-power system in mind, these mere differences in timing suddenly become very important. Gusting, for instance, serious for a single small generator, can be virtually smoothed out by adding the outputs from an array of dozens of turbines spread over a square kilometre or so. Changes over a few hours, or local weather variations, will be at least partially smoothed if you feed power into a national grid from installations a hundred kilometres or so apart. But sunset is sunset within about twenty minutes for a country the size of England, and long periods of calm or windy weather, or the annual variations, are likely to affect most sites in rather similar ways.

Thus it seems that a system based mainly on wind power would need back-up in two respects: reserve capacity capable of producing power at a couple of hours' notice and then, for longer periods of calm, a virtual duplication of the entire system. We would indeed have to be desperate about the consequences of our present methods to adopt such a costly alternative. The generally accepted view is that 20 per cent of the national total is about the maximum that wind could contribute without risking serious supply shortages at times. Not quite the solution to everything suggested above, but nevertheless a great deal more than we have at present. All the current wind-power projects in the UK—including those still to be built—amount to no more than a half a per cent of the total generating capacity, so there is room for a forty-fold increase before we need to start worrying about 'too much reliance on wind power'. Even in Denmark, with the world's highest proportion of wind energy, only 2 per cent of electricity comes from this source.

If we know one thing in the world of energy, it is that predictions about the state of affairs ten years from now will be proved wrong—overall and in detail. Twenty-five years ago wind-power experts were predicting larger and larger turbines: 5 MW, 10 MW, or even more. But the response from wind power to the energy crises of the 1970s was met by modest machines generating a few hundred kilowatts. The main driving force came from California, where tax incentives designed to reduce dependence on fossil fuels encouraged a rapid expansion in the early 1980s. Manufacturers jumped in, not with new experimental turbines but with reasonably well-tested machines in the middle range. Danish companies in particular, who could already offer reliable 200–400-kW turbines, took advantage of the situation, with the result that about half the 10 000 or so constructed in California in less than a decade came from Denmark. The Californian growth has now slowed, following changes in the political and economic climate; and although governments throughout Europe and elsewhere are supporting wind power to some extent, the scale is still very small, as we've seen. Nevertheless, it remains the case that of all the alternative energy sources—tidal power, wave energy, solar power, etc.—the one with the fewest technical, economic, and environmental obstacles to overcome before it can make an appreciable contribution to national supplies is that somewhat surprising example of high technology, the windmill.

11

Solar Energy

A Very Large Source Indeed

The attractions of solar energy are easy to see. Sunshine delivers energy as heat and light to the Earth at a rate of some 15 000 times our entire primary energy consumption, or to put it another way, enough for every man, woman, and child to sit surrounded by a third of a million 100-watt light bulbs. Yet this is only a tiny part—less than a billionth—of the total power that the sun radiates continuously in all directions into space, and on our human timescale this massive total drain on its reserves has hardly any effect. The unimaginable 4×10^{26} watts radiated away means that the mass of the sun is decreasing by over 4 million tonnes a second (see Chapter 8, 'Energy and mass') but it will still take several million years to lose one-millionth of its present mass. For once we need not worry about diminishing resources: it seems that we have at last an energy supply that is enormous, continuous, and free.

But with solar energy as with other free offers, you need to read the small print carefully to see exactly what you'll get. On your individual patch of the Earth it may well turn out to be not all that enormous, it certainly won't be continuous, and it's free only if you don't propose to do anything but sit in it. The first of these claims may seem surprising in view of the figures quoted above, so let's look more closely.

One problem is that the solar energy arriving at the Earth is not very concentrated. To receive solar energy equivalent to the output of a 500-MW power station, at mid-day and in the sunniest parts of the world, you would need to spread out an array of collectors over an area of a couple of square miles; and if you wanted the output as electric power you'd need ten times this space. Even at its brightest and best, sunshine doesn't actually make things very hot. True, eggs can be fried on the streets of New York, and there's an old New England recipe for strawberry jam that tells you to put the fruit and sugar in a flat pan with a sheet of glass on top and leave it in the sun for a few days. (The glass is important, and we'll return to it.) But if you want to use the heat to generate electricity the usual Second Law limit applies and as we've seen (Chapter 5, 'Heat Engines') you need temperatures of several hundreds of degrees Celsius to achieve reasonable conversion efficiencies.

Perhaps the point of solar energy is that we don't need huge power-stations? Let's try a smaller scale. As we saw in Chapter 6, the average British household uses more than 20000 kWh a year of energy in all forms. The solar energy received by a square metre of average British horizontal surface is about 900 kWh a year. So even if you could convert as much as a third of this into useful energy, you'd need nearly 100 square metres, 1000 sq ft, of collector to provide your annual total. Definitely not as compact as a gas boiler. (An average Californian household, with twice the solar input but twice the consumption as well, would be no better off!)

A further well-known feature of solar power is that the sun doesn't always shine. It is missing at night, and in most parts of the world is more visible at some times of the year than others. Consider again the poor Britons, shivering on a grey winter's day. Only one-sixth of their annual solar energy arrives during the half-year from October to March, and on a typical December day each square metre of collector would receive perhaps half a kilowatt-hour of heat, none of it of course in the chilly early morning or during the long dark evening. That is the problem for solar space heating: when you need the heat you often haven't got the sun. This remark is rather misleading, however. Provided your house is not over-shaded by other buildings or large trees, the 900 kWh a year mentioned above falls on every square metre of space it occupies. Even during the winter six months, the total reaching all the surfaces of a typical house in Britain could be some 6000 kWh, enough to have made a considerable difference to the heating bills. (See also the discussion in Chapter 6, 'Solar Gain'.)

In the remainder of this chapter we look at active solar systems. The first is the solar hot water system, undoubtedly the most widespread current use of solar energy, and already mandatory for new houses in some of the sunnier parts of the world. As we'll see, the initial cost makes the economics doubtful in regions such as northern Europe. Our second main topic, the generation of electric power using sunlight, is not so much a system as many different ones. A few large solar thermal power-stations have been in operation for some years, but the main current interest is in photovoltaics, so we'll look at both these technologies to see what they might offer for the future. We start as usual by looking at the energy itself. What exactly is this gift from the sky?

Electromagnetic Radiation

Almost all the solar energy reaching us over the intervening 92 million miles of empty space comes in the form of electromagnetic radiation. (There is a tiny contribution from high-speed particles, mainly the almost undetectable neutrinos; undetectable because they shoot straight through nearly everything, including the Earth. So we shall not consider them further.) Electromagnetic radiation carries energy in the form of waves—electromagnetic waves. In an earlier chapter we met the idea that electric and magnetic effects are produced by electric charges and electric currents. In another chapter we saw that water waves carry energy. Now you can 'generate' water waves by paddling something up and down or to and fro in the water (your toe for instance). So it might not be a surprise to learn that electromagnetic waves are generated by wobbling electric charges. This happens in a TV transmitter, for instance, producing the electromagnetic waves that carry the information to make pictures and sound. It also happens in the sun.

The solar energy sequence is roughly as follows. Nuclear fusion (see yet another earlier chapter) releases huge quantities of energy in the sun's interior, maintaining its temperature of millions of degrees. The energy travels outwards and is eventually radiated as electromagnetic waves by the rapidly oscillating electrically charged particles of the hot surface region. The next stage involves a very important feature of these waves: they will travel through nothingness. Unlike the water waves, they don't need a substance to travel in. If they couldn't travel through empty space we wouldn't see the sun, moon, stars, etc., because light is of course one form of electromagnetic radiation. The final stage of the sequence, when the radiation reaches the Earth, is that the electrically charged particles which make up atoms and molecules are pushed around by the electric effect, picking up energy from the waves. And so you sit, warming yourself in the sunshine.

Everyday experience helps us to add further details. Think what happens as you gradually heat something—a piece of metal, for instance. Before there is any visible radiation to see, you can feel that it starts to radiate heat. This invisible radiation consists of infra-red electromagnetic waves, 'infra-red' meaning 'below the red': the oscillations producing the waves, and correspondingly the wave oscillations themselves, vibrate more slowly than the slowest of visible oscillations, which are those of red light. As you continue to heat the metal, its particles vibrate with more energy and it begins to glow, first red, then yellow, and eventually white-hot. It is now sending out all the colours of the rainbow, all the visible radiations from red to violet—and a lot of infra-red still too, as you can tell by holding your hand near it. Finally, at extreme temperatures approaching the 6000°C of the sun's surface, a few per cent of the energy is ultra-violet radiation, waves oscillating even faster than violet light. Figure 11.1(a) shows the spectrum of radiation from something as hot as the sun, and the very different one from an object of the same size at the temperature of a bright light bulb.

If this is what happens as something gets hotter, what does it do as it gets colder? The answer is that it continues to radiate, but less and less and with waves further and further into the infra-red.

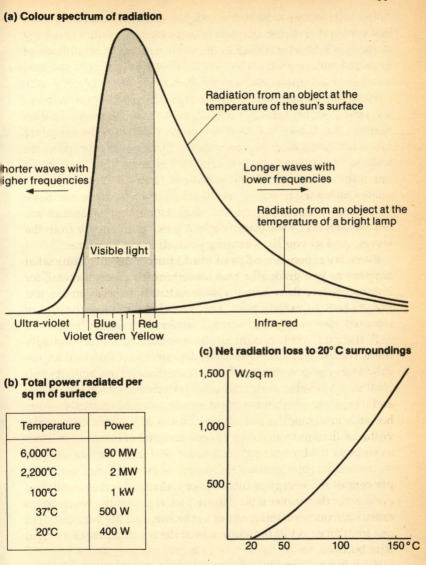

(a) Colour spectrum of radiation

Radiation from an object at the temperature of the sun's surface

horter waves with igher frequencies ←

Longer waves with lower frequencies →

Radiation from an object at the temperature of a bright lamp

Visible light

Ultra-violet | Blue | Red
Violet Green Yellow

Infra-red

(b) Total power radiated per sq m of surface

Temperature	Power
6,000°C	90 MW
2,200°C	2 MW
100°C	1 kW
37°C	500 W
20°C	400 W

(c) Net radiation loss to 20° C surroundings

1,500 W/sq m

1,000

500

20   50   100   150 °C

Fig. 11.1 Radiation from hot objects

All the data are for 'ideal' surfaces. Real objects will radiate slightly less power at the given temperatures.

The radiation curves for objects in the range 20–100° C would be far in the infra-red and only a thousandth as high as those in (a).

Unless your surroundings are very hot, you don't notice this radiation from everything, because you too are radiating. If you are in a room where everything is at 20°C, you are receiving a few hundred watts continuously; but if you are at 37°C you are radiating back about 100 watts more than you receive. (As it is your surface that radiates, this is strictly true only if you are wearing no clothes.) Your net radiation loss, then, is about 100 W. As we'll see shortly, this radiation loss is very important for solar collectors. On a different scale, it is also important for the Earth, which must radiate into space as much energy as it absorbs from the sun, if it is not to over-heat (see 'Global Warming', in Chapter 13).

So much for the energy radiated by objects. How about the receiving process? Any of four different things can happen to electromagnetic radiation when it encounters matter. It can bounce straight back, reflected as in a mirror. It can be scattered, with its energy going off in all directions. It can be transmitted, passing on with little loss, as light does through a window. Or it can be absorbed, in which case the absorbing substance gains energy and is warmed. All these things happen to sunlight in its interactions with the Earth and its atmosphere.

A spacecraft just outside the atmosphere would receive solar energy at a rate of 1350 W on 1 square metre of collector facing the sun. The very best that can be done at sea-level, on an extremely clear day with the sun vertically overhead, is about 1000 W per square metre. So about a third of the original energy is gone, including most of the ultra-violet. (What is left is known as Air Mass 1 radiation.) For present purposes we don't need to consider most of the processes accounting for this loss, but one is quite important for solar systems—and very important for all of us. The atmosphere scatters light, which is just as well, because if it didn't, we'd see nothing but a blazing sun with an almost black sky in other directions (as on the moon, which has no atmosphere). The sky has its beautiful blue colour because the tiny particles scatter the blue and violet light—the faster vibrations—more than the yellow and red. And we see spectacular sunsets because the light coming to us from the low sun passes through a greater length of atmosphere and loses even more of the blue and violet. Clouds, on the other hand, are white because their relatively large water droplets scatter all colours equally.

One important result of all this is that as the sun moves lower in the sky and the path of its rays through the atmosphere increases, the energy reaching us is reduced (Fig. 11.2). At 30° above the horizon its light travels through twice as much atmosphere as when it is vertically overhead (i.e. Air Mass 2), and the maximum energy reaching a collector facing it falls to 800 W at best. This is why the intensity rises and falls in the course of a day, and usually falls at higher latitudes. It rises, of course, at higher altitudes, by about 4 per cent for every 300 metres in European latitudes. Finally, the scattering means that we receive appreciable radiation from directions other than the sun, or on cloudy days. This diffuse contribution can amount to as much as a third of the total reaching a collector in a European city, even on a 'clear' day.

Hot Water

In this study of solar water heating we'll deal mainly with its potential in Britain, or to be more precise, in southern England. The reason for the choice is that this region is, as we shall see, just on the margin: a few hundred miles further north and the contribution is probably too small to be of general interest; a few hundred miles further south and it is certainly useful. At the start of

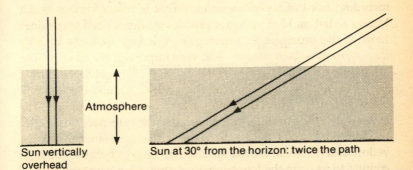

Sun vertically overhead

Sun at 30° from the horizon: twice the path

Atmosphere

Fig. 11.2 The angle of the sun

this chapter we saw some rather discouraging figures, but those were concerned with total household energy consumption. Here we'll confine ourselves to the energy needed to produce hot water. After allowing for tank and pipe losses, this is about 5000 kWh a year for the average household (Table 6.4), so we'll use 14 kWh a day as a target.

Now let's look again at the solar energy. Suppose that you have flat collectors with a total area of 5 square metres (about 50 sq ft) on your south-facing roof in southern England. The total solar energy which might reach the collectors on an average day in each month of the year is shown in Fig. 11.3, and we see that it is by no means negligible compared with the 14 kWh required for hot water. For about half the year it is more than enough. Winter looks poor, but the annual total of just over 5000 kWh is certainly not to be despised.

So much for the incoming energy; but if we've learnt one thing it is that there's many a slip 'twixt primary energy and consumer. How many of those kWh will reach the hot water tank? The answer depends on the collector and the hot water system. A few yards of black hose-pipe coiled on the roof may have provided the hot water for rural Californians eighty years ago, but on a fresh spring day in England the heat losses could equal the solar gain before the water was even lukewarm. The old method has one thing right. Black surfaces are indeed good absorbers of radiation. Where the method fails is in doing nothing about heat losses, and they are almost equally important.

A Flat-Plate Collector

How does the design of a modern flat-plate solar collector reduce heat losses? Looking at a fairly simple version (Fig. 11.4), we see that it has four main parts:

- an outward-facing absorbing surface—the face of the collector plate,
- pipes to carry the heated fluid,
- insulation on the sides and back,
- a sheet of glass on the front.

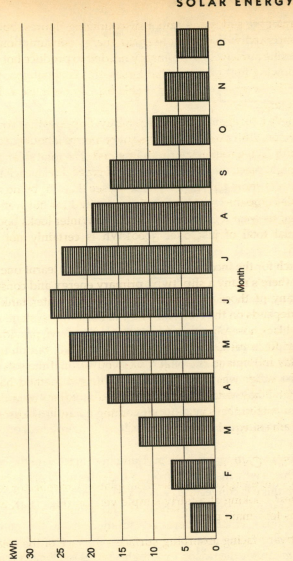

Fig. 11.3 Average daily energy reaching a solar collector
The bars show, for each month, the average energy per day reaching a 5 sqm collector on a south-facing roof in southern England.

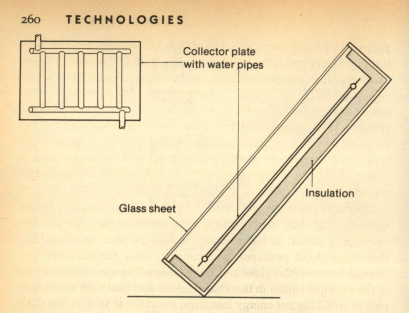

Collector plate
with water pipes

Insulation

Glass sheet

Fig. 11.4 A flat-plate collector

The principle is pretty obvious. Solar energy is absorbed by and warms the collector plate, which in turn warms the circulating fluid. Good thermal contact between plate and fluid is clearly important, and although the fluid can be a liquid or a gas, liquids are generally thought to be more efficient. We'll return to the fluid, but first let's study the ways the collector might lose heat once it is warm.

There is conduction through anything in contact with the collector, and this is why insulation around the sides and back is important. Then there is convection, when air in contact with any warm surface rises and carries away heat. (Wind strength has a marked effect on this.) Finally, there is radiation from the collector surface.

Now we can see the reason for the sheet of glass. First, it reduces convection losses because its outer surface will be cooler than the surface of the collector plate itself. Any sheet of material would do this, of course, but glass has the well-known and very useful property of being transparent to visible radiation: it lets the sun-light in. Moreover, it has another equally useful if less well-known property. It is opaque to infra-red radiation (except for a small region of waves just longer than visible light). Remembering the discussion of radiation from heated objects, we know that the collector plate, being warm but nowhere near red-hot, will radiate its energy almost entirely as infra-red waves. So the glass sheet will allow through most of the incoming solar energy but trap nearly all the out-going radiation. (This is the famous 'greenhouse effect'.)

Of course the outer surface of the glass itself will radiate to the surroundings, but much less than the collector plate would, be-cause it is cooler. If we mentally cancel the sun for a moment (behind a cloud perhaps), and consider only the radiation ex-change between the glass and the surrounding environment—as in the example earlier in this chapter—we find that with surround-ings at 10°C, the net energy loss from a surface at 35°C is less than half that from one at 60°C.

The not very surprising result of all this is that heat losses will be less the cooler the outside surfaces of the solar panel. Naturally we want the circulating fluid inside to reach a reasonably high tem-perature, so the whole art—or science—of designing these collec-tors is to get the inside as hot as possible while keeping the outside as cool as possible. Apart from ensuring that the system won't leak water through the roof, rust to pieces in eighteen months, or blow away in the first gale, this is what you pay for. Now let's see what you get.

Inputs

Solar collectors may look rather simple, but a detailed treatment of how they behave is surprisingly complex. We'll therefore consider what happens to the energy reaching our collector surface in the course of one particular day: one hour-by-hour pattern of sun-shine. To see the best that might be achieved, we'll make it a sunny mid-summer day. We start with the input: the watts reaching each square metre of collector at successive times during the day. Then, by carefully allowing for all the losses at each time, we eventually

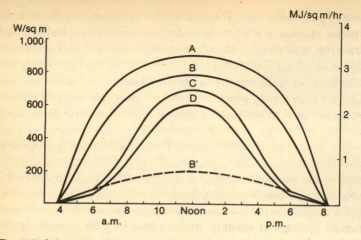

Fig. 11.5 Solar intensity during a summer day
See text for explanation.

reach the useful output: the rate at which energy is being transferred into the hot water system. From this we calculate the total kWh of useful heat during the whole day.

Apart from the weather, which we've decided is cloudless, the energy collected will depend on a number of factors:

- the height of the sun above the horizon, which as we've seen determines the strength of the radiation when it reaches the collector surface,
- the state of the atmosphere: clear, hazy, etc.;
- the angle at which the incoming solar radiation reaches the collector surface;
- the fraction of energy transmitted by the glass;
- the fraction of energy absorbed by the absorber.

Figure 11.5 shows the sad decline of the watts—the gradual reduction as we take into account each of the above factors. It is quite important to distinguish between these in discussing the use of solar energy, so we'll take them in turn.

The outermost curve (A), with the highest intensity at all times of day, shows the maximum possible energy that could be received in this location. The weather is very clear and the collector rotates so that it always faces the sun. (This is called a 'fully-tracking' collector.) Curve B is more realistic; it still assumes a fully-tracking collector but takes into account the fact that there is always a layer of dirtier air over Europe, scattering the sunlight. On the other hand, there will be some contribution from this scattered light reaching any collector. This is included in B, but the dashed line B' also shows it separately.

Tracking collectors are complex and expensive, so it is unlikely that they would be used in a simple domestic system. Curve C shows the kilowatts reaching a fixed collector, mounted on a south-facing roof. We assume that it is tilted at $51\frac{1}{2}$ degrees, which is the latitude at the location. This means that it will face the noon sun in spring and autumn, at the equinoxes. So at noon on our mid-summer day the rays from the sun come a little slantwise on to it, delivering just over 700 W/sq m rather than the full 780 W/sq m of B. When the sun is further to the east or west the slant is of course greater, and at 6 a.m. and 6 p.m. the direct illumination is cut off altogether for this tilt. (A horizontal collector would receive more energy during a long summer day, but very much less in winter, with the sun low in the sky.) The final reduction is for energy reflected away or absorbed by the glass, a loss of perhaps 15 per cent if it is a good collector. The remainder is curve D, and we see that the input rises to a maximum of about 600 W/sq m at midday. The total for the whole day, however, is no more than 5 kWh/sq m.

The sad object in Fig. 11.6 is the mid-winter version of curve D, giving a total daily delivery of little more than 1 kWh/sq m. And

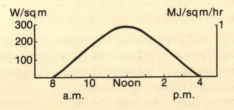

Fig. 11.6 Energy collection rate during a mid-winter day

we haven't yet taken into account the heat losses from the panel itself.

Heat Losses

In looking at the ways a solar panel can lose heat, we saw that the loss rate depends on the temperature of the outside of the panel and the temperature of its surroundings—not surprisingly. Figure 11.7 shows how the total loss from a reasonably good collector might depend on the difference between these two temperatures. (Without the sheet of glass, the loss rates would be roughly twice as much.) To use the graph, we need to make decisions about the temperatures. Let's assume that we want hot water at 60°C. We could circulate the water directly through the collector, but this has two drawbacks. It means a continual supply of new water depositing 'fur' and other odds and ends in the pipes, and it means that the system must be drained in freezing weather—unless you don't mind anti-freeze in your shower water. There is some additional heat loss with a closed-circuit indirect system (Fig. 11.8), but nevertheless it is the most common for the above reasons. (The circulating fluid is likely also to be water, but to avoid confusion with the water in the tank, we'll continue to refer to it as the fluid.)

To maintain the required 60°C in the tank, the circulating fluid must leave the collector at, say, 65°C. If it returns at 55°C—allowing for further losses—its average temperature while in the collector will be 60°C. Suppose now that the outside temperature is 18°C. The average temperature difference is 42°C, and Fig. 11.7 tells us that each square metre of panel will be losing heat at a rate of about 250 W—a quarter of a kWh every hour.

Daily Cycles

Now let's see what happens in the course of a day. To avoid further complexity, we'll assume a constant surrounding temperature of 18°C throughout the day; not very realistic, but we are only after the total energy, so any errors should cancel to some extent.

The remaining factor is that it takes energy to heat the collector

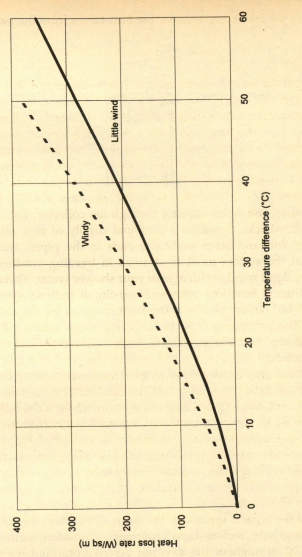

Fig. 11.7 Heat losses from a collector

The curves show how the total losses depend on the temperature difference between the collector and its surroundings.

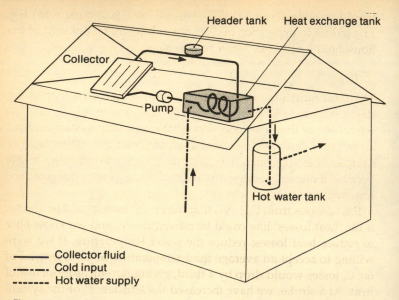

Header tank   Heat exchange tank

Collector

Pump

Hot water tank

——— Collector fluid
—·—·— Cold input
------- Hot water supply

Fig. 11.8 An indirectly heated hot-water system

itself, assuming that it has cooled down overnight. How much depends on how massive it is, and we take a figure of about 3 watt-hours (10000 joules) per degree temperature rise, for each square metre of collector. Assuming that the solar energy entering the panel follows curve D of Fig. 11.5, we find that it takes until a little after 8 a.m. to warm up the system with no circulation (Fig. 11.9).

Once the system is hot, we start circulating the fluid at a rate that maintains the chosen temperature. The losses now stay constant at 250 W/sq m and any excess is useful heat. At mid-day this reaches a peak of about 370 W/sq m, then falling until at about 4.30 p.m. the input is only just replacing the losses. After that, except for a little heat to be gained as the system cools, it makes sense to stop the circulation to prevent heat being carried from the hot water tank to the collector.

The total heat gain in the course of our summer day is a little over 2 kWh per sq m of collector, so our original 5 sq m system would provide about 12 kWh of useful heat. Not quite what Fig. 11.3 led us to expect for mid-summer, but still 60 per cent of the household's daily hot water requirement.

'Efficiency'

The total radiation reaching the 5 sq m on this particular sunny day, calculated using curve C of Fig. 11.5, was nearly 30 kWh, so we could say that the 'collection efficiency' of our system is about 40 per cent. But if we've learnt anything from this rather lengthy exercise it is that such a figure has no general meaning at all, because it depends entirely on the conditions. Two brief comparisons will emphasize the point.

It is obvious from Fig. 11.9 that the useful heat would be greater if the 'heat losses' line could be moved down, and we know how to reduce heat losses: reduce the water temperature. If we were willing to accept an average fluid temperature of 50°C instead of 60°C, losses would drop by a third, giving two-fifths more useful heat. At a stroke, we have increased the 'efficiency' of the system to 56 per cent!

On the other hand, if we carry out the detailed analysis above for the midwinter input of Fig. 11.6, assuming an average outdoor temperature of 6°C, and a fluid temperature of 60°C, there is no useful heat output at all. Still the same collector, but the 'efficiency' is now zero.

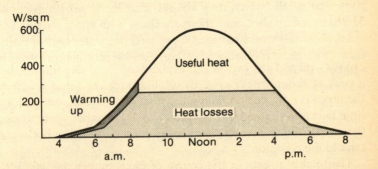

Fig. 11.9 One day's useful heat

Is it Worth it?

So our 50 square feet of solar panel just fails to provide enough hot water for the average household in mid-summer, and then gets worse. But perhaps we are asking it to do the wrong thing. From the point of view of losses, as we've seen, cooler is better. So rather than trying to squeeze out a few litres of very hot water at very low efficiency, a more efficient way might be to use this system to pre-heat the water to 35°C or so; not eliminating other fuel but perhaps halving the amount needed and therefore the cost.

Is it worth it, then? Some people evidently think so, because there are an estimated 40 000 solar collectors in Britain now. Year-round, a collector like the one studied above might achieve a 40 per cent reduction in the fuel and/or electricity needed for hot water, an annual saving of about £80–100 for a typical household—or as much as £200 if you use full-price electricity for all your hot water. The cost of the system would be at least £4000, which means that, even ignoring any interest paid or lost on the investment, the system would need 40–50 years to cover its cost—or about 20 years as replacement for electrical heating. The fact that over 1000 solar hot water systems are sold each year in the UK suggests that there must be many people in the latter situation—or perhaps people selflessly spending their money to reduce CO_2 emissions, or who haven't done their sums, or are spending someone else's money. But if fuel costs rise (as they surely will) and system costs fall (which they should with increased production) the balance may shift, and there are those who argue that half of Britain's houses could have solar-assisted hot water within thirty years or so, reducing national carbon dioxide production by some 6 million tonnes a year.

Elsewhere in the world the situation is already approaching this stage. In the 1980s solar water heaters became mandatory for new houses in parts of California, as they are in other sunny places such as Cyprus. A sixth of all houses in Greece are estimated to use solar systems and the proportion is growing in other countries around the Mediterranean and in the Middle East. With collectors available for less than a quarter of their UK price and sales climbing towards 50 million systems a year, this appears to be one form of renewable energy destined for growth.

Solar Power

Let us design a solar thermal power-station. The principle will be the same as a fossil fuel or nuclear plant: the input energy is used to produce hot steam which drives a turbo-generator. Figure 11.10 shows the general idea. As we know, the maximum possible conversion efficiency is given by the heat engine rule (Chapter 5), which means that it depends critically on the temperature reached in the 'boiler'—in this case the collector. Now this leads to a perfect Catch 22 situation. As we've seen above, the heat losses from a solar collector increase steeply as its temperature rises. So hotter means better and hotter means worse.

Consider an example. Suppose that the solar input is a reasonably healthy 800 W/sq m. Looking back at Fig. 11.1(c), we find that the net radiation loss to surroundings at 20°C is just this much if the temperature of the (unshielded) collector surface is about 110°C. So once the collector reaches this temperature there is no

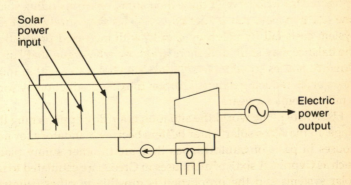

Fig. 11.10 A solar power-station?

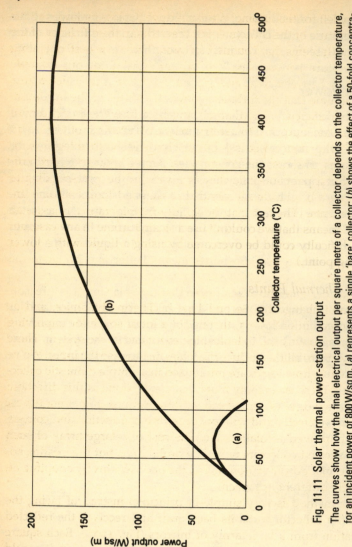

Fig. 11.11 Solar thermal power-station output

The curves show how the final electrical output per square metre of a collector depends on the collector temperature, for an incident power of 800 W/sq.m. (a) represents a single 'bare' collector; (b) shows the effect of a 50-fold concentration of incident power and a well-insulated collector.

energy left for the turbine! We can reduce the loss by lowering the temperature of the collector—but this reduces the efficiency of the turbine. It seems that you just can't win. There is a 'best' operating temperature between the two extremes: 65°C for our example (halfway between 20°C and 110°C). To obtain a realistic picture, let's assume that the turbine achieves two-fifths of the maximum possible efficiency, and that the generator converts 80 per cent of the turbine output into electric power. Curve (*a*) of Fig. 11.11 shows the final electrical output for different collector temperatures. The best is 30 W/sq m, an overall solar-to-electric efficiency of 4 per cent—and this for a solar input corresponding to noon on a bright day! It seems that we must look for some improvements. (The fact that the optimum temperature is less than 100°C means that we couldn't use a steam turbine in any case; but that difficulty could be overcome by using a liquid with a lower boiling point.)

Solar Thermal Plants

We can't change the Second Law of Thermodynamics, and as we've seen in Chapter 5, there's not a lot of scope for improving turbines. So we need to look at the input end of the system. There are two possibilities: reduce the losses or increase the input. We've seen above how losses are minimized in a simple domestic collector, and there is certainly more that can be done in this direction: special window materials and surface coatings, removing the air between collector and window to reduce conduction and convection, improved insulation, etc. The cost of a large array of such sophisticated collectors would be prohibitive, but the existing solar thermal power-stations avoid the need for this by adopting an entirely different approach.

The method is very simple in principle: instead of facing the sun, the collector turns its back on it and receives the reflected radiation from a large array of mirrors (Fig. 11.12). Each square metre of collector now receives many times the power it would receive directly. It is important to understand that this is not at all the same as spreading out a larger number of collectors. The total power is *concentrated* at the collector, with the result that this can

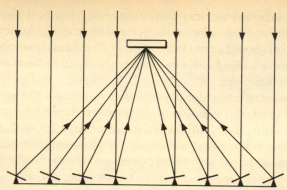

Fig. 11.12 Concentrating the power with a mirror array

reach a very much higher temperature before the losses balance the input. Fig. 11.11(*b*) shows the output under the same basic conditions as (*a*) but with 50 times the power reaching the collector, and insulation to reduce its heat losses by half. The result is a solar-to-electric efficiency of nearly 40 per cent at a collector temperature of some 400°C.

There are now half a dozen or so solar thermal power-stations around the world. The first, Solar One at Barstow in California's Mojave Desert, has several hundred mirrors reflecting the solar radiation on to the boiler on top of the 'power tower'. There a heat transfer fluid is heated to 500°C and carries the heat to the steam generators of the power plant. Solar One's peak output of 10 MW was overtaken in the late 1980s by another plant in the Mojave Desert, operating rather differently. This one concentrates the energy by having its mirrors in the form of long hollow troughs with the heat transfer fluid running in pipes along their centres. Each trough is parabolic in shape, which means that when it is tilted sideways to face towards the sun, the reflected radiation from every part of its mirror surface focuses on to the central pipe. In the largest plant, transfer fluid running through half a million square metres of these collectors carries enough heat to provide steam for a power output of 80 MW. As we've seen above, the overall solar-to-electricity conversion efficiency will depend on the solar intensity (the watts per square metre). Achieving an average of about 14 per cent, this plant even proved economically viable for a while; but the fall in energy prices in the early 1990s changed this.

However, all the solar plants of this type must be regarded as experimental, and it would be surprising if their costs were competitive at this stage. Although the fuel is free, it seems likely to be some time before large-scale solar power-stations are producing really cheap power, even in the sunniest conditions.

Saline Solar Ponds

One way around the problem that simple flat collectors are not very efficient and therefore need large areas is to use large areas. The idea of using sheets of water has been considered for a long time, but the difficulty is that hot water rises to the top, so the heat losses will be high (mainly by evaporation in this case). However, if the water is very salty this stirring-up doesn't happen. A dense, very salty layer forms at the bottom, and stays there even as it gets hot. With most of the absorption of solar radiation occurring near the bottom, an appreciable temperature difference can therefore be maintained.

Experiments with saline ponds have been carried out for some years, particularly in Israel, and temperatures up to 100°C have been reached. The very hot water can be drawn off and used to vaporize a low boiling-point fluid to drive a turbine. The turbine efficiency will be very low, for the reasons mentioned in the previous section, but if the area is large enough this need not rule out the system. The main problem is that the most easily available large areas not used for other purposes and with good sunshine tend to be deserts, and deserts tend to be short of water. Nevertheless several plants have been constructed, including one generating 50 MW. The idea of combining a solar pond with a desalination plant has received some attention in several Middle Eastern countries, and at present this seems the most likely direction of development for this particular form of solar power.

Photovoltaics

From the power towers and turbines of the solar thermal installation to a tiny flake of silicon a few millimetres across, generating a voltage when light falls on it. From the bludgeon to the rapier. If our technological instincts are right this simple direct conversion from solar radiation to electric power must surely be more efficient. Sadly, they are wrong. The rapier is no more efficient than the bludgeon. The millimetre solar cell generates only microwatts, and for megawatts we need hundreds of square metres, just as before. Yet of all the new energy systems the solar cell in many ways shows the greatest potential for really widespread use. Countries with plentiful sunshine, who have not yet developed full national power systems, can avoid all the paraphernalia of large power-stations, transmission networks, and the rest by installing clusters of solar cells to supply power as and where it is needed, for a town, a village, a factory, or even a single household. No one has yet adopted this alternative as policy for a full national system, but it is estimated that in Kenya, for instance, half of all electricity already comes from photovoltaics, and in other sunny countries there are many thousands of small plants supplying power for water pumps, local hospitals and schools, home and street lighting—and of course battery-powered TV sets.

Naturally there is a catch, or rather, there are several. The first is cost. At present you would pay about £3 per peak watt for a set of solar cells (usually called a module). If you bought a nuclear power station instead, it would only cost you about £2.50 per watt. As we'll see, there are many questions about the second of these figures, but this is almost as true of the first. What is a 'peak watt'? It is a very carefully defined quantity: the power output from a cell when the intensity of the radiation reaching it is 1000 W/sq m with an Air Mass 1.5 colour spectrum (see 'Electromagnetic Radiation', above). Now this is an interesting definition, because the specified conditions can never exist! In practical terms, it means that an array of cells with an output specified as 100 W(p) would actually produce no more than 80 W even when pointing straight at the sun on a bright day. Then there is of course the fact that the sun doesn't always shine. Consider Britain, where the average total solar energy reaching a horizontal surface in a year is about 900 kWh/sq m. As there are 8760 hours in a year, we'll treat this as a constant 100 W/sq m—a tenth of the 1000 W/sq m needed to give the peak output. The average output of the 100 W(p) array would therefore be no more than 10 W, so you are paying not £3 but £30 per useful watt.

In practice the average output will be even less than 10 W, partly because we haven't allowed for any losses, and also because the solar-to-electric conversion efficiency falls off at low light levels, so we can't simply scale down the output to match the different input. Before looking further at the processes in a solar cell, it may be worth asking about this conversion efficiency. The above 100 W(p) array probably has a total cell area of a little over three-quarters of a square metre—say 0.8 sq m, so it receives an annual input (in Britain) of 720 kWh. Its annual output, on the basis of a constant 10 W, would be about 88 kWh, which means an average solar-to-electric conversion efficiency of about 12 per cent. Not quite as good as the best of the solar thermal power-stations—but that was in California, so the comparison is not very fair.

Electrons and Photons

The relatively high cost of solar cells is certainly not due to scarcity of raw material. Silicon is the second most common element in the Earth's crust, and reserves tend to be listed as 'unlimited'. The cost rises in two steps. The first is the production of extremely pure silicon—one 'wrong' atom in a million would be regarded as extremely poor. Then this must be melted and re-formed very slowly and carefully so that its atoms are in an almost perfect crystalline array. This need for large high-quality single crystals is the real difficulty, and much effort is going into attempts to produce efficient photovoltaic cells with less demanding structures.

To explain exactly why crystalline perfection is so important would require a more detailed picture than can be developed in a brief paragraph or two, but a simple outline of the processes in a solar cell will perhaps show why the conversion efficiency can never be really high. The name is a good starting-point: 'photo-voltaic', because when light falls on the cell a voltage is generated. Like a battery, the cell will then send an electric current around any circuit connected to its terminals (Fig. 11.13). In Chapter 7 we saw that an electrical supply does two things: it maintains a voltage difference so that electrons will flow round the circuit from one terminal to the other, and it 'lifts up' the electrons, continuously replacing the energy they have given up in the circuit. In the photovoltaic cell this energy comes from the light, and the basic process is that it constantly releases electrons from their state of atomic bondage, freeing them to move off through its crystalline lattice. Solids that need just a little energy to free their electrons are the semiconductors: silicon, germanium, and various compounds such as cadmium telluride, gallium arsenide, etc.

Unfortunately there is a very fundamental reason why photo-cells can't convert all the energy of the light into useful output. It has to do with the well-defined quantity of energy needed to free

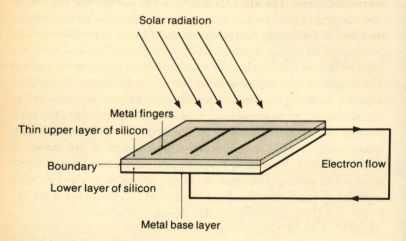

Fig. 11.13 A photovoltaic cell

Electrons are released near the boundary by solar radiation which penetrates the thin upper layer of silicon. Both silicon layers are single crystals, but they incorporate very small amounts of different 'impurity' elements and this leads to a voltage across the boundary, which maintains a flow of electrons around any external circuit.

an electron. If the amount offered by the light is too small the electron stays bound, and if it is too much the excess is wasted as heat. And at this point we meet one of the truly revolutionary ideas of twentieth-century physics. Light, it seems, is not the smooth flow of radiated energy that we have been picturing. There is a great deal of evidence (including the behaviour of these photocells) that it delivers its energy bit by bit, in very precisely defined chunks. And the size of the chunk, the **photon**, depends entirely on how fast the light wave is vibrating. As we saw above, red or infra-red waves vibrate more slowly than blue or ultra-violet waves; so each photon of red light has less energy than a photon of blue or UV.

The consequence for the photocell follows at once. There will be just one type of radiation, one 'colour', whose photons provide exactly the right energy to free an electron. The others deliver either too little or too much. But solar radiation includes the whole spectrum from far infra-red to ultra-violet, so there is bound to be appreciable loss. The ideal for silicon is just outside the red end of the spectrum, in the near infra-red. About a fifth of the energy arriving at the Earth's surface is beyond this and therefore useless, and over half the remainder is in the other direction and becomes wasted excess. So even in principle, a silicon cell can never convert much over a quarter into useful energy. And this is in the best possible case, which means an almost perfect single crystal. Any impurities or imperfections cause the loss of mobile electrons and further reduce the efficiency. In cells developed for special purposes such as the space programme, efficiencies of just under 25 per cent have been achieved under ideal conditions, but the 12 per cent of our example above is more characteristic of the everyday world.

A Small PV System

Returning to the practicalities, what happens when a cloud moves across the sun? Suddenly there isn't enough power to run your equipment. The result is just like trying to start a car on a flat battery: the voltage falls dramatically. For some items, such as a refrigerator motor, brief changes like this are not very important, but sophisticated electronic equipment may not like it at all. Then there are longer sunless periods: how can you use the output of your PV system to watch TV after dark? The answer is, of course, storage, which in this case usually means rechargeable batteries. Car batteries are familiar objects, presenting no new technical problems, and you can even get 'inverters' to convert the 12V DC output of the batteries into 230V AC so that you can run normal appliances. Many small PV systems have operated like this for years, but the additional bits and pieces certainly add yet more to the cost (and batteries, unlike the solar cells, will need replacing every few years).

Let's make an estimate of the total cost. Suppose you want a system able to run a few lights and low-consumption appliances consuming perhaps half a kWh a day: radio, fridge, TV perhaps, but certainly not an oven or washing machine. One car battery would provide reserve for a couple of sunless days, but two would be safer, depending on your location and how important the supply is. There will be losses in charging and discharging the battery, etc., so let's assume an annual demand of 200 kWh. At 12 per cent efficiency, this means a solar input of 1700 kWh. At which point we need to know where you are. In England, you'd need about 2 square metres of cells, less in a sunnier place. Total cost, £2000–3000; maybe more if you want to include an inverter rather than running low-voltage appliances. And a couple of hundred pounds every five years to replace your batteries. Definitely not cheap electricity.

PV Prospects

New types of cell, using different materials, or silicon in other forms, or new cell structures, could reduce the cost per peak watt, but at present none of the cheaper types can match single-crystal silicon in efficiency. Despite the present high cost and low efficiency, photovoltaics is a growing industry, with world-wide production of cells now approaching 100 MW(p) of output a year, having quadrupled in the past decade. There are even some large photovoltaic power-stations feeding electricity to national grid systems.

California, with the first megawatt plant, now has several with outputs in this range. Europe has yet to build a plant this size, but there are several in the 300–500 kW range. One of the earliest, designed as a test-bed for different cell types, has been in operation since 1988 high above the confluence of the Mosel and the Rhine in Germany, whilst Italy, Switzerland, and Spain all have plants of similar size.

We shouldn't leave the subject of PV power-stations without mention of the Satellite Solar Power System (Fig. 11.14). This scheme, beloved of the space industries in the 1970s, would consist of an orbiting satellite with huge thin wings, 12 km ($7\frac{1}{2}$ miles!) across, covered with PV cells. The 5000 MW of power these would generate would be beamed back to Earth as microwave radiation. The solar intensity outside the atmosphere is, of course, excellent, and the sun would hardly ever set on the array; but the possibility

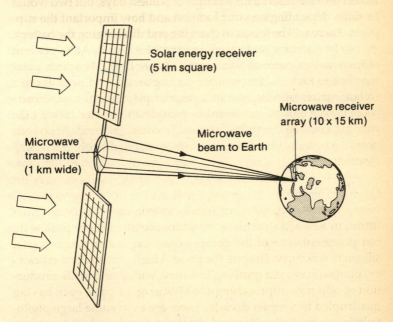

Fig. 11.14 A satellite solar power system

of the beam wandering off target and microwaving the local population has caused some unease—as has the estimated cost of fifty billion dollars.

Returning to Earth, the most interesting current development in the European context is the installation of solar cell arrays as elements of buildings or other structures. Typically these feed a few tens of kilowatts to the grid, and examples include cladding on the sides of buildings, such as that completed on a University of Northumbria building in Newcastle in 1995. Switzerland in particular has developed the idea of arrays along the sides of motorways and railways, and on routes such as the N3 near Chur they ingeniously serve a double purpose as power supplies and sound barriers. On an even smaller scale, grid-connected roof-top arrays generating just a few kilowatts, in some instances replacing the tiles on an entire side of a roof, are encouraged by subsidies in both Germany and Switzerland.

Other PV applications have left the world of science fiction but not yet entered the world of everyday fact. Solar-powered vehicles not only exist but hold races—across Australia and also over the Alps—every year or so. However, they are probably as interesting for their extremely low energy consumption as for their solar cells. A solar-powered aircraft even crossed the USA in 1991 (in twenty hops) using only power from the 700 cells that coated its long thin wings. Looking for more normal vehicles, we can find solar-assisted buses in public use (again in Switzerland), but the PV cells covering their roofs contribute only a small fraction of their total energy. It is not difficult to see why. A normal small car, travelling at say 50 mph and consuming a gallon of petrol every 50 miles, is using 160 MJ of energy an hour: an average rate of about $4\frac{1}{2}$ kW. You are invited to estimate the area of solar cells needed for this output power—and then decide where to put them!

PART III

The Future

The future starts, of course, with the present. In the earlier parts of the book we've seen what the present looks like. We know how much energy we use, where it comes from, and in what forms and for what purposes we use it. We've looked at the present technologies—the machines and systems that make up the world of energy today. We've also studied a few alternatives: sources and technologies which don't yet play a major role but might in the future. And we've taken a glance or two backwards, in case history could also carry lessons.

This, then, is what we've got. There may be new, totally unknown sources of energy or new, totally uninvented technologies; but history suggests that, for the next half-century or so at least, any serious contributions will come from the sources and the systems we already know. Whether we like it or not, these, with all their potentialities and all their problems, are the raw material of our immediate future. The subject of this final part of the book is what we might make of them.

We start with some questions about quantities. How much oil is left in the ground? How much electricity could the wind provide? These resource issues are the subject of Chapter 12. In the next two chapters we look at possible constraints on development: the undesirable penalties of using each energy source and the costs of energy. Finally, Chapter 15 introduces a few options for the future, some scenarios, and other ideas for the period until the middle of the next century.

12

Resources

―――

The Future for Oil

If consumption continues to follow past patterns, present world oil reserves will be exhausted in under 20 years.

If this statement is correct why aren't we in a state of panic? We do tend to be a little short-sighted, planning for the next election rather than the next century, but surely we should be very worried indeed at a claim that our major fuel will disappear so soon? There are causes for concern, but the situation is a little more complex than the above statement suggests. Let's look at the facts behind it in more detail.

Exponential Growth

Figure 12.1 shows the background to the present situation. It uses the same data as Fig. 1.1, at the start of the book, but in a way that is both more and less informative. Figure 1.1 is valuable in giving an instant vivid picture, showing the dramatic rise in oil consumption during the half-century to 1980, and the much more varied pattern since. Figure 12.1, by contrast, makes everything look rather peaceful, smoothing out the dramatic changes into little bumps. It is easy to see how it does this, if we observe the vertical scale. On this scale, a single step means ten times as much oil, two steps a hundred times, and so on. A mere doubling is then a small difference, and a drop in production of as much as one-tenth is hardly visible. On the other hand, the advantage of drawing the graph this way is that it shows us in detail what is happening to

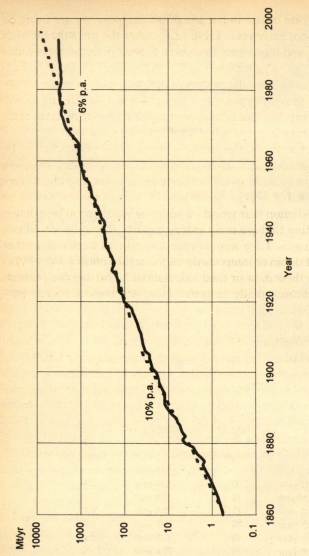

Fig. 12.1 World oil production and annual rates of rise

Each step on the vertical axis corresponds to a ten-fold increase in production. The dotted lines show steady annual growth at the rates indicated.

the annual rate of rise in our use of oil. Suppose we are using 10 per cent more each year. Table 12.1 shows the growth, for each year at first and then every five years. Plotted directly, these numbers would give a graph like Fig. 1.1. But in Fig. 12.1, because each year's output is the same *multiple* of the previous year's, a steady 10 per cent growth appears as a straight line. Growth at a steady percentage rate like this is called exponential growth, and the scale that straightens it out is called a logarithmic scale.

As Fig. 12.1 shows, the annual growth of oil production in its first few decades was indeed about 10 per cent, doubling the consumption roughly every seven years. The consequences were soon appreciated, and in the very early years of the century came the first prediction that world oil supplies would soon be exhausted. According to these early energy experts, the wells would run dry by the 1930s. They were of course wrong, as were many other prophets of doom at intervals throughout the century. Why? Was the fault in their data or their calculations? And are the present-day predictions equally in error? How are these forecasts produced?

Reserves and Resources

Witches and incantations over boiling cauldrons have fallen from favour in recent years, and today's heads of government expect their advisors to provide some scientific justification for their fore-

TABLE 12.1. *Exponential growth*

	Output (Mt)		Output (Mt)
1st year	1.00	10th year	2.36
2nd year	1.10	15th year	3.80
3rd year	1.21	20th year	6.12
4th year	1.33	25th year	9.85
5th year	1.46	30th year	15.86
6th year	1.61	35th year	25.55
7th year	1.77	40th year	41.44
8th year	1.95	45th year	66.26
9th year	2.14	50th year	117.39

casts. To do this, they need two things: some data and a theory. Suppose it is 1970 and you are trying to predict how much longer the oil will last. You have good data showing that for the past 50 years oil consumption has been rising at a fairly steady 6 per cent a year—doubling about every 12 years. You also have a reasonable theory: that this pattern will continue for at least a few more decades. But you still need one more piece of information. In order to predict when the oil will run out, you need to know how much there is: all the oil in the world—the **total resource**.

The author of the early prognosis mentioned above may have been wrong in predicting a continuing rise at 10 per cent a year instead of the 6 per cent which actually occurred, but a much more serious handicap was the fact that he knew little or nothing about the oil-fields of the Middle East, South America, Africa, Siberia, Alaska, or the North Sea—over nine-tenths of today's known reserves.

What do we now know about the amount of oil still in the ground? We are told by the oil companies, that the world's **proved reserves** are about 140 billion tonnes, which is the figure behind the claim at the start of this section. But it is important to understand that this term has a special meaning. The 'proved reserves' are the oil that the oil companies know about. More formally, they are

> those quantities of oil which are known to be in place and are considered to be economically recoverable with present technologies.

In other words, oil that has been carefully investigated by the geologists, with an assessment of the amount and the cost of getting it out of the ground and into the refinery. Figure 12.2 shows some of the possessors of this valuable commodity (and incidentally explains a lot about world politics). But the important point is that this total represents only the sources of oil that have been investigated in detail at the time the data are presented. We have, for instance, already consumed several times the 'proved reserves' of the 1960s.

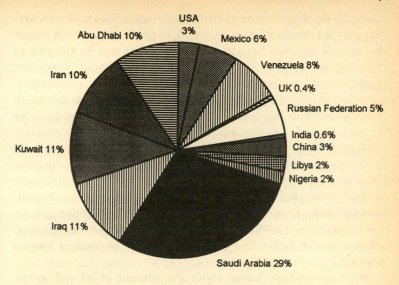

Fig. 12.2 Proved reserves of some oil-producing countries

The 'total resource' is very much more difficult to specify. The general view is that present geological knowledge is good enough to rule out further large unknown oil-fields, but that still leaves us with at least two major uncertainties. Essentially these are related to the two terms used above: 'economically recoverable' and 'present technologies'. A reservoir of oil is not a large pond to be bailed out with a bucket until it's empty. There is no pond at all, just a mesh of tiny channels in porous rock. Oil, gas, and water migrate through these until they are captured under a dome of impermeable material where they remain, held under pressure, in the pores of their rock. If the overlying material is punctured—naturally or by drilling—the oil–gas–water mixture is propelled towards the surface, often with some violence. The total amount of oil recovered then depends on the conditions underground and the way the well is operated. The quickest and cheapest method collects just the oil that propels itself out, and then moves on to the next well, leaving at worst nine-tenths of the oil underground. Re-injecting gas (or water) to maintain the pressure helps to increase the fraction recovered, to as much as three-quarters at best. Then there are even more sophisticated methods, involving, for instance, heating the oil underground to make it flow more easily; but these are very expensive. Given this situation, it becomes obvious that 'how much there is' depends critically on how much we are willing to pay to get it out.

Another complicating factor—or set of factors—is the existence of 'oil' in quite different forms. In the Canadian province of Alberta, for instance, the Athabasca tar sands, occupying an area nearly the size of Switzerland, have an oil content which could be close to the total of the world's conventional proved reserves. But extraction is not proving easy. Northern Alberta has a fierce climate, hot and mosquito-ridden in summer and so cold in winter that the tar becomes a hard glass, facing developers with the problem of huge surface-mining machines which sink into boggy peat in the summer and break their steel teeth after a day's use in winter. Another potential resource which presents even greater extraction problems is the huge volume of oil shales in—or rather under—Colorado and adjacent states in the USA, and in parts of Africa and China. Oil shale is a rock containing a solid hydrocarbon called kerogen, and has to be crushed and heated to some 400°C in order to produce liquid fuel. Moreover, to obtain one tonne of oil, up to thirty tonnes of rock must be mined and processed, leaving a burnt residue which can't even be re-buried because its volume is a third larger than the original shale!

What can we say, then, about the world's total resource? Oil company figures, based on estimates of the unproved amounts in known fields together with 'probable' fields not yet explored, suggest a remaining total of 250–350 billion tonnes, i.e. two to three times the proved reserves. This, however, still refers only to oil which could be recovered at not much greater cost than at present. Even more uncertain estimates which include the more expensive recovery methods and sources such as the tar sands and oil shales might double this to 600 billion tonnes—but at very great economic and environmental cost.

How Long will it Last?

Having made a decision about future growth and a choice of 'total amount', it is not difficult to calculate the number of years until supplies run out. Figure 12.3 shows the approach. The solid line represents the total cumulative production at the end of each year, the sum of all the oil extracted up to that date. Above this are two slightly hazy horizontal lines representing the proved reserves and the estimated total resource, both in this case for 1994.

The two dotted lines show the continuation according to two different sets of assumptions about what happens next. The upper projection shows the consequence of growth at 6 per cent a year. This is the pattern that would probably have been used (with an earlier starting point, of course) by someone making predictions in 1970. In the present graph, it reveals what will happen if we return in the coming few years to the growth rate characteristic of most of the twentieth century. The statement at the start of this whole section is indeed true: the proved reserves of 1994 will have gone in less than twenty years. Worse, the total resource of conventional oil will be exhausted only a few years later, and then we'll be looking at the delights of tar sands and oil shales.

The more modest projection of the lower dotted line shows the effect of continuing at the present mid-1990s production rate, with no further rise in consumption. The justification for this is that it's roughly what we've done for the past fifteen years. It gives us about 45 years before today's proved reserves are exhausted. But the real reason for worry is that even in this case it looks as though we'll have used up the total resource in well under a century—not a long time in which to revolutionize the largest contribution to the world's energy systems. In any case, is it reasonable to assume no further increase in consumption? The world population, between $5\frac{1}{2}$ and 6 billion in the mid-1990s, will (short of a catastrophic plague) pass 9 billion in the next fifty years. Just to keep pace with this growth, oil production would need to rise at about 1 per cent a year, effectively halving the time we have left. And then what about demand from the developing countries for a little more of their fair share?

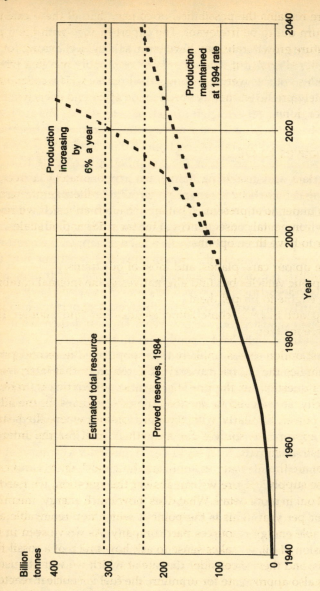

Fig. 12.3 Cumulative world oil production

There remains the possibility, of course, that all these calculations turn out to be irrelevant. The expert in 1970 with his 6 per cent future growth rate may have been, as they say, 'wrong for all the right reasons'; but where he failed very badly was just where Macbeth's witches were most successful. Those wise women very accurately predicted the unexpected, something no energy expert has ever done.

Alternatives to Oil

If the data and reasoning above are approximately correct, it seems that there'll be no more oil within the lifetime of anyone who is under 30 at present. What are the alternatives? If we reject the environmental consequences of the tar sands and oil shales, we appear to have three options:

- Give up our cars, planes, and most of our trains.
- Keep our vehicles but find alternatives to the internal combustion engine to propel them.
- Keep our internal combustion engines but find another fuel source for them.

The first option seems unlikely to be popular. The second probably implies the electric car and we'll return to that later; but it raises a question for the present discussion. Electric cars require electricity, so we need to ask about possible sources for the additional power. Similarly with the third option, where the search is for appropriate sources for a synthetic fuel for the internal combustion engines.

What are the alternatives to oil, and how much energy can each of these supply? Before we can answer this question, we need to spell it out in more detail. What does 'how much energy' mean? In total, or per year? This is the point at which non-renewable and renewable energy resources part company. As we've seen in the discussion of oil, it makes sense to ask how much of a fossil fuel there is, and then to consider the rate at which we want to use it. This is also appropriate for uranium, the fuel for nuclear reactors; but the question, 'How much solar energy is there?' is obviously different. We are not enquiring how long the sun will last. What we really need to know is the rate at which we can obtain useful energy from the sun: the *annual* contribution we can expect. So we'll look at the two types of resource separately, and then see later whether their contributions can be brought together into an overall assessment.

Other Finite Resources

Natural Gas

The process of assessing the total quantity of natural gas is similar to that for oil, and in the mid-1990s the proved reserves of the two are much the same. Our present rate of consumption is only a little over half that of oil, so the predicted life of known reserves should be nearly twice as long. However, while world consumption of oil has remained fairly constant over the period since 1980, gas consumption has risen by nearly 50 per cent, and all the indicators suggest that this is likely to continue. Gas seems to be the preferred fuel for everything today: heating buildings, generating electricity, manufacturing chemical products, and so on. So, although methane would be a useful raw material for synthetic oil, or even an alternative fuel for engines, it would be most unwise to assume that it can take on either of these roles as well. Indeed, we might be looking in the other direction, towards reducing one of its present roles by finding ways to generate electricity which don't use up this valuable heating fuel.

Coal

The one fossil fuel of which there is plenty is coal. Estimates suggest a total world resource of perhaps 10 million million tonnes, enough to sustain present production for more than 2000 years. Unfortunately it seems that we don't really like coal very much. World consumption is still just rising (at less than 1 per cent a year), but this is due mainly to high rates of increase in countries such as China and India which have relatively cheap supplies and limited choice of other fuels. Most industrialized countries have seen a fairly steady drop over recent decades, although the USA, with enormous coal reserves and concerns about oil supplies, has moved slightly against this trend. It is possible of course that we'll see a total reversal everywhere within a few decades, because coal has two further great merits. Not only is there plenty of it, but coal-mining is a developed technology, so production could be increased rapidly if need arose. And secondly, as we've seen in Chapter 4, coal is a potential source of synthetic oil. If the oil-wells really do run dry before we can replace our present vehicles by electric cars, a crash programme of coal-conversion plants is probably the only practicable option. Moreover, if we do change to electric motors for transport, it is coal, already the fuel for about half the world's power-stations, that is the most likely candidate for the necessary expansion of generating capacity.

Coal is, of course, a dirty fuel, but modern liquefaction and gasification methods can greatly reduce the emission of particulates (smoke) and the sulphur and other compounds that lead to acid rain. Unfortunately, one potentially serious problem remains. No matter what we do with the coal, we are going to produce a great deal of carbon dioxide. We can use all manner of sophisticated and elegant processes to produce a more acceptable final fuel, but the fact remains that if we start with a certain number of carbon atoms, we'll finish with a corresponding number of CO_2 molecules, and apart from producing a few fizzy drinks, there is little we can do but release them into the atmosphere. So if global warming really is leading to catastrophe, we must with great regret leave this most plentiful of fuels in the ground.

Uranium

Which leaves the fourth and last of the non-renewables: nuclear power. Twenty years or so ago, in anticipation of rapid growth in the number of nuclear power-stations, there was concern that the technically and economically accessible reserves of natural uranium, estimated as several million tonnes, would last for no more than a few decades. This was one argument for the development of breeder reactors (see Chapter 8). More recent years saw this concern much diminished, initially because the nuclear industry did not develop as fast as expected, and then because, as someone has said, we are currently 'awash in uranium and plutonium'.* A slight exaggeration, perhaps, but the decommissioning of nuclear weapons has certainly increased the availability of these two fuels, and initially at least, removed the urgency from breeder programmes. This particular pendulum may however already be swinging the other way. One argument is that breeders could help dispose of the surpluses (but see Chapter 13), and another is that if we begin to run out of oil and gas, and coal proves to be the forbidden fuel, nuclear power is the remaining 'conventional' resource. There is even the possibility of a 'hydrogen economy' (Chapter 15), with electricity from nuclear plants supplying the energy to generate this fuel as a replacement for both gas and oil. There may be public reservations about its cost and its hazards, but nuclear power has the great advantages that it produces almost no CO_2 and that the technology is there. We have already lived with it, happily or not, for over half a century.

So much for the non-renewables. We've seen two resources which will almost certainly be in short supply before long and two which are plentiful but give cause for environmental concerns. Can the renewables do any better?

The Renewables

We know what we need: fuel for vehicles, fuel for heating, and sources for electric power. We've discussed the technologies for most of the renewables in earlier chapters: biomass, heat from the sun, electric power from water, winds, waves, tides, and again the sun. The questions here are to do with the amounts of energy they can provide. It is important to note at the start that the resulting estimates represent the total energy that is technically available and are likely to be severely reduced by practical issues such as cost and how these contributions would fit together to make a complete energy supply. We return to these matters later.

---

* 'Return of the Breeder', *Scientific American*, January 1996.

Biomass

As we saw near the start of the book, biomass probably supplies about a seventh of the world's present primary energy. The total annual contribution of just over 50 EJ represents some 3 billion tonnes of assorted materials, or about half a tonne per head of population. The distribution is, of course, very uneven, with bio-fuels providing as much as 90 per cent of all energy in some developing countries and a very small fraction in most of the industrialized world. There are a few exceptions, such as Sweden and Austria, both with about a tenth of their primary energy coming from these sources. Nevertheless, most of the present uses involve fairly simple technology, very different from the systems needed if biomass is to make an appreciable contribution to the energy uses listed above.

How large a resource is this? The total mass of all the world's land plants is thought to be about 1800 billion tonnes, with the forests making up nine-tenths of this. A more relevant figure for our present purposes is that the biomass is constantly renewed by natural processes at a rate of some 400 billion tonnes a year. (It is of course this natural cycle that makes biomass CO_2-neutral if grown sustainably, and therefore a valuable replacement for fossil fuels.) Allowing for the fact that rather more than half the mass is water, we find that the 400 billion tonnes represents about eight times our total annual primary energy consumption. So it appears that in terms of the annual 'total resource', biomass should be able to make an appreciable contribution. But of course we can't use everything that grows, nor would we want to, so even the most optimistic estimates suggest no more than a twelfth of this: perhaps 200 EJ a year, or about half our present primary energy. To give an idea of scale, this would mean making good use of about half the residues of all agricultural and forestry activities world-wide and growing 'energy crops' on about a fortieth of the total land area of the Earth. This is not, of course, something which could be brought about overnight, and even with enthusiastic international effort, it would be fifty years or so before the above contribution could be reached.

Once we've got it, can we use it? Given time to develop the systems, the answer seems to be yes. We saw in Chapter 4 how biomass could be the raw material for both liquid and gaseous fuel, and in Chapter 5 how electricity can be generated using integrated gasifier combined cycle systems. Optimists suggest that the motor fuel might be produced at an overall efficiency of 60 per cent and electricity at 40 per cent, so we find biomass contributing maybe 100 EJ of energy in the forms we need. How does this compare with the other renewables?

Hydroelectricity

Hydroelectricity makes the second major renewable contribution to world energy at present, with an annual output of 2400 billion kWh (roughly 8 EJ). When we ask about the total annual resource, we find very much the same situation as with biomass. The energy delivered in each year by the flows of all the world's rivers is perhaps 40 000 billion kWh, but even the most enthusiastic developers consider no more than half of this to be technically accessible: 20 000 billion kWh, or 70 EJ, of electricity—about twice the world's present total electricity production.

Wind Power

Estimating the total energy carried by all the world's winds is possible but not very useful for our present purposes. Even looking fifty years ahead, it doesn't seem sensible to include winds a mile above the surface of the Earth or in the middle of the larger oceans, and the remoter regions of the Arctic and Antarctic are not usually included at present. Without these, and considering only sites on land or in coastal waters, the total is large enough: 500 000 billion kWh or 1800 EJ—over four times world present primary energy consumption. So perhaps wind is the answer to all our problems? Needless to say, it's not. If we eliminate areas where the winds are so poor or unreliable that the investment wouldn't be worthwhile, and decide not to cover every remaining piece of ground with wind-farms, the figure falls to about one-tenth of the above total: 50 000 billion kWh, or 180 EJ, of electricity.

Tidal Power

Tidal power is another instance where a simple calculation of the total energy flow is not very helpful, but for a rather different reason. Tidal plants will probably be worthwhile only in places where the tidal range is particularly large, which means that estimating a 'world total' involves not a general assessment but careful site-by-site investigation. Using this approach, the potential output of the most promising sites is considered to be about 300 billion kWh, or about 1 EJ.

Geothermal Energy

One further 'semi-renewable' resource not discussed at all so far is geothermal energy. There is a constant flow of heat from the hot interior of the Earth, and a corresponding rise of temperature as you go deeper underground. In most places this is too little to be useful with present technology, but some parts of the world are particularly favoured, with very hot water or even steam only a few hundred metres below the surface. Where the hot fluid breaks through naturally, hot springs or geysers are found, and these have been used as heat sources for thousands of years. The first generation of electric power using geothermal steam was in 1904 at Larderello in Tuscany, and this original source is still in use, with an output now approaching 1000 MW. Because the resource varies so much from place to place, the situation is rather like that for tidal power, with a 'world total' obtained by detailed investigation of possible sites. Locally, the contribution can be significant: in the Philippines, for instance, geothermal plants already supply nearly a quarter of all electricity. But the world output of about 50 billion kWh of electricity a year is well under 1 per cent of all electricity, and an estimated direct heat contribution of similar magnitude is tiny compared with the heat from other sources. The most optimistic estimates see the electrical output as increasing four-fold in the next fifty years, and if the heat use shows similar growth, the annual total becomes 400 billion kWh, or about $1\frac{1}{2}$ EJ.

Solar Energy

Coming finally to the source of nearly all the other renewables, we have yet another problem in estimating the useful contribution. A nice simple calculation goes as follows. The annual energy reaching the surface of the Earth as solar radiation is about a billion billion kWh (4 million EJ). An appropriate mix of solar panels and photovoltaic cells would be able to convert this to any desired combination of heat and electricity at an efficiency of perhaps 10 per cent. So the total annual potential is 100 000 000 billion kWh! Fine, until we ask a few practical questions, such as whether we want to cover the entire surface of the globe with panels and photocells. (This would certainly eliminate not just the biomass contribution but the biomass itself.) And if all the nation's energy supplies come directly from the sun, what happens when it's night-time in our part of the world? The idea is obviously absurd, but there is a serious purpose behind the reasoning. It reflects the current situation, which is that solar heating and photovoltaics offer potentially very large sources of energy in the forms we want, and the technology to use them already exists, but we aren't at all sure how to integrate them with other supplies. There are some interesting ideas, however, and we'll look at these later; but for the moment we must leave a question mark against this contribution.

Summary

Table 12.2 summarizes the situation. The absence of several sources discussed in earlier chapters calls for comment. For some, such as solar ponds, this is because the contribution seems likely to be local and relatively small on the world scale. Other systems, such as wave power, OTEC, or fusion reactors may offer enormous potential for the future, but the full-scale technology doesn't even exist yet, and for this reason we must regard it as unlikely that they will make an appreciable contribution within the time-scale of our study.

TABLE 12.2. *World resources*

| | Main final-use form | Present primary contribution (EJ/y) | Total potential[a] | |
			Resource (EJ)	Final-use contribution (EJ/y)
Finite resources				
Oil	Motor fuel	135	10 000	
Natural gas	Heating	79	11 000	
Coal	Electricity	91	>100 000	
Nuclear power	Electricity	8	(see text)	
Renewable resources				
Biomass	Motor fuel + electricity	52		100
Hydroelectricity	Electricity	8		70
Wind power	Electricity	0.02		180
Tidal power	Electricity	0.002		1
Geothermal energy	Heat + electricity	0.3		$1\frac{1}{2}$
Solar energy	Heat + electricity	0.005[b]		(see text)

[a] See the text for discussion of the data in these columns.
[b] Solar electricity only.

The information in Table 12.2 is certainly necessary if we want to plan for future energy supplies, but it is by no means sufficient. The figures for the 'new' resources are estimates of the maximum practical annual contributions we could possibly extract within the next forty or fifty years, and in the next few chapters we'll encounter many reasons why their acceptable contributions are bound to be smaller—in some cases very much smaller. There are the environmental and safety aspects to take into account, and we certainly need to know something about the cost of the energy from each source. (These two factors should come in this order, because the overall cost of any scheme may depend heavily on the expense involved in avoiding pollution and reducing the risk of accidents.) Further questions arise when we consider total energy supplies, for the world or for one country. Is the source located where the energy is needed? If it is in some other part of the world, what are the financial and political consequences? How large a role can we afford to give the unreliably intermittent sources such as sun and wind? And we must not forget the most important 'alternative supply' of all: can we use less energy?

13

Penalties

___

Introduction

Any plan for the future must take into account not only the potentialities but the penalties of energy from the different sources.
Table 13.1 lists many of the current concerns, and presents a rather
depressing picture of hazards to health, devastation of the environment, and the risk of catastrophic accidents. The aim of this
chapter is to provide a little of the scientific background to some of
these concerns and to assess what we actually know about the
effects. It is then left to you, the reader, to make the decision.
Which penalties are you willing to accept as the cost which accom-
panies all the benefits of plentiful supplies of warmth, electricity
and motor fuel?

. . . and Statistics

One thing becomes obvious as soon as we start to look at the
health and environmental effects of energy systems. The available
information, the factual background, is often very different from
the facts about, say, the efficiencies of turbines or generators. The
difference is that often the data are essentially statistical. We've
met statistical data before, of course, but usually in the form of
simple averages: average UK household energy consumption, for
instance. Here, they play a much more central role—or rather two
different roles.

First, there is the question of the effects of the by-products of our energy systems. These effects, or at least the ill-effects, commonly appear at low levels, or are diffuse, or distant in space or time from their original causes. (Foolish we may be, but we usually have enough sense not to use systems which are obviously and instantly lethal.) Quite often the only way to link an effect with its cause is to look carefully for correlations in the variations of the two. It is believed, for instance, that one particularly bad smog in London in 1952 caused 4000 deaths in five days. Not because that number of otherwise healthy people fell gasping in the street and expired on the spot, but because there were 4000 more deaths from respiratory and related diseases than normal for that population in that place during that period. It could, of course, have been a random fluctuation, or the effect of a wicked fairy or a conjunction of planets, but because there was other statistical evidence relating air pollution and respiratory illness, and at least the beginnings of an understanding of the link, the smog was held responsible.

Now 4000 extra deaths in London in a few days is a pretty obvious effect; but what happens when the scale is much smaller? You may feel that something should be done about the emissions from power-stations or internal combustion engines even if they 'only' cause 100 extra deaths a year in the whole country; but detecting such a subtle effect would be like looking for a hundred extra pieces of hay in a haystack. At these levels, we must ask whether statistics will allow us to detect the effects—reliably.

The second role of statistics is in the assessment of risk. Suppose that we have satisfied ourselves that none of our energy systems is detectably harmful in normal use. This still leaves the possibility that something can go wrong with catastrophic results. The assessment of risk is a controversial subject, but the results have played—and are likely to continue to play—such a role in the comparison of different energy systems that we must attempt to look at the issues, the difficulties, and a few of the predictions. You need only think of the everyday phrase 'the *chances* of an accident' to see that statistics will be central to this discussion.

Space doesn't permit a detailed account of every item in Table

13.1, so selection is inevitable, and we'll look at two specific concerns and two general questions, choosing four topics which exemplify the particular problems that arise in assessing the side-effects of any technology. The first is the general issue of pollution of the atmosphere—an important factor in comparing present and potential fuel sources. Then there are two specific concerns about our present energy sources: the greenhouse effect and the nature and effects of radioactivity. Whatever the final

TABLE 13.1. *Environmental and social concerns*

These are the main concerns expressed in current discussion of our energy supplies. See the text for more detail.

Source	Causes of concern
Oil	Global warming, air pollution by vehicles, acid rain, oil spills, oil rig accidents
Natural gas	Global warming, pipe leakage, methane explosions
Coal	Environmental spoliation by open-cast mining, land subsidence due to deep mining, spoil heaps, ground-water pollution, global warming, acid rain
Nuclear power	Radioactivity (routine release, risk of accident, waste disposal), misuse of fissile material by terrorists, spread of nuclear weapons
Biomass	Effect on landscape and biodiversity, ground-water pollution due to fertilizers, use of scarce water, competition with food production
Hydroelectricity	Displacement of populations, effect on rivers and ground-water, dams (visual intrusion and risk of accident), seismic effects, downstream effects on agriculture
Wind power	Noise, visual intrusion in sensitive landscapes, bird strikes, TV interference
Tidal power	Destruction of wildlife habitat, reduced dispersal of effluents
Geothermal energy	Release of polluting gases (SO_2, H_2S, etc.), ground-water pollution by chemicals including heavy metals, seismic effects
Solar energy	Sequestration of large land areas, use of toxic materials in manufacture of PV cells, visual intrusion in both rural and urban environments

outcome, these will certainly enter into decisions about energy in the coming decades. Finally, we'll investigate the methods used to assess risk.

Atmospheric Pollution

What is atmospheric pollution? Like any form of pollution, it is the presence of substances that are potentially harmful to the health and well-being of the human population or of other living things, or even inanimate objects such as buildings. The pollutants in the atmosphere are gases, vapours, and aerosols, and it may be worth distinguishing between these. Both gases and vapours consist of separate individual atoms or molecules. In everyday terms we tend to call the oxygen and nitrogen of the air 'gases' but regard any water molecules as forming a 'vapour', but this turns out to be only a reflection of the temperatures at which we happen to live. Any gas can be turned into a liquid under the right conditions, but for oxygen and nitrogen this means cooling down to about minus 200°C. Under pressure, they can be liquefied at somewhat higher temperatures, minus 100°C or so; but at room temperature no amount of pressure will change these gases into liquids. This is the technical distinction between a gas and a vapour: if the substance is at a temperature where it can be liquefied by pressure, it is technically a vapour. If not, it's a gas. An aerosol is quite different. It consists of tiny particles, perhaps a thousandth of a millimetre across but nevertheless each containing millions of atoms; much larger than the individual free atoms or molecules of a gas or vapour. What are these pollutants, then? The five main constituents and their principal sources are as follows.

Sulphur Dioxide

Sulphur dioxide (SO_2) results from combustion of almost any fuel, because almost all—not only fossil fuels but biofuels too—contain some sulphur. But the amounts vary greatly, and so does the ease with which the sulphur can be removed before using the fuel. For these reasons coal-fired power-stations are the main producers of SO_2. The main polluting effects result from the conversion of SO_2

into sulphuric acid (H_2SO_4) in the atmosphere. If it remains in the air, this can produce an aerosol of sulphate particles which we see as an unattractive haze; but its best-known effect is when it comes to earth as 'acid rain'.

Nitrogen–Oxygen Compounds

The NOXs (see 'Flue Gases' in Chapter 4) are an inevitable result of burning any fuel in air. The chief sources are motor vehicles, a result of the nature of the combustion in internal combustion engines, and the main effects are similar to those of SO_2. In the atmosphere, the NOXs become nitric acid (HNO_3) and provide a further contribution to acid rain. But because, unlike SO_2, they are generated near the ground and often in close proximity to people, their immediate effects on the respiratory system are more obvious.

Carbon Monoxide

Carbon monoxide (CO) is a result of incomplete combustion of a fuel. (Full combustion would lead to CO_2.) Although usually produced in small quantities, it is a very undesirable pollutant because it is a poison. A badly adjusted combustion system such as a household gas boiler can produce enough CO to kill someone in a matter of hours in an ill-ventilated room. The toxicity of carbon monoxide is related to the fact that it is chemically very active—an important difference from a gas such as carbon *di*oxide which produces immediate physiological effects only when there is so much that we begin to suffocate through lack of oxygen. By far the major producer of carbon monoxide is the internal combustion engine. The toxic effect is of course less dramatic out of doors, but whether inhaled or forming unpleasant compounds with other pollutants, CO is certainly an undesirable by-product of motor vehicles.

Volatile Organic Compounds

This category, the VOCs, embraces a range of chemical compounds of different kinds and from different sources. There are hydrocarbons, mainly another result of incomplete combustion in internal combustion engines. Then there are vapours from solvents and similar materials used in, for instance, the plastics industries. Many of these are carcinogenic, and they contribute to the 'chemical' smog of Los Angeles or Mexico City.

Particulates

As the name suggests, this group includes anything in the form of solid particles: the visible products we usually call dust, smoke, or soot. There are always small particles in the air, of course: the 'motes' visible in a beam of sunlight in even the cleanest parts of the world. But as we'll see, there is considerable evidence linking the density of particulates with a variety of respiratory illnesses.

Ozone

An important indicator of atmospheric pollution is ozone. This gas, whose molecules consist of three oxygen atoms (O_3 rather than the O_2 of normal air), features in our environmental concerns in two entirely different ways. At or near ground level, ozone is produced by the effect of sunlight on mixtures of some of the pollutants listed above, so it is a by-product rather than a direct product of our use of motor vehicles. Nevertheless it usually appears as a sixth item on the list, and is often used as a general indicator of the level of pollution.

Much further up in the atmosphere, at twenty to thirty thousand metres, is the natural phenomenon known as the ozone layer. This ozone is also produced by the effects of sunlight, but unlike the ozone near the ground, it is of great positive value to us because it absorbs much of the ultra-violet part of the solar radiation reaching the outer atmosphere. Too much ultra-violet is harmful to our eyes and may lead to skin cancer, so the recent discovery of 'holes' in the ozone layer is giving rise to concern. For once, however, it is not our energy systems that are the main cause of the problem, but other organic materials, so the ozone hole remains outside the scope of this book.

The Sources

The six items above are the main, but by no means the only, atmospheric pollutants. (Carbon dioxide is not listed here because its main environmental effect is quite different, and we'll discuss that later.) Identification of the pollutants is only the first step in comparing the effects of different energy systems. It is obviously necessary to monitor the quantities present in different locations, and this area of investigation has advanced very rapidly in recent decades. (Data on atmospheric concentrations even appear regularly in some newspapers.) Unfortunately, these reliable measurements do not go back very far, which limits the extent to which levels of pollution can be related to either their causes or their effects. Let's start by asking about the causes.

We know that combustion produces toxic or otherwise harmful substances. The fact that air consists of four-fifths nitrogen and one-fifth oxygen means that burning any fuel, even pure hydrogen, will produce some NOXs. Other fuels are much more complex, but provided we know the composition and the furnace conditions, we should be able to make reasonable estimates of all the combustion products. The section 'Furnaces' in Chapter 4, for instance, included an inventory of materials leaving the boiler of a coal-fired power-station, and similar information is available for other power-plants, internal combustion engines, domestic boilers, other industrial processes, etc. So it should be possible to estimate the emissions from each source in a particular country in a year. Figure 13.1 gives the annual UK emissions of SO_2 and NO_2 (as well as CO_2) and shows the sources believed to be responsible. It is interesting to note that in greater Los Angeles, with about one-quarter of the UK population, annual SO_2 emissions are only 50000 tonnes, whilst nitrogen oxides, nearly half a million tonnes, are more in line with UK values. The use of natural gas or oil rather than coal in power-stations and industry is in part responsible, but the figures also reflect the greater number of vehicles, with about two-thirds of the total LA emissions coming from transport.

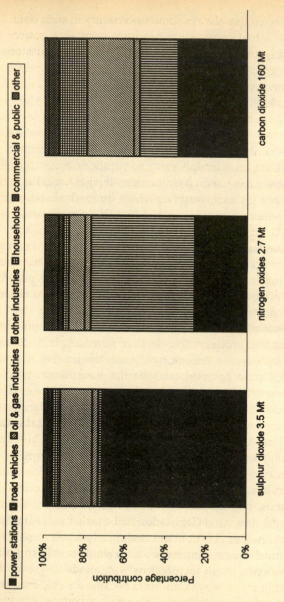

Fig. 13.1 Sources of some atmospheric emissions, UK 1994

There is of course always some uncertainty in such data. Determining the actual combustion products from each source is not easy. Most countries have regulations governing emissions from large power-plants, and an increasing number also regulate motor vehicles; but no one can constantly check every furnace and every vehicle exhaust. Nevertheless, the results of efforts to reduce pollution do support the general view of the probable sources, as the following examples from the histories of our two cities suggest.

During the great London smog of 1952, the levels of both particulates and SO_2 in the air reached several parts per million (ppm). The result was a yellow-grey blanket so thick that pedestrians were feeling their way yard by yard and a motorist could make a complete U-turn in the road without realizing it. The average levels of these pollutants in London in the early 1950s were less than 0.5 ppm, so the severe smog represented a ten-fold increase. Its catastrophic consequences led to action, and the Clean Air Act of 1956 totally prohibited the burning of untreated coal in London. As a result, the annual average particulate level fell below 0.04 ppm within twenty years, and whilst London still has the damp foggy days characteristic of a low-lying city, it is now several decades since the last real 'pea-souper'.

The Angelinos of Southern California were also worried about air pollution in the mid-1950s. The LA smog, a thin yellow-brown, throat-catching, eye-watering haze in which the presence of hydrocarbons is only too evident, was quite unlike the London version. The causes were different too; not coal burning but gas-guzzling automobiles (the average fuel consumption in the 1950s was 13 mpg (US)—about 15 miles per UK gallon), together with heavy industry and an absence of controls exemplified by the fact that most households disposed of all their domestic rubbish by burning it. Emissions legislation had a rather more bumpy ride in the next few decades than in London, in part because the situation was much more complex, with no single source of pollution. But the backyard trash incinerators were made illegal in the late 1950s, and in many ways California became a world leader in the control of vehicle emissions. Catalytic converters, for instance, were mandatory for all new cars from 1975; 'clean gasoline' has reduced the VOCs, and overall, the mid-1990s car emits only a tenth of the pollutants of its predecessor twenty years ago. An intriguing approach to industrial pollution is the 'emission off-set' requirement: if your new scheme is going to produce X additional tonnes of pollutant a day then you must somehow reduce emissions from existing plant by the same amount. Air quality in the Los Angeles area still fails to meet the US federal standards for much of the time, but a reduction of the maximum ozone level from 0.6 to 0.3 ppm over a period when the population rose by 40 per cent and the number of cars by 60 per cent is not to be despised.

Health Effects

What about data on the effects of the different pollutants? In which ways and at what levels are they harmful? These are much more difficult questions, and the main concerns are centred on two areas: the health effects on people who live close to the sources of pollution—near industrial complexes or in large cities, and the environmental effects experienced many miles or even hundreds of miles from the sources. There are many other possible effects but we'll confine ourselves to these two, and to just a few pollutants.

Once more, we start with the great London smog. The suggestion is that concentrations of SO_2 and particulates of about 3 ppm caused 4000 extra deaths in a few days in a population of about 10 million. Say 1000 deaths per day, or roughly 1 death per day per 10000 people. But this case is well-known precisely because it is not typical. Can we apply the results to today's much lower levels? Can we say that at 0.01 ppm, a three-hundredth of the above level, these two pollutants will cause 3 deaths per day per 10 million people (about 100 a year per million people)? This question, whether the results obtained from the effects at high concentrations still apply at levels hundreds of times smaller, has been the subject of much debate, with some experts holding that the effect is proportional to the exposure down to the lowest levels and others claiming that there is a threshold below which the pollutant has no effect at all. It is almost impossible to decide by observation which is true for the above death rates. The annual death rate in industrialized countries is about 10000 per million people, and even a 10 per cent increase in present SO_2 concentration would mean adding only 10 to this figure, a change that would almost certainly be lost in other fluctuations.

One possibility might be to look not at death rates, but at more frequent effects, to find any relationship with pollutant levels. Figure 13.2 shows one set of data for a particular effect at low SO_2 concentrations. (Note that 13 µg per cubic metre is 0.01 ppm by weight.) The line shows the relationship that was deduced from the data: no effect up to a threshold of 7 µg/cu m and then a rising incidence of asthma attacks. It certainly requires the eye of the believer (or blind use of a computer) to decide that this particular line follows from this information.

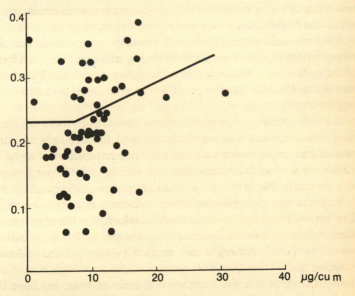

Fig. 13.2 An effect of air pollution?

Each point shows the rate of asthma attacks in a group of sufferers and the concentration of SO_2 at the time. See text for discussion of the graph.

Then there are other problems. How do we know that the recorded death rates or asthma attacks were not affected by any number of other changing factors—the weather, a flu epidemic, changes in other pollutants. And there are further complications when two pollutants are frequently found together. Is it the SO_2 or the particulates, or some combined effect, or the sum of two individual effects, that causes harm? Then can we assume that exposure for a year produces 365 times the effect of exposure for a day? And how about time: are there delayed effects, appearing many years later?

Acid Rain

We now add to the problems by considering effects that might be acting hundreds of miles from their sources. This is certainly the case with acid rain. It is well established that power-stations emit SO_2 and motor vehicles NO_2, and that these can produce sulphuric and nitric acids by reactions in the atmosphere. Measurements in clouds have detected water drops with the acidity of vinegar or lemon juice (acid drops, perhaps?). It has been observed since the 1960s that lakes in some regions in both Europe and the USA have become so acidic that they can no longer support life. However, connecting the effect to the possible cause in detail is not so easy, and for many years accusations and denials flew to and fro between the owners of power-stations and the owners of dead lakes. The situation was particularly vexed in Europe, where the victims and the accused were often in different countries. As techniques for tracing pollutants through the atmosphere improved, it became possible to link sources and emissions much more closely, and it is now generally recognized that the change from gases to acids takes place in long plumes which can stretch over a thousand miles downwind from the source; which means eastwards for North America, the northern Atlantic, and western Europe.

The late 1970s saw growing signs of an even more widespread potential disaster: Europe's forests were dying. By the mid-1980s, along a huge swathe from Scandinavia through the Low Countries, Germany, and Poland, and into the Czech Republic, up to half of all forest trees were reported to be damaged in varying degrees; about one in twenty seriously so. Similar effects were being observed in the eastern regions of North America. The fact that all these appeared when SO_2 emissions were already falling has led to two rather different interpretations: one school of thought holding that it could be a delayed effect of the acid rain of earlier years, and another believing that it has nothing to do with acid rain at all. This remains a controversial issue today. No other single cause for the damage has been found, and the majority view is that a number of factors come into play, many experts holding that acid rain entering the soil initiates the process, ultimately weakening the trees and making them vulnerable to other stresses.

Conclusions

We've now looked at just one possible penalty of our energy systems. What have we learned? To be sceptical about invitingly simple sound-bites, certainly. Epidemiological and environmental studies are not simple. Interpreting them requires care, and we must certainly do our best to take into account all the possible 'interfering' factors which might offer alternative explanations for the observed effects. This is not, however, to say that we should sit back and do nothing until we have rock-solid data. No one wants a return to pre-1950 London; and if no measures at all had been taken to reduce air pollution in LA, its inhabitants—if any—would all now need gas-masks. The moral is rather that we shouldn't claim better data than we've got, but neither should we wait for certainty until it is too late. It is sometimes advisable to act even on inadequate information to be on the safe side.

Biological Effects of Radioactivity

To assess the environmental effects of a nuclear plant we need to know what its emissions are, how they are distributed in the atmosphere, how much is received by individuals or the population, and what are the health effects of these amounts. In other words, just as for the other pollutants discussed above; and it is partly to avoid covering the same ground twice that we concentrate here on the last stage: the health effects. There are other reasons too. Unlike SO_2, radioactivity is not a single substance, and it is important—particularly in such a controversial area—to be clear exactly what we are talking about. Then there is the significant difference that the range between 'routine emissions' and 'worst possible emissions' is many orders of magnitude greater for nuclear reactors than for fossil-fuel plant.

The routine emissions from a properly run reactor are, as we'll see, very low; that is, they add only slightly to our normal exposure to radioactivity. It is arguable (if not universally agreed) that they represent less hazard to health than the normal emissions from the equivalent coal-fired plant. However, the total radioactive content of a reactor is a million or more times its normal annual discharge, so concern centres less on routine emissions than on the potential for accidents. We return to this later, but here we'll accept without much comment the 'routine' data and look in some detail at the health effects over a wide range of exposures.

Measuring Radioactivity

In order to discuss its effects at all, we need to be able to measure amounts of radioactivity. The three main 'radiations' were introduced in Chapter 8, and one way to characterize a radioactive source is to state which type it emits and give the number of decays per second. This is its strength in **becquerels (Bq)**.* A piece of anything with an activity of 1 MBq emits one million particles a second, and so on. Table 13.2 shows the half-lives and activities of a few radioisotopes. To put this in context, we might note that 1 gram is the mass of half a tea-bag; that a microgram (μg) is a millionth of this—a speck of dust; that 50 parts per million,

---

* The becquerel replaced the earlier unit for the strength of a source, the curie. A one-curie source would emit 3.7×10^{10} particles a second, so the conversions are very roughly $1\,\text{Ci} \approx 40\,\text{GBq}$ or $1\,\text{TBq} \approx 30\,000\,\text{Ci}$.

TABLE 13.2. *Half-lives and activities*

Isotope	U-238	U-235	Pu-239	Sr-90	I-131
Type of particle	α	α	α	β	β
Half-life	4.5×10^9 years	7×10^8 years	24 000 years	28 years	8 days
Activity of 1 gram[a]	12 000 Bq	80 000 Bq	2000 MBq	5 TBq	5000 TBq
Mass for 10 000 Bq	1 g	0.1 g	5 μg	0.002 μg	2 μμg

[a] These are the activities of the pure samples, before they have had time to produce 'daughters' which would change the sample.

million, million of iodine-131 in air produces an activity of 400 Bq per cubic metre (the maximum permitted concentration for workers); and that the encapsulated sources considered safe for school laboratories have activities of perhaps 10 000 Bq.

Does this mean then that 10 000 Bq is 'a safe level of radio-activity'? Absolutely not! First, it isn't a level but the strength of a particular source. And secondly, safety depends on what the source is and where it is. An encapsulated course used correctly in the laboratory adds a negligible amount to the natural radioactivity that we all receive continuously; but 10 000 Bq of plutonium in soluble form entering the bloodstream through a scratch is serious enough to justify cutting away flesh to prevent its spreading. To assess safety—or potential danger—we need something other than the strengths of sources.

One relevant quantity is the energy deposited by the high-speed particles or penetrating radiation as they pass through any material, living or otherwise. The particles tear apart the atoms or molecules of the material, and one measure of the damage they do is the energy dissipated in doing this. So we have a new unit:

- One **gray** is the quantity of radiation that deposits one joule of energy in each kilogram of material.

Notice that this is a total amount, not a 'per second' rate. We have moved away from the source and its strength to the recipient and the dose; and we can see at once why a nicely enclosed 10 000 Bq source on the laboratory bench is very different from a 10 000 Bq source in the bloodstream or lungs. You could hold your geiger counter at the side of the first for a long time and not detect any difference from the normal background rate of clicks, whilst every particle from the second could be absorbed in a small volume of tissue—very different numbers of grays. Damage can of course come from external sources, particularly if they produce the penetrating gamma rays. In discussing the 'radiations' we should also include X-rays, which are similar to gamma rays but come from the surrounding electrons rather than the nuclei of atoms. Then there are the neutrons which, as we've seen in Chapter 8, are bound to be present in large numbers in a reactor. Both of these must be included in any estimation of total dose.

The dose in grays is not the end of the story, however, because not all grays are equal. The biological damage resulting from a particular dose in grays is about ten times greater if it comes from heavy particles—alphas or neutrons—than from betas, gammas, or X-rays. It also depends on the type of tissue receiving the dose and on the rate at which the energy is delivered. The unit that takes all these factors into account, giving the best measure of the possible damage, is the **sievert** (Sv). We shall adopt a usual practice and simplify the definitions as follows:

- The dose in sieverts is taken to be equal to the dose in grays, as defined above, for beta particles, gamma rays, and X-rays.
- The dose in sieverts is taken to be ten times the dose in grays for alpha particles and neutrons.

It is this dose in sieverts which is the subject of assessments of potential harm and regulations about permitted exposure.*

Doses and Effects

How large a dose is 1 sievert? What effect does it have? Data come from three main sources: laboratory experiments on tissue samples or on animals, studies of those unfortunate groups of people

---

* It is still common to find two older units, the rad and the rem. Conversion is easy, because 1 gray is 100 rads and 1 sievert is 100 rems.

who have been exposed to high radiation levels, and epidemiological studies of larger populations at low doses. (One hopes that every effort is being made to record in detail the effects of the Chernobyl accident, so that at least some good can come from that disaster.) Collectively, the existing studies suggest that radiation in large single doses can produce acute effects with symptoms appearing in hours or days, and that—over a wide range of doses and exposure times—it can also produce longer-term effects: cancers, and also mutations, genetic changes which may appear in later generations.

To summarize the often controversial results of many studies over many years may mean dangerous over-simplification. Nevertheless, it seems useful to give some idea of at least the orders of magnitude. The following indicators refer to whole-body doses and will not necessarily apply to, for instance, doses concentrated in a single organ.

- A dose of 10 Sv or more in a short period almost certainly means death within hours or days.

- Doses of 1–10 Sv over a short period lead to radiation sickness and disability for weeks or months, and can be fatal.

- For doses below 1 Sv received within a short period, the symptoms decrease, until at about 0.1 Sv there may be no immediately obvious effects.

- Over a wide range of doses, whether received by a few people or a large population, in a single dose or over a long period of exposure, the long-term rate of induced cancers appears to lie in the range *between one and two cancers per 100 person-sieverts*.

- The total number of genetic effects down to about the tenth generation is thought to be of the same order as the number of cancers. (This figure, coming mainly from studies on mice, is recognized as being very tentative and subject to correction by at least a factor of five each way.)

- The annual radiation dose to which we are all subjected continuously lies in the range 1–3 millisieverts. (Table 13.3 shows some details of this for the UK.)

TABLE 13.3. *Annual radiation dose, Britain*

The figures are population averages; the dose to a particular individual could be greater or less than that shown in all cases. The figures are 'body averages'; the dose to a particular organ could be greater or less than that shown in all cases.

Annual dose to an average person		Microsieverts
From natural sources		
Cosmic radiation	250	
Environmental radioisotopes[a]	650	
Radioisotopes in food	300	
Total, natural background		1200
Medical contributions, total[b]		400
Non-medical contributions		
Miscellaneous industrial	10	
Fallout[c]	5	
Nuclear power industry[d]	7	
		22
Total		1622

[a] Mainly from radioactive materials in the ground and in building materials. Locally, this can be much greater, with an individual average in Cornwall, for instance, of about 7000 μSv.
[b] Including X-rays and radioactive materials used diagnostically and for treatment.
[c] Fallout from past atmospheric nuclear weapons tests together with residual fallout from the Chernobyl accident.
[d] Based on dose to total population including workers in nuclear industries.

The figure for the rate of induced cancers plays such an important role in discussions of nuclear power that it is worth spelling out its meaning in more detail. It implies that, in a group of people receiving doses of 5 Sv (roughly the maximum received by Hiroshima survivors) between 1 in 10 and 1 in 20 will eventually develop cancers. At the other extreme, it means that the 2 mSv a year of natural background radiation will be responsible for 1000–2000 cancers for each year of exposure in the population of the UK. (The annual death rate from all cancers in this population is of the order of 100000.) We must note, however, that this says nothing about when the cancers will appear. In the case of the whole population, the calculation also assumes that the effect is proportional to the total dose, no matter how small, and as discussed earlier in this chapter (see 'Health Effects'), not everyone believes that such extrapolations are valid.

Discharges and Exposures

Figures such as those above provide the basis for international standards (Table 13.4) which are used by many countries in legislation governing permitted exposures and permitted discharges from nuclear plants into the air or water. The latter must of course take into account the nature of different isotopes. Are they airborne? What is their half-life? By what routes, if any, can they enter the human food chain?

To see in outline how permitted exposures and permitted discharges are related, we'll consider just one fission product: I-131, a beta-emitter with a half-life of about eight days. Iodine is a solid at room temperature but vaporizes easily and is a gas within the reactor. Discharged into the atmosphere, it can reach us either directly in the air we breathe or by a more circuitous route when deposits on grass are eaten by cows whose milk we drink. It is a health hazard because iodine concentrates in the thyroid gland, and concentration of any radioisotope means an increased dose to the surrounding tissue. On the other hand, the short half-life means that within a month over nine-tenths of the activity will

TABLE 13.4. *Recommended allowable doses*

These limits are recommended by the International Commission on Radiological Protection. Doses to particular organs are the subject of more detailed recommendations.

Maximum cumulative dose in one year	Millisieverts
Occupational, to any individual	50
Population, to any individual	5
Population, average dose	1.7

have disappeared. Estimates of routine emissions of I-131 from power-stations tend to fall in the range 1–10 MBq a day. To convert these figures into health effects requires data on weather, population distribution, etc., and a more detailed analysis than is possible here; but the general conclusion is that such low levels of discharge are unlikely to lead to even one cancer over the life-time of a power-station.

I-131 is of course only one of a number of radioisotopes in routine discharges to the atmosphere, to ground-water, and to the oceans. And these discharges are only one of a number of sources of environmental radioactivity associated with the nuclear power programme. Fuel fabrication and transportation contribute. Reprocessing, if carried out, is thought to produce greater emissions than the power-plants themselves. Then there are the uranium mines. Lung cancer due to inhaling radioactive radon gas, released when uranium ore is broken up, is a classic example of occupationally linked disease, and emissions from mine tailings have been responsible for some of the highest routine exposures of population groups. This exposure will not, of course, appear in the statistics of countries that import their uranium, such as Britain, but this can hardly justify ignoring it.

The data for annual radiation doses resulting from nuclear power have been the subject of much debate, and as elsewhere in this section, the figures we give must be treated with caution. One point to bear in mind is that whole-body population doses are averages on two senses. They can hide large variations between different groups of people, and large variations in doses to different organs. The figures given here come from estimates of total emissions and studies of critical pathways, records of levels near nuclear plants, and data from monitors worn by workers. Subject, then, to all these reservations, the present annual level of whole-body exposure due to the UK nuclear power industry may be expressed in two ways:

- The total annual exposure of the entire population, including workers in the nuclear industries, is about 400 person-sieverts.

- The overall average annual exposure per member of the population is about 7 μSv (microsieverts).

Nuclear power accounts for about a quarter of Britain's electricity. We can therefore say that, even if all power came from nuclear plants, the total exposure would represent only a 3 per cent addition to the natural background radiation which we all receive in any case. Or, using data earlier in this section, a fully nuclear electricity industry might add 20 or 30 cancers a year to the present 200 000 or so. These are the reasons justifying the claim that routine operation of present nuclear power-stations does not constitute a major hazard to health. (We'll come to non-routine events later.)

Global Warming

Short History of a Small Planet

Billions of years ago the Earth was a mass of very hot material. Then it cooled and became solid on the outside with some water and a layer of carbon dioxide gas around it. Then came plants, using the carbon dioxide and water to grow, and producing oxygen in the process. When plants died they decomposed, taking up the oxygen and returning the carbon dioxide and water to the atmosphere. But some plants became buried and didn't use their share of oxygen, so the amount increased until there was enough for animals, who breathed oxygen in and carbon dioxide out. Some of the buried plants became coal. Some animals died and became oil and natural gas. Others became humans, who first burnt the plants and then found the coal and oil and gas and burnt them too. Then there was only carbon dioxide and the Earth became very hot again and the humans disappeared.

The Greenhouse Effect

The fairy-tale above is perhaps a little over-simplified but it does include one important point: the temperature of the Earth is critical in determining the life-forms it supports. We know how to calculate the temperature of any object, because it is always the result of a balance between its heat energy inputs and outputs. For the Earth, an object floating in space, by far the major input is solar radiation and the output is the energy radiated away by the Earth in all directions into space. We saw in Chapter 11 ('Electromagnetic Radiation') that everything radiates energy, and the hotter the object the more it radiates. So the temperature of the Earth will remain steady when the energy radiated away from it exactly balances the solar input. It is a self-adjusting system: if it becomes too cold, it radiates less and therefore warms up; if too hot, it radiates more and cools down. Putting numbers into this reasoning and taking into account the fact that the surface of the Earth is better at absorbing sunlight than it is at radiating infra-red, we find that the average temperature should be about 250K—roughly minus 20°C!

There is clearly an error somewhere, and it doesn't take long to find it. We've forgotten that the Earth is surrounded by an atmosphere, and this makes a very great difference. The sequence of events is thought to be roughly as follows. When the solar radiation reaches the outer atmosphere, about one-third of the energy is reflected away. Some of the rest is absorbed, warming the atmosphere as it passes through, and about 50 per cent reaches the Earth's surface. The warm surface radiates back, but—and this is the important part—because it is only warm and not white-hot, it radiates mainly infra-red radiation, and almost all of this is absorbed by the atmosphere, warming it still more. Finally, the warm atmosphere radiates enough energy away into space to maintain the balance, but also radiates an appreciable part back to the surface. When everything is in balance, the surface finally receives only about two-thirds of the original solar radiation, but its average year-round temperature is a comfortable 17°C. This action of the atmosphere is called the greenhouse effect because glass also behaves like this, transmitting visible light but absorbing the infra-red. (It doesn't actually play a great role in a real greenhouse, where the main function of the glass is to keep the wind out and the warm air from escaping.)

The final important point is that this infra-red absorption by the atmosphere is due to the presence of the so-called 'greenhouse gases': not only carbon dioxide but methane, water vapour, nitrous oxide, and others. And the reason for all the concern is that if we increase the concentrations of these gases we are likely to change the present balance, causing more infra-red to be absorbed and increasing the radiation back to the surface, with a resulting overall rise in the average temperature. Molecule for molecule, carbon dioxide is one of the less effective greenhouse gases, but this is more than compensated by the fact that there is far more of it in the atmosphere than any of the others.

The Carbon Dioxide Balance

The burning of fossil fuels inevitably produces carbon dioxide—a few tonnes for every tonne of fuel burnt—and our present consumption of fossil fuels releases into the atmosphere nearly 800 tonnes of CO_2 in each second. Carbon dioxide already accounts for about one three-thousandth of normal air, and the annual release by our energy industries is a little over 1 per cent of the amount already there. But it is enough to cause concern.

As the 'Short History' above suggests, the pre-industrial CO_2 concentration in the atmosphere is thought to be the result of a number of processes operating simultaneously. Every growing plant is using CO_2. The total mass of all the land plants is some 1800 billion tonnes, or about 1300 billion tonnes if we exclude the water they contain. (Nine-tenths of the total mass is in the world's forests, so each of us is responsible for the maintenance of about 300 tonnes of tree.) Plants are estimated to recycle about 400 billion tonnes of CO_2 a year, taking it from the atmosphere as they grow and returning it in respiration and decomposition. The oceans also contain a very large amount of CO_2, and constantly release it into and re-absorb it from the atmosphere, recycling about the same quantity each year as the biomass. Animals of course take in oxygen and breathe out carbon dioxide, but their overall effect is relatively small. The CO_2 concentration in the atmosphere resulting from the balance between these natural processes, before human activities intervened, was about 270 ppm by volume (about one gram of CO_2 in every five cubic metres of air).

In the past 100 years we have changed this state of affairs in two ways. The first is the release of carbon dioxide into the atmosphere from burning fossil fuels, currently some 24 billion tonnes of CO_2 a year. The second is the destruction of the tropical forests, reducing the amount of CO_2 taken out of the atmosphere. As much as one-fifth of the area of tropical forest has been destroyed in the past 50 years and the present rate of deforestation removes a further 200000 square kilometres a year. The reduction in the net take-up of CO_2 is estimated to be 10 billion tonnes each year.

So we are effectively adding 24 billion tonnes to one side of the CO_2 balance-sheet while subtracting 10 billion tonnes from the other side. The inevitable result of re-establishing equilibrium is that the concentration of CO_2 in the atmosphere must rise. There is good evidence that this is indeed happening, and has been happening for over a century. Increasingly reliable records show an annual increase of about $1\frac{1}{2}$ ppm, corresponding to some 10 billion tonnes of CO_2 (Fig. 13.3(a)). This restores a third of the above imbalance. The oceans are thought to account for about another third. If there is more CO_2 in the air above the water surface then more will be absorbed until that equilibrium is also re-established. The fate of the remaining 10 billion tonnes is still the subject of debate. Some authorities believe that the contribution from deforestation is an over-estimate that fails to take into account other factors, such as the replacement of trees by other plants. Others think that absorption by the oceans removes more than the 10 billion tonnes suggested above. A third view is that the greater concentration of CO_2 in the atmosphere enhances plant growth and therefore increases the take-up—an interesting example of 'negative feedback'.

It is obviously important to understand the processes leading to the increasing level of CO_2 in order to be able to control it if necessary, and a great deal of research effort is being devoted to the problem. But even if we don't yet fully understand the processes, the facts seem to be well-established, so our next question must be about the effects of this annual increase.

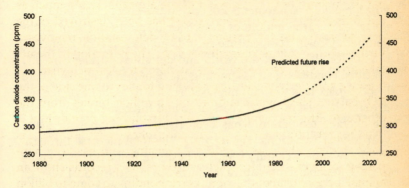

(a) Concentration of carbon dioxide in the atmosphere

(b) Temperature trends and predictions

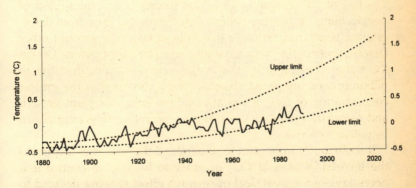

Fig. 13.3 Carbon dioxide and global temperature
In (b) the solid line shows how the global average air temperature has changed from
year to year over the past century. The smooth curves show the range of predicted
increases due to rising concentrations of greenhouse gases.

Is the Earth Warming?

It is by no means easy to tell whether the temperature of the Earth is rising. For one thing, what do we mean by 'the temperature of the Earth'? We obviously need a properly calculated average, which means measurements not only at the easy places, but in the polar regions, the middle of deserts or tropical forests, or in the Southern Ocean. Temperature records go back several centuries, but not for all parts of the world and not always under carefully specified conditions, so assembling the data into a reliable record is a complex task. Careful analysis has led to global average figures for the past hundred years or so and the general view is that the average temperature has been rising, although with many year-to-year variations (Fig. 13.3(b)). The total increase throughout the twentieth century seems to be about half a degree Celsius ($0.5°C$). Reliable temperature readings can take the global average back no more than 150 years, but there is a great deal of more local information on earlier periods. There was the Little Ice Age of the sixteenth and seventeenth centuries, with winter fairs on the frozen Thames. Evidence from tree growth and boreholes suggests that this cooling, followed by a relatively rapid rise during the nineteenth century, was not limited to Europe. At even earlier times, tens and hundreds of thousands of years ago, there were of course the real Ice Ages. On this long time-scale, variations in the Earth's average surface temperature seem to have been common. The causes are by no means well understood, but there is some evidence that concentrations of CO_2 in the atmosphere did rise and fall with these widespread temperature changes.

Cause and Effect?

So we have good evidence for increased atmospheric CO_2 (and also other greenhouse gases such as methane). There is some evidence for global warming. And there is a possible mechanism connecting the two. The next thing is to develop the theory in more detail in order to make firmer predictions, but this has unfortunately not been as successful. The weather, or the longer-term pattern we call the climate, is the result of interactions between solar radiation, the atmosphere, the oceans, and the land masses of the Earth; and constructing a mathematical 'model' to reflect and predict the behaviour of this very complex system is fraught with difficulties. So it shouldn't surprise us that the predictions don't always agree—and are not infrequently wrong. Present theories suggest that the increase in atmospheric CO_2 together with other greenhouse gases should already have led to an average temperature rise in the range 0.5–1.5°C. As we've seen, the measured rise seems to be about 0.5°C—only just on the border of the range. Several reasons have been put forward for the discrepancy. (One idea is that the sulphur dioxide haze in the atmosphere acts to reduce the temperature at the surface; the villain of the acid rain story thus becoming a rather surprising hero.) A factor which certainly enters is the huge 'thermal inertia' of the oceans. It could be that the atmospheric conditions for much greater warming already exist, but the change is being delayed as the oceans very slowly follow. Theories taking this delay into account suggest that the temperature rise should at present be between one-third of a degree and one degree, in much better agreement with the measurements. It will indeed be unfortunate if this particular theory proves accurate, because the same long delay would affect changes in the other direction, and we could find the heating continuing for many years, even if we have mended our habits and reduced our CO_2 output.

The detailed pattern of change is even less predictable. There is general agreement that the temperature changes will be different in different parts of the world, with smaller effects in the tropics than at higher latitudes. Rainfall patterns are also expected to change. Most theories suggest that some of the polar ice will melt, but how much, and when, is very uncertain. (The melting of the *Arctic* ice should not raise the levels of the oceans. This ice is floating, and Archimedes told us long ago that a floating object displaces its own mass of water. So when an iceberg melts, the resulting water just fits neatly into the hole in the sea that the iceberg occupied. The situation is quite different for the Antarctic ice, which rests on land.)

If this is as far as predictions about the climate can take us, it is not going to be easy to assess the effect of global warming on the world's ecosystems. Some optimists point out that a slightly warmer Earth might be an improvement: increased rainfall could mean that the deserts bloom again; tropical and temperate forests might expand; food crop yields could increase; and regions at present habitable only by Inuit might become living space for less hardy people. Most climatologists, however, are far less sanguine. A doubling of the CO_2 concentration leading to a temperature rise of a few degrees would mean a rise in ocean levels even without melting of the ice caps, because water expands when heated. Changing rainfall patterns could increase the area of desert or semi-arid land in the lower latitudes and rising temperatures could destroy the northern boreal forests, further increasing atmospheric CO_2. A warmer atmosphere might also be more turbulent, with increased numbers of severe storms and tornadoes.

So there is no simple theory and there are no firm predictions; but as with the case of the other atmospheric pollutants discussed above, this does not necessarily mean that we should do nothing. We may complain about our present climate, but we've learned to live with it and perhaps we should be doing our best to keep it rather than continuing towards an unknown and possibly catastrophic alternative.

I Think that I Shall Never See . . .

As a footnote to the discussion of carbon dioxide, the following idea might appeal. A hundred metres of a busy six-lane motorway could be carrying as many as forty vehicles at any moment. Averaging 60 mph and 30 mpg, these would consume petrol at a rate of 80 gallons an hour. In doing so they would use about a tonne of oxygen an hour, releasing roughly the same amount of CO_2. Plants use CO_2 and release oxygen, and a large tree can recycle perhaps 2 kg an hour. So we need to plant all motorways with 500 large trees per 100 metres to maintain the balance.

Assessing Risk

It is proposed to build a nuclear power-station near your home. When you express your concern about the possibility of a serious accident, you are informed that the chances are only one in ten million per year of an accident serious enough to cause perhaps ten immediate deaths and 10000 ultimate deaths from cancer. How do you react?

A. That would be terrible. I'd rather live without electricity.
B. So what? In ten million years I'll be dead anyway.
C. Place your bets! £5000 to a penny that it'll survive ten years.
D. How do they know?

Accidents are not of course confined to nuclear reactors. Until recently they still caused some fifty deaths a year in Britain's coal-mines. And oil-rigs can catch fire, liquefied natural gas tanks explode, and dams burst, sometimes killing hundreds in a single incident. Air disasters bring similar numbers of fatalities, and of course we kill ourselves in our thousands on the roads every year. In contrast, there has not yet been even one immediate fatality in Britain or the USA resulting from a reactor accident in a public supply nuclear power-station. (The careful qualifications in this statement limit it to situations where we believe the available information to be accurate.) None the less it is the thought of such an accident that causes much of the public concern about nuclear power. In Chapter 8 we looked briefly at possible reasons for this, and now we must try to see whether there is any rational justification for it.

Probabilities and Consequences

It is not the intention here to assess the probabilities of particular accidents, or their consequences if they do occur. Only experts with very detailed information can do that. What we can do is to ask in general terms how the experts reach their figures. What sort of methods are used and what sorts of factors are taken into account? In other words, we'll play person D in the responses above.

Chances mean probabilities, and we can start with the obvious point that probabilities are not certainties. The chances are 1 in 6 that your dice will show a 2; but this doesn't mean that every sixth throw will be a 2, nor even that a 2 will turn up once in every six throws. It is perfectly possible that you get no 2s at all in a dozen throws, or that you throw half a dozen in succession. In this sense, respondent B above shows a poor appreciation of probabilities, whilst the bookmaker C understands what they mean (and hopes, like the National Lottery, to make a profit).

How does anyone reach a figure for the probability of a certain type of accident? One rather simple method is to use past history. You can ask, 'What has been the average life of this type of light bulb?' or 'What proportion of these cars have been arriving without steering wheels?' You can then plan on this basis, keeping appropriate stocks of spare light bulbs or steering wheels. The method is not foolproof. For one thing, history may not repeat itself. One minor reactor accident in the USA was complicated by switches which stuck, a fault traced to the fact that a previously reliable supplier had moved, taken on new inexperienced workers, and failed to notice the quality deterioration. On the whole, however, the approach has proved sufficiently reliable to be used routinely by designers of many complex systems.

Risk assessment like this has moved from the design office to the public domain largely with the rising concern about reactor accidents; indeed it could be seen as a counter to the response of person A above. As people became aware of the appalling consequences of the worst conceivable accident, it became necessary to point out (or to find out, according to your view) just how small the probability was that such an accident would occur. A rational person, it is argued, will reach decisions on a basis of *probability multiplied by consequences*. If I'll accept a situation with a one in a thousand chance of five fatalities a year, then I should accept a one in a million chance of 5000 fatalities, and so on. And similar reasoning should determine my choice between alternatives.

Accidents in complex systems like power-stations are caused by combinations of circumstances, so we need combinations of probabilities to assess their likelihood. If one in every 500 meat pies has no meat and one in every 2000 jam doughnuts has no jam, then the probability that your lunch will consist of a meatless pie and a jamless doughnut is one in a million. If we know the individual probabilities we can calculate overall probabilities for complex sets of events—like a switch failing to open and a valve failing to close and . . . The reasoning can run either way. You can say that, in order for the core to melt, the following and the following and the following must all happen, and then calculate the probability of this conjunction. Or you can ask what happens if X fails, and in addition Y fails, and so on, and in this way find the probabilities and consequences of all possible accidents.

There are complications of course. If your meat pie and jam doughnut were made by the same baker, who was having a bad day, the coincidence of two missing fillings would be more probable than the calculation suggested. Your lunch would be the unfortunate consequence of a **common mode failure**. Allowing for common mode failures is essential in assessing risk, and eliminating them is an important aspect of design. The best-known example of what not to do is probably the 1975 BWR accident at Brown's Ferry in Alabama, where a single fire affecting hundreds of cables put out all the carefully planned emergency cooling systems in one go.

Two other difficulties are 'unknowns' and people. There can be parts of the system for which probabilities based on past history are not available. Risks must then be assessed by calculation, by analogy with similar cases, and where possible by experiment. The behaviour of the massive steel pressure vessel of a PWR under the stresses which might result from an accident, and the behaviour of emergency cooling water as it hits the hot core, are examples where there is little history to go on (fortunately); but this has led to controversy over both.

People present similar problems. Brown's Ferry is only one of many cases where human ingenuity prevented serious consequences, but the incident at Three Mile Island (see Chapter 8 and below) seems initially to have been the result of a determined effort by all present to counter the actions of the safety systems, and the Chernobyl catastrophe was also in part the result of human error. (It is only fair to add that the TMI engineers were in a control-room with at one moment over a hundred alarms sounding and lights flashing. Like those at Chernobyl who lost their lives or subsequently put themselves at severe risk, they were heroes to be there at all.) Any risk assessment that ignores the human factor will obviously be of little value, yet to give figures for the chances that people will behave in certain ways clearly introduces a whole new spectrum of uncertainties.

Despite all these difficulties, estimates are made. The Rasmussen Report of 1975* remains the most comprehensive risk assessment exercise for any major part of the nuclear industry: three years' work, at a cost of three million dollars, producing a huge multi-volume analysis of the probabilities and consequences of accidents in light-water reactors. Its conclusions have been much criticized for the degree of certainty they claim, but nevertheless the data have featured in many subsequent analyses. The Report and its successors have also been attacked on the more general ground that most major industrial accidents have been caused by totally unforeseen factors rather than combinations of known possibilities. This may be so, but the detailed step-wise assessment could still be useful; not only as an aid to designers but because it offers an idea of the likelihood of at least some events. After all, if the analysis showed a 1 in 3 chance of a particular accident within a year, we'd surely do something about it.

So, with all these reservations, we'll look at a few of the Rasmussen figures. Table 13.5 shows simplified versions of the probability-times-consequences conclusions for three potential accidents: a core meltdown with little or no release of radioactivity, a meltdown with an explosion violent enough to breach the containment, and the second of these again but with the reactor in a densely populated area and weather conditions that maximize the effect, exposing a population of 10 million or so. The first column of figures reflects the type of event. The next three take into account all the uncertainties about doses and their effects

* The National Research Council, *Reactor Safety Study: An Assessment of Accident Risks in US Commercial Nuclear Reactor Power Plants*, US Nuclear Regulatory Commission, 1975.

TABLE 13.5. *Estimates of accident probabilities and consequences*

See the main text for further explanation and comment on these figures.

| Event | Activity released (curies[a]) | Total dose to population (person-sieverts) | Consequent number of deaths | | Probable number of events per million reactor-years | Predicted number of deaths per thousand reactor-years |
			Immediate	Delayed		
Meltdown without major breach of containment	0–10000	0–1000	0	0–10	10–100	0–1
Meltdown with breach of containment, under average conditions	10–100 million	0.1–1 million	1–10	1000–10000	0.1–10	0.1–100
Meltdown with breach of containment under worst conditions	10–100 million	1–10 million	1000–10000	10000–100000	0.001–0.01	0.001–1

[a] To obtain orders of magnitude in TBq, divide the numbers given by 20.

discussed above. The figures in the fifth column are determined by combining the probabilities of many small events to give ranges of probabilities for the specified accidents. Finally, the sixth column shows the result of multiplying probabilities by consequences. It should be noted that this is just a small part of a very much larger set of conclusions—and that this analysis is for essentially one type of reactor.

The Evidence

Fortunately, the number of serious reactor accidents has been far too small for any proper test of these estimates, but it may be worth looking briefly at three known events in this context—noting that only one of the three was in fact in a light-water reactor. The first is the fire in 1957 in the graphite moderator of the Windscale reactor in Cumbria, in north-western England. The containment was not breached in the usual sense, but there was a release of radioactive gases including some 1000 TBq (roughly 20 000 curies) of iodine-131. As a precaution, milk from herds grazing in the locality was destroyed for a few days, and the accident was subsequently claimed not to have caused a single death. If the relationship between activity released and consequences shown in Table 13.5 is at all correct, this seems statistically unlikely (a point noted in the first edition of this book in 1980). In the late 1980s the official view changed, with the statement that the release in 1957 probably led to a few tens of deaths from cancer—far too small a number, of course, to be detected in the mortality statistics, but now in rough agreement with the Rasmussen consequences for that release. What about the probability of the event? An event with similar release of radioactivity is given a probability of 10–100 per million reactor-years, and Windscale had been in operation for about one year. Does this tell us anything? Yes, it tells us that the chances are greater than zero. Otherwise extremely little; not because this was a Magnox reactor rather than a PWR but because a single event says very little else about the statistical chances, one way or the other.

In the minds of the public at least, iodine-131 features largely in concerns about reactors. As we have seen, it is an isotope that easily enters the food chain and that presents particular health hazards. But we also saw earlier in this chapter that routine emissions, of the order of millions of becquerels a day, are unlikely to cause much harm to anyone. However, the total I-131 content of a reactor can be exabecquerels: several million, million times these routine amounts; and it is the possibility of an appreciable fraction of this escaping that causes concern. It certainly featured in our second example, the accident at the Three Mile Island plant near Harrisburg, Pennsylvania in 1979. Here a combination of improbable events—a switch failing to open, a valve failing to close, misinterpretation of meter readings—resulted in a chemical explosion within the reactor. To the credit of the designers, the containment was not breached, but about 1 TBq of I-131 was released, less than a millionth of the total content. Although this was a million times the daily norm, Table 13.5 suggests that it should not have caused even a single additional cancer or death. TMI is, however, an interesting case when we look at probabilities. One accident like this per 300–30000 reactor-years was the prediction, and by 1979 these PWRs had accumulated a total of about 400 reactor-years. We cannot, however, agree with the statement (in a major energy study, surprisingly) that 'the range has proved to be correct'. The fact that your sixth throw of the dice is a 2 does not confirm the view that 1 throw in 6 will be a 2.

The most serious accident known to date in a nuclear power plant was at Chernobyl in the Ukraine in 1986. The particular design of reactor played a role in this, but the immediate causes were the interruption of a testing procedure in order to meet an unexpected demand for power, and a subsequent operator error on resumption of the tests. The consequence was an uncontrollable rise in power until pipework ruptured under pressure and blew out the 'lid' of the reactor, which fell back tilted, leaving the interior exposed. (The floor was also blown downwards, as mentioned in Chapter 8, and was eventually found four metres lower, in the sub-structure.) The cloud of radioactive material released was traced over the following days as it swept across Europe on a long looping path, driven north-west and then south again by the winds. A number of people at the plant received lethal radiation doses in the first few days. (These included pilots who flew helicopters low over the open reactor in an attempt to drop neutron absorbers into the core; a useless action, as almost no fuel remained there—but this wasn't known until later.)

Conclusions

The death rate for any population is well-known: it is one per person. Try again. If you are the average inhabitant of an industrialized country your chance of dying in the coming year is about 1 in 100. About 500 000 people die each year in Britain, some 100 000 of them from cancer. If the figures earlier in this chapter are correct, about 1000 of these are the result of natural background radioactivity and perhaps five are due to the nuclear power industry. If we take the 'worst case' from Table 13.5, with the present number of reactors, accidents might add another 1 or 2—on average. And there's the rub. In the last two words. When all the sums are done, how do we respond to probabilities? Is one of the first three responses at the start of this section the 'correct' one?

- If the rational response is to compare probability-times-consequences for different alternatives, then as far as routine emissions and reactor accidents are concerned, the figures—if even remotely reliable—place nuclear power amongst the safest energy sources, and the bookmaker C is on good ground.

- But perhaps this response is not appropriate for very large-scale low-probability catastrophes? It has been argued that, as individuals or societies, we normally don't bother at all about risks whose chances are less than perhaps one in a million a year; that we do in practice adopt the light-hearted approach of person B.

- On the other hand, there are those who argue for response A: that if the consequences are sufficiently awful we shouldn't accept the risk at all, no matter how low the probability.

To dismiss any of these views as 'not rational' seems, to this writer at least, neither justifiable nor particularly useful.

14

Costs and Prices

Introduction

We are all agreed that the price of energy is important. (Table 14.1 shows some data on energy prices, on the large and small scales.) However, our views on the precise nature of its importance are likely to depend on where we stand. As consumers— householders or factory owners—we look at our fuel and electricity bills and complain that energy is too expensive. Wearing other hats, and thinking about dying forests and global warming, or wondering why it isn't worth investing in double-glazing, we sometimes ask whether energy isn't too cheap. If we are an electricity generating company, we may be concerned to establish whether coal, nuclear, or wind power will produce the cheapest electric power in the future. And if we own an oil field, we'll need to think about price trends in deciding how much to invest in developing new wells.

This chapter will look only briefly at just three aspects of energy costs and prices. We'll start with the relationship between price and demand, because this is central to the sort of economic reasoning behind many plans for energy in the future. We make no attempt to discuss economic forecasting itself. The methods used by the economists in constructing their projections are beyond our scope, but a look at this particular link may help us to understand a little of the basis for some of the scenarios described in Chapter 15.

TABLE 14.1. *Energy prices*

Fuel	World market prices		
	In traded units	Per kWh[a]	
Oil	$16 per barrel (bbl)	1.0¢	0.07p
Coal	$50 per tonne	0.6¢	0.04p
Natural gas	$70 per 1000 cu m	0.7¢	0.04p
Electricity (UK pool price paid to generators)			2–3p
	Prices paid by UK domestic users[a]		
Heating oil			5p
Coal etc.			2p
Natural gas			2p
Electricity			9p

[a] In the case of fuels the prices are per kWh of heat produced.

In contrast to the broad sweep of economic theory, our second item is a matter of detailed accounting. How does the owner or prospective owner of a power-station work out the cost of the electricity it will produce? We've mentioned the cost of electricity from different sources several times in earlier chapters, as though it was a simple matter of fact. As we'll see, this is not necessarily the case. Calculating the total cost should in principle be fairly straightforward; but in practice it has been the cause of much debate and discussion. For many years, the costs of power from coal-fired and nuclear plant were the subject of furious shouting matches between the supporters of the two sides. Then the past decade or so has seen the 'dash for gas' in the UK, and renewable energy sources entering the field in many countries. Why is the gas turbine everyone's pet project while the renewables struggle for a foothold?

Finally, returning to the very broad picture, we look at the question of 'externalities'. Is it desirable—or even possible—to take into account the environmental and social effects of our energy systems in assessing their cost?

Elasticities

If your income rose by 10 per cent next year, how much more electricity would you use? Your answer indicates your **income elasticity of demand**. If you used 5 per cent more electricity as a result of your 10 per cent rise, then your income elasticity of demand for electricity would be 5 per cent divided by 10 per cent, or 0.5. (Of course, you might invest in better insulation and therefore use 20 per cent *less* electricity—giving an elasticity of minus 2.)

Price elasticities, rather than these income elasticities, are our main concern. If an 8 per cent increase in the price of electricity meant that you used 2 per cent less, then your **price elasticity of demand for electricity** would be minus two-eighths (–0.25). Or if you are determined that your total bill won't change, and therefore take care to reduce your consumption by 8 per cent, your price elasticity of demand will be minus one.

A complication in relating demand for energy to price is 'inter-fuel substitution'. When electricity prices hit the roof, you go back to your old coal fire, or buy a gas water-heating system. Except that you may no longer have a fireplace, and few people buy complete heating systems on the spur of the moment. So there is another factor: the time delay between a change and its effect. If the forecast of energy demand in the year 2020 is to take into account all these factors, it will need a price-elasticity-of-demand-for-electricity-in-2020-assuming-that-all-other-energy-prices-are-unchanged, and so on. This sounds complicated, but is no more than the way we all behave. If the price of electricity doubles, you are likely to make more use of your gas boiler—but not if the price of gas has trebled.

When the consumer is a whole country, we are more likely to be interested in the effect of world prices on national consumption. In Chapter 3 we met the idea of the energy/GDP ratio: the amount of energy used for each pound or dollar earned in the country as a whole. Many economic forecasts have used the reasonable assumption that when prices rise, efforts will be made to use energy more efficiently so the energy/GDP ratio will go down. In other words, just as for the individual above, the price elasticity of the energy/GDP ratio will be some negative quantity. Or if we plot a graph to show how the ratio depends on price, it should be a downward sloping curve.

The upper graph of Fig. 14.1 is an attempt to do this. The points

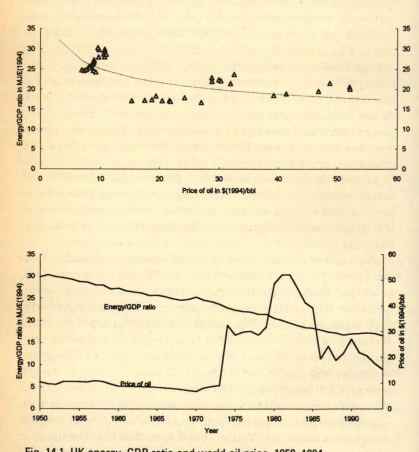

Fig. 14.1 UK energy–GDP ratio and world oil price, 1950–1994

The pounds and dollars have been corrected for inflation and are expressed in 1994 values.

cover the years from 1950 to 1994, each one showing the UK energy/GDP ratio and the world price of oil for a particular year. As you can see, they hardly lie on a nice smooth line. Indeed, it would be very difficult to decide which, if any, line to draw as the 'best fit' (we'll return to this in a moment). The lower graph is much more informative, showing what was actually happening to each of the two quantities year by year. We now see the pattern: a more or less steady fall in energy/GDP ratio, not really affected in any obvious way by the wildly changing price of oil. We looked at possible reasons for differing energy/GDP ratios in the national comparisons in Chapter 3, and some of these are probably relevant here. Industrial and other consumers are becoming more efficient and using less energy, and the UK pattern of use is undoubtedly changing, with the decline of manufacturing industry and growth of the service sector. We must also remember that the energy/GDP ratio is just that: the ratio of two quantities, and Fig. 14.1 doesn't tell us what happened to the two separately. It could be that energy demand and GDP both fell when oil prices rose. (Figure 2.4 in Chapter 2 supports this view to some extent.) Whatever the explanation, the scattered points of the graph certainly illustrate the uncertainties in this particular elasticity.

We could of course proceed quite differently. If instead of contemplating Fig. 14.1, we simply feed all the data into a computer, it will obediently fit them to any formula we choose and give us a value for the elasticity. (It won't of course point out how badly they fit, unless we ask.) The dotted line through the points shows the result of fitting—or should it be forcing—the data to the relationship expected if there is a constant elasticity. Moreover, the computer will give us the value: the oil price elasticity of the UK energy/GDP ratio is –0.197. As someone said in another context,* 'Given a formula, many people can calculate the unknowns with any desired precision (even with much undesired precision, if a computer is available).' You can use this method to find values for a wide variety of elasticities. To return to our earlier example, you

* Editorial, IEE Transactions on Reliability. R28 (1979).

can find the income elasticity of demand for household electricity. Indeed, depending on your source of data, you can find almost any figure you like for it, from values greater than 1 down to zero, or even, as one writer said plaintively, 'of the wrong sign'. (Is it so obvious that wealthier people are bound to use more electricity?)

So we shall not finish this section with a nice table of elasticities. The justification for it lies not in particular numerical results but in the fact that many predictions of future energy demand involve assumptions about elasticities, and we should at least know enough to recognize them—particularly when they are not spelled out. The moral is that we need to look carefully at the data and assumptions behind any figures we are offered—and that we shouldn't be fooled into believing that any number of pages of mathematics can produce reliable predictions from uncertain data and doubtful assumptions.

The Cost of Electricity

It should be very straightforward to calculate how much each unit of electricity from a power-station costs to produce. We know all the items of expenditure:

- Initial costs involved in purchasing the site, obtaining planning permission, etc.
- Construction costs.
- Regular annual operating and maintenance costs.
- Fuel costs and any others that depend on the output.
- The costs of decommissioning, restoring the landscape, etc. when the useful life of the plant is over.

We also know the output, the number of kilowatt-hours of electricity sold during each year—or for a proposed plant, we make suitable assumptions about this. So all we need do is to add together all the costs and divide by the total lifetime output. Converted to suitable units, the result will be the cost in pence per kilowatt-hour (p/kWh).

Counting the Costs

Unfortunately it isn't quite so simple in practice. First, the list of cost items above is open to a variety of interpretations. There are the two 'etcs.', for instance. Are there costs arising even earlier that are not mentioned above? How about all the development work that went into designing the plant? Who paid for that? The cost of the machines for, say, a wind-farm is likely to include a sum to cover the research and development costs of their manufacturer. Many governments are supporting renewable energy to some extent, so in part this may have been paid for by public money. Should this be included when we compare the cost of power from the wind-farm with that from other power-stations? Where large public utilities provide the power, as was the case in Britain until recently, the situation is even more difficult. There have been long and bitter arguments about the extent to which past R & D expenditure on coal-burning plant and nuclear reactors should feature in present cost estimates. Fuel costs raise similar problems. If the coal-mines or uranium processing plants are subsidized by the taxpayer, is this another item to add to the final cost of power? Then there is the last item on the list above, one of the two most difficult financial issues for nuclear plants in particular. (Insurance against the risk of accidents is the other.) Closing any large power-station involves costs if the landscape is to be restored to an acceptable state, but dealing with the radioactive contents of a reactor will probably require a different order of expenditure. In the absence of any agreed method yet for disposing of highly active wastes, this particular issue is featuring largely in the privatization of the more profitable parts of Britain's nuclear generating capacity, and at the time of writing it seems likely that buyers will be forthcoming only if there is a fairly open-ended commitment to cover the decommissioning costs from public funds.

Discounting the Payments

An entirely different source of debate, and the main reason why our simple method of costing isn't used, is that the value of money changes. Suppose I ask you to lend me £100, and promise to return it by paying you £20 a year for five years, starting in a year's time. You would probably not regard this as a very good offer, for two reasons:

- If inflation continues, it will mean that the successive payments of £20 will buy less and less.
- You could have invested your money and had *more* than £100 in five years' time.

It is usual to separate these two factors. If we start by allowing for inflation, we can then see whether there have been 'real' changes in costs or prices. The oil prices in Fig. 14.1, for instance, are in '1994 dollars'. The actual price per barrel in 1950 was only $1.70, but due to inflation you would need $10 in 1994 to have the same spending power. Doing this allows us to look at the past in present-day terms, rather than having to remember each time that, 'a penny would have bought much more in those days.'

Suppose now that I offer to repay the borrowed money in instalments that allow for inflation: £21 next year, £22 the year after, etc., depending on the annual rates of inflation. Would this be satisfactory? It shouldn't be, because we certainly hope that interest rates on money we invest are high enough to provide a real gain after allowing for inflation. The difference, the real rate of interest, is the figure we need to know in deciding whether to lend—or borrow—money. It is also critical in determining the costs of electric power, or any other commodity bringing a future return on a present investment.

Returning to your £100, suppose you know that you could invest it at a real interest rate of 2 per cent a year. After one year you would have £102. If you left it in place, that would become £104.04 after another year, £106.12 after the third, £108.24 after the fourth and finally £110.41 at the end of the five years. To put it another way, £100 today is worth £110.41 to you in five years' time. But you can also stand this argument on its head, and calculate that a sum of £100 that you expect to receive in five years' time has a present value of only £90.57. You have discounted the future figure, at a discount rate of 2 per cent a year.

This is where the power-station calculations come in, because the initial construction costs must be paid now, but the running costs and the income from the sale of electricity only appear in later years. So if we want to calculate a total present value, all these later annual amounts must be discounted as described above. Moreover, if this is a commercial enterprise, the expected discount rate, effectively the rate of return on the investment, is likely to be a lot greater than 2 per cent. Figures of 8 per cent a year or even more are not unusual in such calculations, and as we'll see, this has a serious effect on the resulting cost of electricity.

Two Power-Stations

The two cases in Table 14.2 are designed to show how discounting can even reverse our view on which of two power-stations produces the cheaper electricity. Using much simplified figures, it calculates the cost of power from two types of plant. They have the same rating and annual output, and the same total cost. The difference is that one has relatively low construction costs but high annual costs, whilst the reverse is the case for the other, which also has a longer lifetime. The first might be a gas turbine plant—relatively cheap to install but with fuel to be included in the annual costs. The second could be a hydroelectric or tidal plant, with heavy construction costs but no fuel to pay for. (The differences between a coal-fired power-station and a nuclear plant would fit a similar pattern.)

The figures in Table 14.2 show very clearly that financial assumptions can make a great deal of difference to the results. Using the simple method of calculating the cost of electricity—effectively zero discount rate—Plant B produces power at two-thirds the cost of Plant A. But this changes dramatically when we introduce the 8 per cent discount rate, with power from B now apparently costing more than from A. It obviously all depends how you do your accounts, or to put it another way, gas turbine plants give you a quick return on your money. This is one reason why they are currently popular with generating companies. The capital cost is low, at least for plants in this range, because they can use what are essentially aero-engine turbines and therefore 'off the shelf' items. Running costs are not too high because gas is still a relatively

TABLE 14.2. *Calculating the cost of electricity*

The aim is to compare the cost of electricity from two different power-stations. Both have a rated capacity of 100 MW, and both produce 700 million kWh a year—about 80 per cent of the maximum possible. They also have the same total lifetime cost: £280 million.

Plant A has construction and pre-construction costs of £100 million and a total annual cost of £9 million throughout a 20-year lifetime.

Plant B has construction and pre-construction costs of £220 million and a total annual cost of £2 million throughout a 30-year lifetime.

The simple calculation

Plant A produces a total of 14 000 million kWh for a total cost of 28 000 million pence. So the cost per unit of electricity is 2 p/kWh.

Plant B produces a total of 21 000 million kWh for a total cost of 28 000 million pence. So the cost per unit of electricity is 1.3 p/kWh.

Discounting the costs

We now recalculate the costs using a discount rate of 8 per cent. As the electricity is also sold in the future, we discount that as well, before calculating the cost per unit.

Plant A

Construction and pre-construction costs	£100m
Total discounted value of £9m a year for the next 20 years	£88m
Total cost after discounting	£188m
Total discounted value of 700 million kWh a year for the next 20 years	6800m kWh
Cost per unit	2.7 p/kWh

Plant B

Construction and pre-construction costs	£220m
Total discounted value of £2m a year for the next 30 years	£23m
Total cost after discounting	£243m
Total discounted value of 700 million kWh a year for the next 30 years	7900m kWh
Cost per unit	3.1 p/kWh

---

cheap fuel. (Whether this growing use of a premium fuel to run power-stations will prove wise in the long term remains to be seen.) Meanwhile, plans for systems that require large initial investment languish on the shelf, in part because the power that they would still be producing in 30 or even 50 years' time literally 'doesn't add up to much' today.

Table 14.3 shows data for power-stations using some of the renewable energy sources discussed in earlier chapters, with the resulting cost per unit of electricity if we assume a discount rate of 8 per cent. As Table 14.1 showed, the current price paid to UK generating companies is 2–3p/kWh, so we see that few of the renewables are financially viable at the 8 per cent discount rate. As an interesting example of the effect discussed above, it's worth noting that with zero rate the unit cost from tidal plant would fall to under 2p/kWh, making it cheaper than landfill gas. Once again, the moral is that you need to look carefully at how the sums are done.

Externalities

We want the energy but we don't want the penalties that come with it. Many people feel that the 'external' effects of different forms of energy should be reflected in their costs, by attaching a

TABLE 14.3. *Electricity from renewable sources*

The table shows data and calculated unit costs for electricity from power-stations using renewable energy sources, assuming an 8 per cent discount rate. All costs are in 1994 money.

Source	See Chapter	Capital cost[a] (£/kW)	Running cost[b] (£/kW/year)	Load factor[c] (%)	Lifetime (years)	Unit cost (p/kWh)
Solar PV	11	3500	35	11	25	38
Large-scale hydro	9	2000	5	50	40	4.4
Small-scale hydro	9	1200	30	60	20	2.9
Tidal plant	9	1400	8	22	50	8.0
Wind-farm	10	1400	10	25	20	7.0
Wave power[d]	9	2000	50	20	30	15
Energy crops[e]	4	1500	300	85	20	6.1
MSW combustion	4	3000	−100[f]	85	20	3.0
Landfill gas	4	800	100[f]	88	10	2.8

[a] The capital costs of construction are mid-range values and could vary by 50% either way in most cases.

[b] The annual running costs include operation and maintenance and fuel production if relevant.

[c] The load factor depends on both the availability of the resource and the pattern of use.

[d] As no full-scale system yet exists, the data for wave power are particularly uncertain.

[e] Energy crops are purpose-grown biomass, used either in conventional steam plant or gasified.

[f] Municipal solid waste, used either directly as fuel or in landfills, carries the fuel 'credit' paid for disposing of it.

cost to items such as those listed in Table 13.1 of the previous chapter. This is by no means a simple exercise. What does it mean, to 'reflect' these externalities in the costs? Who pays what to whom? How is it to be done?

Causes and Effects

Before considering the problems of making estimates of external costs, we might usefully analyse the type of situation in which they could arise, and consider some possible methods of dealing with them. The simplest case is a deleterious effect that occurs locally, where both the cause and the effect can easily be identified. Examples might include the after-effects of strip-mining, spoil heaps remaining after deep mining, or plants emitting thick smoke or releasing poisons into a river. If there is a known technical remedy to eliminate the effect or reduce it to a harmless level, and if environmental regulations exist which require the polluter to restore the landscape or install clean-up systems, the so-called external costs become 'internal'—a normal element in the cost of building, maintaining, and decommissioning the plant. Even in this straightforward case, there can be disagreement about acceptable levels, and it does of course depend on the existence of the necessary regulations.

Suppose again a deleterious effect, but one that is widespread and comes from many separate sources. Obvious examples are the atmospheric emissions from fossil-fuel plants and internal combustion engines. If technical remedies are again available, any environmental regulations requiring pollution-abatement systems will spread the costs over all sources, regardless of their individual contributions to the specific effect. This can lead to complications, particularly if the causes and/or the effects extend over several countries with different environmental regulations.

Both the above cases deal with those deleterious effects that can be eliminated by technical means. What about those for which there is no remedy? The example causing most concern in the early 1990s has been carbon dioxide, with its possible consequence of global warming. There is no practicable way to 'remove' the millions of tonnes of CO_2 released each year, so the only way to reduce it is to burn less fossil fuel. A number of countries have considered imposing a 'carbon tax' to bring this about. This would tax energy systems according to the amount of carbon dioxide they produce. (Most proposed versions have in fact combined the carbon tax with a more general energy tax.) The aim is to persuade people to change to less harmful energy sources, or to reduce their overall energy consumption; but the tax has been resisted, in particular by the heavy energy users in industry. Some countries, or states in the USA, do have forms of energy tax designed to encourage conservation and thus reduce consumption. In the UK, the imposition of VAT on domestic heating fuels has been justified on these grounds. However, a full carbon tax has yet to be implemented anywhere at the time of writing.

CO_2 isn't the only effect for which there is no remedy. Oil refineries or wind-farms can't be rendered invisible. A valley can't be both flooded and unflooded. It seems to be no coincidence that these examples concern aesthetic and social effects. If we found that a system was releasing pollutants that couldn't be prevented and were known to be harmful to health, it wouldn't be allowed to continue in operation (one hopes). Again, people may be compensated for financial loss if they are deprived of their land or livelihood. But we appear to take a different view of other types of effect. There are of course planning regulations to take into account these issues in many countries, but once permission is granted, that is usually the end of the matter. Ought there to be a continuing cost as long as there is a continuing effect? Do we want a visual amenity tax, or perhaps compensation payments because you no longer like the view? Or to take an entirely different case, should there be a tax on gas turbine power-stations because they are using up reserves of a premium fuel?

It has also been argued that beneficial effects should be rewarded, perhaps by a form of negative tax. Many countries provide support for some forms of renewable energy, usually in its early stages of development. Extending this idea, should there perhaps be some way to take account of the fact that a particular power-station is very flexible in supplying power when we need it? Or should indigenous sources be supported to help them compete with cheaper imported supplies, for strategic reasons?

This list is by no means exhaustive, but the examples show that 'including externalities in the costs' is by no means a simple process. Indeed, there seem to be at least three separate concepts at work. The first and most straightforward is that the energy providers should pay to avoid undesirable effects when this is possible. Then there is the view that polluters should pay something to society at large, perhaps associated with the idea that the resulting tax income would be used to ameliorate the undesirable effects. And finally there is the attempt to change the situation by rewarding the 'good' and punishing the 'bad'.

Assessing the Damage

The past half-century has seen many different attempts to estimate the external costs of energy systems. It should be said at the outset that some of these exercises have been rather too evidently designed to support the claims of one system against another. (Can the cost of injuries to people struck by coal-carrying trains on level crossings really be a significant factor in the coal vs. nuclear debate?) The more general issue, however, is how to assess the cost to be associated with each ill-effect. The value of a life or a limb is to some extent standardized. In Britain, for instance, a life is worth between three-quarters of a million and about two and a half million pounds, figures obtained by assessing how much we would be willing to pay for, say, a road improvement that saved five lives a year. To take a very different case, how do we quantify clear air? The mountains around Los Angeles, hidden by a brown shroud, are invisible from a distance of a couple of miles in midsummer. In Alaska, glaciers seventy miles away can be seen in crystal-clear detail. What is the monetary value of this difference? Then there is the question whether such assessments should include the possible results of catastrophes with very low probability (see for instance the section 'Risk' in Chapter 13). Add the further difficulty that not all studies have embraced the same range of effects or the same set of sources, and the value of any summary becomes rather uncertain. For this reason, we offer in conclusion only some broad indicators of costs rather than detailed figures for individual sources.

The estimated external costs for the energy sources and systems for which assessments have been made lie between about 0.02 p and £10 per kilowatt-hour of energy used. To appreciate these figures, it is useful to look at the data in Table 14.1, showing 0.04–0.07 p/kWh as the world price paid to the original producer, and 2–9 p/kWh paid in the UK by the final consumer. What then are we to say about a claim that £10 per kilowatt-hour should be added for external costs? Investigation shows that this is a 'catastrophe' figure, reflecting the overall cost of global warming if the worst predictions prove correct, with the oceans rising and climate change ruining the environment. In similar vein, one much-quoted calculation shows that the Gulf War added $24 a barrel to the external costs of oil in the USA. Whilst it is interesting, and perhaps important, to reflect on these figures, we should note that most estimates tend to suggest external costs in the range 1–4 p/kWh for the main present fuels and types of power-plant. These have usually confined themselves to the main 'penalties' discussed in Chapter 13: air pollution, global warming, and the risk of major accidents, although some consider other aspects such as water and land use, and occasionally, social and aesthetic effects. In studies that include the renewable resources, the costs for these are usually somewhat lower, with large-scale hydroelectric plant as the occasional exception. However, in many ways the most interesting observation to come from this work is that the energy 'sources' with the lowest overall external costs are conservation measures: systems designed to reduce energy demand instead of increasing the supply.

15

Future Alternatives

Introduction

This final chapter looks at some options for the future, so we'll start by going back to the beginning and asking a few questions.

First Question

Why do we want energy? Here are a few reasons.

- Those of us who live in cold climates must keep warm in order to survive.

- Many of us who are chemical workers, metal workers, etc., and all of us who cook, need a different sort of heat in order to change materials.

- Most of us, whether we are building workers, factory workers, farmers, foresters, household workers, or even office workers, want mechanical aids to help us in our work.

- We'd all like to be able to travel in comfort.

- Many of us have become accustomed to continuing our normal activities after sunset or before sunrise, so we like to have some form of light other than the sun.

- Very many of us, it seems, have become addicted to gizmos: we want to watch TV, play disks, tapes, or computer games, talk to someone in California or on Mars, and so on.

To summarize, we need warmth, heat, machines, transport, light, and communications. This may all seem very obvious, but the point lies in what the list does not say. It does not say that we need oil, coal, gas, or any other specific energy source. It probably implies that we need electricity, but otherwise most of us don't care where our warmth and other benefits come from as long as they are convenient to use and affordable.

Second Question

Where does our energy come from today? We know the answer to this, and it doesn't even need a list, because apart from tiny fractions from hydro and nuclear power, almost all of it comes from burning fossil fuels or biomass.

Third Question

How much energy are we going to need tomorrow? Here are a few facts that might be relevant.

- The population of the world is about 6 billion and will very probably continue increasing at some $1\frac{1}{2}$ per cent a year, reaching 9 billion in about 2025. Much of the growth is expected to be in the developing countries.

- The average energy consumption per person in the industrialized countries is about ten times that for the rest of the world. Per capita daily consumption in the country that uses most energy is two hundred times that in the country that uses least.

- In the decades after World War II, before the oil crises and recessions of the 1970s and 1980s, world energy consumption was rising at about 5 per cent a year while the population was growing at about 2 per cent a year. In the same period, world oil consumption was rising at about 6 per cent annually and electricity consumption at $7\frac{1}{2}$ per cent.

Fourth Question

How much energy is available for tomorrow? Chapter 12 discussed this in some detail, and concluded that we have approximately

- enough coal for several centuries,
- oil for nearly a century at the present rate of consumption but only 30 years if growth at 6 per cent returns,
- natural gas for over a century at the present rate, but less if we continue to use it increasingly for everything,
- nuclear power for several centuries if breeder reactors and the surpluses from decommissioned nuclear weapons are used,
- hydroelectric power equivalent to about twice the world's present annual electricity consumption if we ignore all environmental and similar constraints.

This is the situation for our present sources. Table 12.2 showed some of the other possibilities and we'll return to them later.

Final Question

Are there reasons, other than limited supplies, for changing from our present sources? Possibly, because

- we may be killing the forests,
- we may be heating the Earth and causing the worst flood since Noah,
- we may be risking the worst catastrophe since the death of the dinosaurs.

For a more measured account of these hypothetical events, see Chapter 13.

Predictions

> *Energy forecasting is easy. It's getting it right that's difficult.**

How *do* we predict what will happen in the future? The discussion of resources in Chapter 12 involved projections of demand, but we didn't really look at the justification for these. Is there a science of prediction? Any science needs rules—scientific laws—so let's investigate a few possibilities, starting with the simplest:

* Graham Stein, in *RENEW*, Mar.–Apr. 1996 (see Further Reading for details).

• Things will be much the same in future.

This may seem absurd, but in energy matters many of us seem to work on this assumption. We expect to need about the same energy next year as this, and we assume that we'll get it. Unfortunately, we've failed to notice that we are actually demanding a little more each year, and a glance back at some of the charts in Chapter 2 shows that this theory, if used forty years ago, would have left all of us in considerable difficulties. So let's move up a step. We look back and observe certain trends, and this leads to a new theory:

• Trends will be much the same in future.

This was the reasoning which led to predictions that the oil would run out by the 1930s. They proved wrong, but mainly, as we've seen, because a great deal more oil was found. Consumption did continue to rise roughly as predicted, but most of us took very little notice, and unfortunately for the scientific method, it wasn't the dawn of understanding that at last made us pause. Wars and politics led to the shortages and price rises of the 1970s, and the lesson we learned was that the world's oil supply is determined by the world's oil producers.

By definition you can't include the unexpected in your forecasts, but governments continue to demand predictions, so the appropriate experts continue to provide them. Predicting energy demand and supply have become part of economic forecasting, with theories, or economic models, which are considerably more complex than our simple rules. These usually play a role in the exercises known as scenarios, whose approach can be characterized by what we might call the optimist's law of prediction:

• The future will be what you choose to make it.

Scenarios

Before 1970 a scenario meant an outline for a play or film. Then groups of people in various countries started thinking about future energy supplies in a new way. Instead of fitting economic theory within the existing framework of habits, attitudes, laws, and regulations to make a prediction, they opened out the whole discussion. 'What if', they said, 'the government introduced regulations cutting fossil fuel consumption by 10 per cent a year?'; or, 'What if no more nuclear plants at all were built?' (The early composers of scenarios did tend to be *rather green*.) These 'what if' exercises, called scenarios to distinguish them from forecasts, proved very popular in the late 1970s and early 1980s. Then for a while there were fewer, perhaps because people looking at the record of energy consumption in the 1980s despaired of finding any pattern. However, several have appeared in the early and mid-1990s, and it is particularly interesting to see that many of the present-day studies by official bodies and large organizations in the energy field now adopt the scenario approach. Another change over the years in almost all forecasts or scenarios is the inclusion of the renewable energy sources in the equation. (Significantly, the term 'alternative', with its 1960s connotation of long hair and strange life-styles, seems to be fading from use.) In the following we'll look at a few scenarios which are typical of different points of view, and then at a couple of systems which are incorporated into some of them, and at a suggestion that is more a concept than a detailed plan.

World Energy in the 21st Century

Figures 15.1–15.3 show possible patterns of world energy consumption over the next fifty years. Each represents in simplified form the results of scenarios that have appeared in the first half of the 1990s, and they are chosen to exemplify three different views of the future. None of them requires dramatic life-style changes and all three would claim to be consistent with continued economic growth world-wide, accompanied by some improvement in the relative positions of industrialized and developing countries. Current concerns about global warming are reflected in the fact that almost no one today offers the type of scenario that appeared frequently only a decade ago, where steeply rising energy demand was to be met by a massive growth in the use of coal.

Scenario 1: Full Steam Ahead

The scenario in Fig. 15.1 assumes that world energy demand will grow at $2\frac{1}{2}$ per cent a year. This is about 1 per cent higher than the expected average rate of population growth over the period, allowing for some 'catching-up' by the developing countries; but it means that total annual consumption in 2050 is four times the present rate. In the picture presented here, world oil consumption peaks in the late 2020s and then slowly decreases, returning to the mid-1990s level at the end of the period. Gas consumption rises to roughly twice its present rate and then remains steady. An element of concern about global warming constrains the growth in coal consumption to some extent, but nevertheless it continues until almost the end of the period. As the graph shows, the three fossil fuels meet only about one-third of the demand in 2050.

The scenario assumes rapid and continuing growth in both hydroelectric and nuclear power, to make up as much as possible of the shortfall. The 3 per cent growth rate for hydroelectric plant means that by 2050 some two-thirds of the world's estimated total potential (see Chapter 12) will have been developed. The nuclear capacity will require several thousand new reactors, which would include both thermal and fast-breeder types. Biomass, using all available wastes together with energy crops as soon as these can be developed, is seen as the only source with the potential to fill the gap in the coming decade or so. Its ultimate contribution, at five times the present rate, is seen as serving the increased population of developing countries and also as a source of liquid fuel when oil supplies are falling. (Note that this is its primary energy contribution, whereas the biomass figure in Table 12.2 is the final-use energy, after conversion.) From about 2020 we see rapidly increasing contributions from wind power and solar energy (solar heating and PV) to meet the ever-rising demand, and by 2050 the contribution required from these sources is a little greater than our total present energy consumption.

This study certainly provides food for thought. The growth in demand is quite modest: a per capita increase of only 1 per cent a

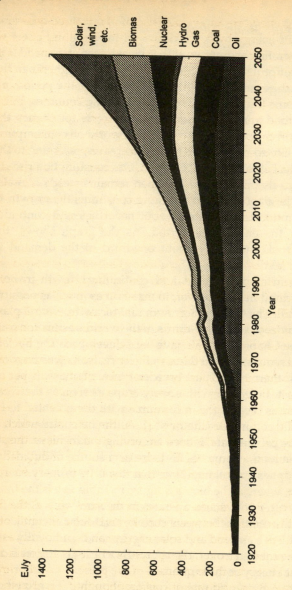

Fig. 15.1 World primary energy consumption 1920–2050, scenario 1

year, giving everyone an average rise of about three-quarters of their present energy by 2050. However, the resulting effect will depend very much on how this increase is distributed. If the wealthier countries receive 'their' three-quarters, then the rich get richer and the others may just manage to rise from one-ninth to one-seventh of the present level in the industrial countries. But if all the increase went to the developing countries, their per capita consumption could reach half the figure for the wealthier parts of the world. So even in this 'high growth' scenario there is still a long way to go before we all have equal shares of this valuable commodity. It is also noticeable that carbon dioxide emissions (Fig. 15.4, below) continue to rise steeply, starting to fall only when both oil and coal consumption start to decrease.

Scenario 2: The Middle Road

The second scenario (Fig. 15.2) has many features in common with the first: the same patterns of oil and gas use and similar growth in hydroelectricity. Nuclear power increases at only half the rate, but the main difference is that Scenario 2 takes global warming very seriously indeed, with a determination to reduce coal consumption as fast as possible. This is to be achieved mainly by fairly dramatic improvements in energy efficiency, leading to an overall growth in demand of $1\frac{3}{4}$ per cent a year instead of the $2\frac{1}{2}$ per cent of Scenario 1. If the economies are to grow at about 3 per cent at the same time, this implies a continuing world-wide decrease in energy/GDP ratios (see Chapter 14). As the countries which are still developing their industries are unlikely to achieve this, the assumed annual energy/GDP reduction in the industrialized world needs to be considerably greater than the $1\frac{1}{4}$ per cent overall average.

For the rest, this scenario operates in the same way as the first. Biomass fills the gap between supply and demand until other renewables such as wind and solar energy can become fully established. They then take over, rising rapidly to a contribution in 2050 that is equal to about three-quarters of the present world primary total. Overall, the world rate of consumption in the mid-21st century is $2\frac{1}{4}$ times the mid-1990s rate, which means that average per

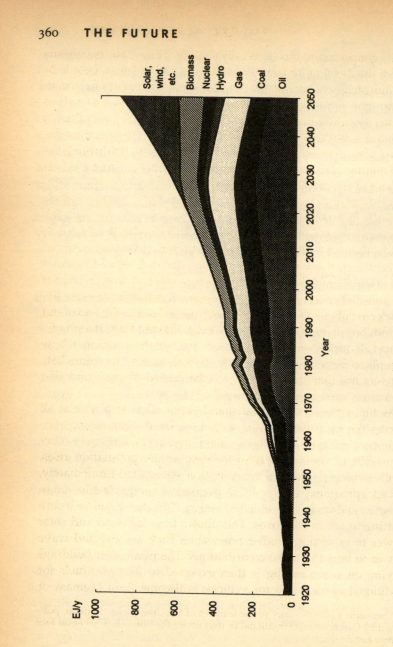

Fig. 15.2 World primary energy consumption 1920–2050, scenario 2

capita consumption increases only slightly. This, of course, means that if the developing countries are indeed to develop, people in the industrialized world will need to accept less energy each year rather than expecting more. It is the aim of Scenario 2 to reduce carbon dioxide emissions, and indeed they are much lower than in Scenario 1. But unfortunately even with the severe restraints imposed here, the annual release of CO_2 continues to rise through the first quarter of the next century and is still above present levels at the end of the period studied.

Scenario 3: Greening the World

The scenario shown in Fig. 15.3 is really different. It sets out to eliminate fossil fuels entirely from the picture within 100 years or so, replacing them with a roughly half-and-half mix of biomass and other renewable sources.* Nuclear power has an even shorter life and disappears within twenty years. Existing large-scale hydroelectric plants are allowed to continue, at least to the end of our period, but no new ones are to be built. Having thus abandoned almost all our present energy sources, we face the question of how to replace them. As with the other two scenarios, the immediate answers are that they are not all abandoned at once and that biomass is used to fill the gap in the early years.

As Fig. 15.3 shows, total demand is not allowed to rise at all during the next decade. This, of course, means decreasing consumption in the developed countries if the share going to the other four-fifths of the world is to increase as the population rises. World-wide, oil and coal consumption start to fall immediately, but gas, producing the least CO_2 per unit of energy, is allowed to grow to just under twice its present rate of consumption before starting to fall in the 2010s. This allows time for wind and solar power to expand and other renewables such as tidal and wave power to begin to make contributions. The number of buildings relying on solar heating is then expected to increase; fuels for additional heating and for vehicles will come from biomass or

* Scenario 3 adopts many of the features of the Greenpeace scenario, published by Greenpeace International in 1993 under the title *Towards a Fossil Free Energy Future*.

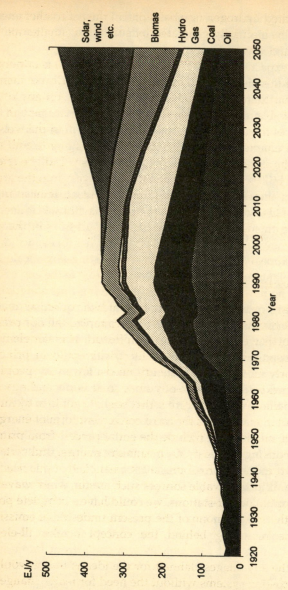

Fig. 15.3 World primary energy consumption 1920–2050, scenario 3

solar-generated hydrogen (see below); and the main other energy carrier will be electricity generated by sun, wind, small-scale hydro, tides, and waves.

The effect on CO_2 emissions is shown in Fig. 15.4. It is important to note that this assumes all the biomass to be produced sustainably and that there are no emissions associated with any of the other renewable sources. Moreover, it takes no account of the consequences for CO_2 levels of further destruction of the world's forests (see Chapter 13). It is therefore disappointing to find that even with the extreme regime of Scenario 3 we shall still be releasing over 10 billion tonnes of carbon dioxide a year into the atmosphere in the middle of the next century—about the same as in the mid-1960s. Hardly a return to pre-industrial days. It will indeed be a very long time before we can reverse the increases of the past century.

The All-Electric Economy

We now leave detailed scenarios to look at two particular 'energy economies'. Neither of these is expected to replace all our present systems, but as we've seen above, both feature as major elements in some proposals for the future. Electricity could in principle supply nearly all the world's energy needs. For many people in industrialized countries it already does so at home and at work, and on the whole we rather like it that way. It provides by far the cleanest and in many ways the most convenient form of energy to the user. Of course, if we include the entire process from primary energy to consumer, it is by no means the cleanest and certainly not the most efficient form, but the argument is that this need not be the case. With renewable sources such as sun, wind, waves, or tides as input to power-stations, we could have a complete power system with virtually none of the present undesirable emissions. This is the reasoning behind the concept of the all-electric economy.

One of the advantages claimed for the idea is that it would fit well into existing systems without the need for major changes. In countries which already have full distribution systems, the power

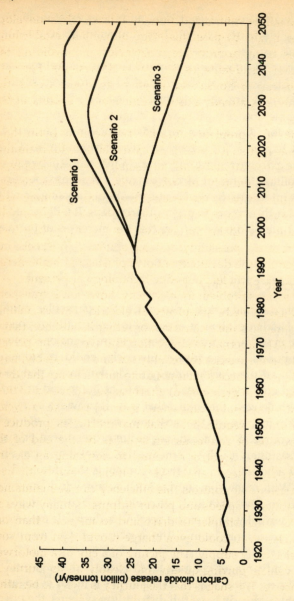

Fig. 15.4 World carbon dioxide emissions

sources could still be centralized, initially at least, whilst developing countries might by-pass this stage altogether, establishing
local supplies using appropriate renewables and avoiding the
costs and other disadvantages of large-scale systems. For consumers, industrial or household, in all parts of the world, the
essential technology already exists: electric motors, heaters, appliances of all sorts.

There are just two problems, or rather, two versions of the same
problem: storage. First, it would need extremely careful planning,
on either local or national scale, to establish a firm supply of
electricity relying entirely on renewables, and some storage
element would probably be essential almost anywhere (see
'Storing Energy' in Chapter 9). If the local geography is suitable,
pumped storage could be the answer. Or for small-scale local
systems, there is the possibility of using spinning flywheels, but
this would require the development of sophisticated high-energy
versions which are still leading-edge technology at present.

The really serious problem for electricity, however, is transport.
Of course, there already are plenty of electric vehicles, mainly
trains and trams. It is the electric car, or rather its absence, that is
the problem. (The alternative suggestion that we give up private
transport altogether would, regrettably but understandably, have
very little chance of success.) It is not quite correct to say that there
are no electric cars. A great deal of effort has been devoted to their
development for several decades now, spurred on in recent years
by the Californian requirement that manufacturers produce a
certain proportion of zero-emission vehicles by the end of the
century. There is no problem of course in designing an electric
vehicle. Electric motors can be very efficient, and with new
designs and electronic controls this efficiency can be maintained
over a wide range of speeds and power outputs. In many ways an
electric car is much simpler to drive and to maintain than our
present vehicles—you could even charge it overnight from your
household electricity supply. The picture of a city or a motorway
with every vehicle purring quietly and cleanly on its journey is
indeed attractive. The snag is that the journey is likely to be rather
short and rather slow.

Consider the petrol tank of a present-day car, viewed as an energy store: say fifty litres of petrol at 35 MJ per litre: 1750 MJ in all. Internal combustion engines are very inefficient, as we've seen, so let's assume that the engine can convert this tankful into only 240 MJ of useful energy to drive the vehicle. The electric car, with its much more efficient engine, might need 270 MJ of electrical input for the same output—about 75 kWh. Now consider normal lead-acid car batteries. A 'battery pack' of these that would fit into the luggage space of a small car might store just about one-tenth of this energy. And there is the further question of the instantaneous power delivered by the engine. When you put your foot down, you expect tens of kilowatts from even a modest present-day car engine, and in electrical terms, tens of kilowatts mean hundreds of amps at hundreds of volts. Where are they all going to come from? It is not surprising that a 'good performance' for any electric car able to carry more than a couple of rather small people means a maximum speed of perhaps 40 mph and a range of less than 100 miles. Nevertheless, a number of manufacturers are developing such vehicles, and if the cost of the car and the replacement cost of batteries is low enough, they may prove attractive as town run-abouts (particularly if pollution regulations were to ban internal combustion engines in cities). Batteries with much better perform-ance than the simple lead-acid one are also being developed, but there are still technical problems to be solved and the cost is much too high at present. So despite all the effort, it seems that there is still a very long way to go before the electric car will be able to go a very long way.

The Hydrogen Economy

Hydrogen is in many respects the ideal fuel. The energy released per tonne in combustion is more than twice that of any hydrocar-bon (Table 4.2), and the sole product is water—no CO_2 because no carbon is involved. The amount of free hydrogen gas existing naturally is very small; it isn't for instance produced by natural processes such as the anaerobic digestion that generates methane.

There are, however, standard methods of producing it commercially, and the world's chemical industries currently use nearly 100 million tonnes a year. Unfortunately the raw material for most of this is methane (or coal) so it is hardly a useful way to reduce dependence on fossil fuels and reduce CO_2 emissions. But the advocates of the hydrogen economy see a much more plentiful source than any hydrocarbon: hydrogen accounts for one-ninth of the mass of all the water in the world.

The plan is as follows. Hydrogen will be extracted from water, distributed as we now distribute natural gas, and burned as heating fuel or in internal combustion engines, in both cases combining with oxygen from the air to form water vapour. It doesn't require deep thought to see the catch in this. You can't start with water, carry out a series of processes finishing with the same amount of water and produce some energy on the way—apparently out of nothing. (We rejected a scheme for methane production on just these grounds in Chapter 4, 'Secondary Fuels'.) The point is that, like electricity, hydrogen is a way of dealing with energy: of transporting it from one place to another, not a way to produce it in the first place. You use energy to extract hydrogen from water and the hydrogen then carries the energy to the final user—just as electricity does. The hydrogen economy is in this sense an alternative to the all-electric economy discussed above.

The best available method for extracting hydrogen from water uses electricity, and in this case the hydrogen economy is better described as the electric economy with an 'add-on'. The method is simple in principle. Two pieces of metal dipping into water—or to be precise, into a very dilute salt solution—form an electrolytic cell. When a voltage is applied between these, the positively and negatively charged ions that exist in the solution are pulled in opposite directions. As they reach the plates, the negative ones give up electrons to the metal while the positive ones collect electrons. The result is that two gases consisting of ordinary uncharged molecules bubble off—hydrogen at one plate and oxygen at the other. The electrons meanwhile are restored by flowing round the circuit connecting the two plates; driven by the electrical supply, they are the current that must be maintained to give the flow of gases. The salt in the solutions, potassium hydroxide for instance, is not consumed, and the sole effect (in the ideal case) is the breaking up of H_2O into hydrogen and oxygen using energy from the electrical supply. Theoretically there is even an energy gain, because the cell will have taken in some heat from the surroundings, so the energy stored in the gases should be slightly greater than the electrical input. In practice, it is about equal at best.

But why go to all this trouble? If you have to produce the electric power in the first place, why not stay with the electric economy? The answer lies in two very important advantages of hydrogen: it can be stored, holding the energy until it is needed, and it can be used as portable fuel in an internal combustion engine. All the necessary technologies exist. Large electrolytic plants have been in use for years, and storage tanks (each equivalent to about ten Dinorwig pumped-storage plants), and hundreds of kilometres of pipeline in industrial complexes like the Ruhr. Vehicles have run on hydrogen. Many countries including Britain used 'town gas', made from coal and consisting of 50 per cent or more hydrogen, in households and industry for over a century before natural gas became available. The scale of production is of course far too small at present. A full electro-hydrogen economy would need a five-fold increase in the world's electrical generating capacity to provide the input for about a hundred times the world's present hydrogen production capacity. So it is hardly an instant answer, and Table 15.1, comparing the two systems, shows that there are a few other potential problems—apart from the obvious one of cost.

There is yet another possibility: to produce the hydrogen using solar energy directly. This requires very high temperatures and the process has not even been tried on a large scale, but it could be an option for the future. Either way, if we could achieve a hydrogen or hydrogen/electric energy economy, with the input coming from renewables, as in Scenario 3 above, we would at last have a clean and inexhaustible energy system.

TABLE 15.1. *The all-electric and hydrogen economies*

	The all-electric economy	The hydrogen economy
Primary sources	Short term: present primary sources. Longer term: renewables.	Short term: as for electric power. Longer term: as for electric power, or direct conversion using solar radiation.
Storage	Short term: pumped storage Longer term: flywheels, batteries(?)	In tanks—under pressure or as liquid hydrogen maintained at very low temperature.
Distribution	High-voltage power lines	Tankers; pipelines.
Advantages	Familiar; clean in use; safety systems well-established	Clean in use; can be stored; can be used in internal combustion engines
Disadvantages	Firm supply doubtful; problems of electric road vehicles (and aircraft!)	Unfamiliar to most users; danger of explosion; existing gas pipelines probably not usable.

Small is Beautiful

Twenty or thirty years ago, as far back as the 1960s, a steady flow of books and articles began to appear whose theme was the need for a radical reappraisal of our attitudes to energy production and consumption. The authors deplored the accepted view that ever-rising demand was natural and inevitable, and in particular repudiated the fashionable belief in economies of scale—that bigger must be more efficient or more cost-effective, and therefore better. In recent years, increasing numbers of people have come to share this unease, and although the more radical ideas remain outside the mainstream, the early proponents of what came to be called soft energy paths* claim that they were often the ones who were right. It is certainly true that current official predictions for the next half-century frequently bear more resemblance to the 1960s

* The name comes from Amory Lovins' seminal study, *Soft Energy Paths*, first published as a Penguin book in 1977.

forecasts of the 'naïve and unrealistic' radicals than to the projections which those same officials were then offering. And as we have seen above, the renewable sources, long considered appropriate only for people with torn jeans and an alternative life-style, are now part of the most orthodox of scenarios.

What are the soft energy paths? One thing is certain: they are many. We are not talking here about a single group of people with one agreed plan for the future. If there is a common view, it is probably best characterized by a set of aims rather than one particular programme. And it is a measure of its increasing acceptance that hardly anyone would today dispute these aims: to achieve the transitions from exhaustible to renewable resources, from polluting to non-polluting technologies, and from energy waste to energy conservation. The differences tend to come in the interpretation of the aims and the assignment of priorities. Which doesn't make them any less different, as we've seen in our three scenarios. But we've looked at these, so perhaps it is more interesting here to concentrate on the other plank in the soft platform, the one that gives this section its title: the belief that the scale of most of our present energy systems is wrong.

The electric power industry, whether public or private, is a major target for this criticism. (Oil is another, but the spread of do-it-yourself backyard oil wells is definitely not an aim.) Power production is crucial because it is seen as offering the greatest contrast between the systems we have and those we might have. The typical modern power-station has an output in the gigawatt range, sufficient for a million households. Its fuel is coal or uranium, and for economic or environmental reasons it is unlikely to be sited in the centre of a town or city. It is seen as large, distant, and controlled by a large, distant organization.

The soft energy version would be different. The demand for electricity would be lower, because resources now spent on devising ever more ways of using energy and persuading consumers to buy as much as possible would be devoted to making houses 'energy-tight' and developing energy-efficient appliances. Prices would encourage conservation, too, with the price per kilowatt-hour increasing rather than decreasing with the amount used. (This pricing policy has been adopted by some utility companies in places where regulations make it attractive.) In general, the idea is to persuade the utilities that their profits would be just as good, or even better, if they saw themselves as selling not electricity but warm buildings. They might then sometimes find that insulating buildings was better business than building new power-stations. (Some small publicly owned utilities have tried this approach, too.)

The 'soft' scenario sees the reduced demand resulting from these measures as being satisfied mainly by renewable resources. Agricultural and urban wastes, energy crops, wind-farms, small-scale hydroelectricity, and photovoltaics would provide the power, and combined heat and power would maximize the efficiency with which the fuels were used (see Chapter 5). Instead of competition between large organizations, each committed to encouraging the use of one form of energy, local control of the full range of available supplies would promote the best use of all resources.

Small-scale systems do already exist, of course. In Denmark, many wind-turbine plants are owned by local co-operatives, and farmers' co-operatives have built small power-stations running on gas from anaerobic digestion of animal wastes. Switzerland now has over 100 grid-connected PV installations, and Britain has increasing numbers of small-scale power-plants, using wind and water, landfill gas and other wastes, and taking advantage of the opportunity to sell power to the grid. The US has similar legislation (although 'small-scale' tends to have a different meaning there), and increasing numbers of cities and local communities are also developing systems that take advantage of all their local resources. But perhaps the strangest allies of the enthusiasts for soft energy paths are the companies in Britain who, for purely commercial reasons, are building small gas turbine plants rather than large power-stations—and thereby making a greater contribution to the reduction of UK carbon dioxide emissions and acid rain than anyone else. Small is beautiful indeed!

Choices

What can we say about the future, then? If one thing is sure, it is that in 2050 the energy world will not be exactly like any of the pictures offered in this chapter. It may not even be remotely like them. The graphs in this chapter, or Fig. 1.1 at the start of the book, show how things have changed in quite unexpected ways in the past, and if history tells us anything, it is that our present energy world is not the result of careful planning but of many individual events and decisions. Should India build a new hydro-plant, displacing thousands from their homes, or a dozen more coal-fired power-stations to pollute the atmosphere? Should the Swiss drown a few more Alpine valleys or construct another nuclear power plant? Should the UK government subsidize energy-saving systems in ten million older houses—at the taxpayer's expense? Will the Californians in the year 2000 actually buy the zero-emission vehicles that the law requires? Should I replace my ancient boiler or do something about the draughty windows?

Then there is technology. Fifty years is just long enough for a new technological invention to take over the world (consider computers). Perhaps we'll find a way to absorb huge volumes of carbon dioxide, bringing coal back into fashion as the answer to everything. Or nuclear fusion will produce clean electricity in large quantities. Or PV modules become so cheap that we can cover the world's deserts with them, using the power to generate hydrogen as a universal fuel. A pollution-free energy world, with plenty for everyone. Now there's a nice idea.

APPENDICES

APPENDIX A
ORDERS OF MAGNITUDE

The problem is how to deal with very large numbers without writing (or even worse, having to recite) large numbers of noughts. There are two solutions: use a shorthand form of arithmetic, or use special names.

Powers of ten

Two million is two times a million, and a million is ten times ten times ten times ten times ten times ten—six of them in all. This can be written mathematically:

$$2\,000\,000 = 2 \times 10^6$$

The quantity 10^6 is called 'ten to the power six' (or ten to the six for short). The advantage of using this power-of-ten form is particularly obvious for very large numbers. Britain's annual primary energy consumption, for instance, is about $9\,000\,000\,000\,000\,000\,000$ joules, and it is certainly easier to write 9×10^{18} (or to say 'nine times ten to the eighteen') than to spell out all the noughts. And you can even observe that 18 is 3 times 6, so the figure is 9 million, million, million.

Prefixes

The powers of ten give us the basis for the special names for large (or small) numbers. With a few exceptions, names are given to the multiples of 1000 (10^3, 10^6, 10^9, 10^{12}, etc.). The table on p. 375 shows these, with some examples. Sub-multiples also have special prefixes and the table includes a few of these.

Prefix	Symbol	Multiply by . . .	Examples
kilo-	k	1000, or 10^3	A typical UK household uses energy at an average rate of about 3 kW.
mega-	M	a million, or 10^6	A 5-MW power-station could supply enough electricity for a small town.
giga-	G	a billion,[a] or 10^9	The output of a large modern power-station is about 1 GW.
tera-	T	a million million, or 10^{12}	The world is consuming primary energy at a rate of about 12 TW . . .
peta-	P	a million billion, or 10^{15}	which is equivalent to about 43 PJ an hour . . .
exa-	E	a billion billion, or 10^{18}	or about 370 EJ a year.
centi-	c	a hundredth, or 10^{-2}	There are about 30.5 cm in a foot . . .
milli-	m	a thousandth, or 10^{-3}	and about 25.4 mm in an inch.
micro-	μ	a millionth, or 10^{-6}	A grain of granulated sugar has a mass of about 1 μg

[a] A *billion* now normally means a thousand million and we use it in this sense throughout the book. (The old 'British' million million seems, like other old British institutions, to have faded away.)

APPENDIX B

UNITS AND CONVERSIONS

Chapters 1 and 2 discussed some of the ways in which quantities of energy and power are measured. This Appendix summarizes the results of those discussions and is designed as a quick reference source for 'energy arithmetic'. It also includes a few conversion factors for quantities other than energy. Many of the conversion factors below are rounded to two digits, reflecting the precision of most of the national and international data quoted in the book.

In addition:

- See Appendix A for the meanings of the multiplying prefixes.
- See the List of Abbreviations at the front of the book for the meanings of other abbreviations.

Energy

The main energy units used in the book are the *joule* and its multiples. The other unit that appears frequently is the *kilowatt-hour*.

Energy units which are still in use in some contexts and some countries include the calorie, kilocalorie, British Thermal Unit, and therm. Table B.1 shows how each of these is related to the joule.

TABLE B.1

1 kWh	is	3 600 000 J	or	3.6 MJ
1 cal	is	4.2 J		
1 kcal or Cal	is	4200 J	or	4.2 kJ
1 BTU	is	1055 J	or	1.055 kJ
1 therm	is	105 500 000 J	or	105.5 MJ

Energy Equivalents

The two tables below give the conversion factors between the principal units used for energy data in the book. Table B.2 shows 'household-sized' units and Table B.3 the larger units that appear in national or world data. The examples following the tables illustrate how they are used.

TABLE B.2					
	MJ	GJ	kWh[a]	toe	tce[b]
MJ	1	10^{-3}	0.28	24×10^{-6}	36×10^{-6}
GJ	1000	1	278	0.024	0.036
kWh	3.6	0.0036	1	86×10^{-6}	0.13×10^{-3}
toe	42 000	42	11 700	1	1.5
tce	28 000	28	7800	0.67	1

TABLE B.3					
	PJ	EJ	TWh[a]	Mtoe	Mtce[b]
PJ	1	10^{-3}	0.278	0.024	0.036
EJ	1000	1	278	24	36
TWh	3.6	0.0036	1	0.086	0.13
Mtoe	42	0.0042	11.7	1	1.5
Mtce	28	0.0028	7.8	0.67	1

[a] The factors for kWh and TWh are direct conversions of amounts of energy, not equivalent power-station outputs. (See the discussions in Chapters 1 and 2.)

[b] The energy content of coal varies. These tables are based on the commonly used international average of 28 GJ per tonne.

Example 1. A household uses 2.5 gigajoules of energy a month for hot water. How many kilowatt-hours is this? To answer this, we find the GJ *row* in Table B.2 and move along it to the kWh *column*. The entry there is 278, which is the required conversion factor. Multiplying by the original 2.5 GJ gives the required result: 695 kWh, or roughly 700 kWh.

Example 2. Biofuels contribute about 8.5 exajoules to India's annual primary energy consumption. How much oil would be needed to provide this energy? Using the above procedure with Table B.3, we find that the entry in the EJ row and Mtoe column is 24, so the answer is $8.5 \times 24 \cong 200$ million tonnes of oil.

Rates

Power is the rate at which energy is consumed, transferred, or transformed. The main units used for power are the *watt* (W) and its multiples. The watt is defined in terms of the joule:

$$1 \text{ watt} = 1 \text{ joule per second}$$

TABLE B.4				
rate	joules ... per hour	per year	kilowatt-hours per year	oil equivalent per year
1 W	3.6 kJ	31.5 MJ	8.76	—
1 kW	3.6 MJ	31.5 GJ	8760	0.75 toe
1 MW	3.6 GJ	31.5 TJ	8.76 million	750 toe
1 GW	3.6 TJ	31.5 PJ	8.76 billion	0.75 Mtoe
1 TW	3.6 PJ	31.5 EJ	8760 billion	750 Mtoe

Table B.4 shows quantities of energy consumed, transformed, etc. per hour and per year, for constant rates in different numbers of watts.

Example 3. A 100-watt lamp runs constantly. What is its annual electricity consumption in kWh? We see that with a power of 1 W, the consumption is 8.76 kWh per year, so the 100-W lamp uses 876 kWh.

Example 4. The world consumes primary energy at an average rate of about 12 TW. What is the equivalent in tonnes of oil? Table B.4 shows that 1 TW is equivalent to 750 Mtoe a year, so 12 TW is equivalent to 9000 million tonnes a year.

Other Quantities

Table B.5 relates a few metric units to their common non-metric equivalents.

TABLE B.5

Quantity	Equivalent amounts	
mass	1 kilogram	2.2 lb
	1 tonne	1000 kg or 2205 lb
length	1 metre	39 in or 3 ft 3 in
	1 kilometre	0.62 miles
	1 mile	1.6 km
area	1 square metre	11 sq ft or 1.2 sq yards
	1 hectare	10 000 sq m or 2.5 acres
	1 acre	0.40 hectares
volume	1 cubic metre	1000 litres or 35 cu ft
	1 gallon (imperial)	4.55 litres
	1 gallon (US)	3.8 litres
	1 barrel	35 gal (imp) or 42 gal (US)
speed	1 metre per second	2.2 mph
	1 mile per hour	0.45 metres per sec
pressure	1 atmosphere	14.7 lb per sq in
power	1 horse-power	750 W or $\frac{3}{4}$ kW

FURTHER READING

This section offers a few ideas for further study and some other sources of information. There is a very large number of books on energy, from primary school picture-books to massive tomes on technical topics. At the time of writing, however, there does not appear to be any suitable up-to-date book that provides the necessary step up from this one, treating the whole subject at a slightly more advanced level. Recent years have seen the usual number of new books on specific technologies, and many on the politics of energy, but the closest approach to a broad treatment at a suitable level seems to be limited to books which concentrate on the renewable energy sources. Three of these are therefore listed below. There are also suggestions for a few journals which might be of interest, and the section finishes with some information on sources of data. First, however, a suggestion which will no doubt already be familiar to many readers.

Searching

New books on particular technologies or aspects of energy studies appear all the time, so rather than offering a list which may soon be out of date, here is a suggestion. Most good libraries have a copy of the volume called *Books in Print*. In the past, individual versions for the UK, the USA, etc. were customary, but it is now common to find these combined on one CD. This makes searching very easy, and typing in a few key words leads quickly to a list of current books on any topic. With the printed versions of the volume, the process takes a little longer, but even browsing through the several pages of titles under the heading 'Energy' can be interesting and illuminating.

Three Books on Renewable Energy

The following are all considerably more detailed than this book, but in general at a level which makes them suitable 'further reading'. They don't, of course, treat the fossil fuels or nuclear power in any detail.

The first offers a little more science and technology, some detailed case studies, and brief histories, and considerably more on the economics and politics of energy. It also has many useful references to more specialized book and articles. (At this point it is only proper to declare an interest.

This is the textbook for an Open University course on Renewable Energy and was written by the course team—which included the present author.)

> Godfrey Boyle (ed.), *Renewable Energy: Power for a Sustainable Future* (Oxford: Oxford University Press, 1996); 479 pp.

The next book would be of value to anyone interested in renewable energy in Britain. It is beautifully produced, with colour photographs and many graphs, and includes good, concise introductions to the renewables. The detailed analyses of the potential contributions are fairly complex, but their results are certainly interesting.

> Energy Technology Support Unit (ETSU), *An Assessment of Renewable Energy for the UK* (London: HMSO, 1994); 308 pp.

On the world scale, there is an appropriately world-sized paperback, the result of a major study prepared for the United Nations Conference on Environment and Development (UNCED) held in Rio in 1992. Again, the details of the energy scenarios may be rather more than some readers wish to work through, but the book is a gold-mine of detailed information on the technologies and the uses of renewable energy in different parts of the world, and its conclusions are certainly very interesting.

> T. B. Johansson *et al.* (eds.), *Renewable Energy: Sources for Fuels and Electricity* (Washington, DC: Island Press, 1993); 1160 pp.

Journals

A number of journals provide interesting material on energy topics. There is of course the *Scientific American*, with its excellent and authoritative articles. The *New Scientist* has useful discussions on topics of current interest, news items, and occasional longer articles on energy matters.

The UK Energy Technology Support Unit (ETSU) produces a nice general magazine on renewable energy called *New Review*. Details of this and other material can be obtained from

> New and Renewable Energy Enquiries Bureau
> ETSU, Harwell,
> Oxfordshire
> OX11 0RA

More informally, a good way to keep in touch with the news—and some interesting gossip—is *Renew*, the bi-monthly journal of the Network for Alternative Technology and Technology Assessment:

NATTA
Energy and Environment Research Unit
Faculty of Technology
The Open University
Milton Keynes
MK7 6AA

Other readable journals in particular fields include *Atom*, published by the UK Atomic Energy Authority and *Wind Power Monthly* from the British Wind Energy Association.

Data

The best concise summary of world energy production and consumption is probably the annual *BP Statistical Review of World Energy*, published each June. It can be purchased from

BP Educational Service
PO Box 943
Poole
Dorset
BH17 7BR

The United Nations and the OECD both publish energy statistics in various forms, but these are probably volumes for libraries rather than individual readers.

For UK data, the monthly *Energy Trends* and the annual *UK Energy Statistics* are both published by the Department of Trade and Industry and available through HMSO outlets.

INDEX

See also the lists of Figures, Tables, and Abbreviations at the front of the book. **Bold** indicates a definition or main item.